e-Discovery

FOR

DUMMIES®

by Linda Volonino and Ian Redpath

T0256653

WILEY

John Wiley & Sons, Inc.

e-Discovery For Dummies®

Published by
John Wiley & Sons, Inc.
111 River Street
Hoboken, NJ 07030-5774
www.wiley.com

For general information on our other products and services, please contact our Customer Care Department within the U.S. at 877-762-2974, outside the U.S. at 317-572-3993, or fax 317-572-4002.

For technical support, please visit www.wiley.com/techsupport.

Wiley publishes in a variety of print and electronic formats and by print-on-demand. Some material included with standard print versions of this book may not be included in e-books or in print-on-demand. If this book refers to media such as a CD or DVD that is not included in the version you purchased, you may download this material at http://booksupport.wiley.com. For more information about Wiley products, visit www.wiley.com.

Library of Congress Control Number: 2009937841

ISBN 978-0-470-51012-4 (pbk); ISBN 978-0-470-58407-1 (ebk); ISBN 978-0-470-58408-8 (ebk); ISBN 978-0-470-58409-5 (ebk)

Manufactured in the United States of America

10 9 8 7 6 5 4 3 2

WILEY

About the Authors

Linda Volonino (PhD, MBA, CISSP, ACFE) entered the field of computer forensics and electronic evidence in 1998 with a PhD and MBA in information systems (IS). She's been a guest lecturer on computer forensics and e-discovery at the State University of New York at Buffalo School of Law, and to attorneys and state Supreme Court justices as part of Continuing Legal Education (CLE). She's a computer forensics investigator and e-discovery consultant with Robson Forensic, Inc. working for plaintiff and defense lawyers in civil and criminal cases. In addition to standard e-mail and e-document evidence, she's consulted on cases involving electronically stored information (ESI) from social media sites and handheld devices as part of e-discovery.

Linda's coauthored *Computer Forensics For Dummies* and four textbooks: two on information technology, one on information security, and one on computer forensics. She's published in academic, industry, and law journals on e-discovery and the need for electronic records management as part of pre-litigation readiness. She's a senior editor of Information Systems Management and was Program Chair for the 2009 Conference on Digital Forensics, Security and Law. Linda can be reached via `lvolonino@aol.com`.

Ian J. Redpath holds a Bachelor's degree from Hillsdale College, a JD from the University of Detroit, and an LLM from the University of Wisconsin. He has 34 years experience in litigation and has been admitted to practice in the states of Michigan, Wisconsin, and New York as well as the Federal and Tax Courts. Ian is also a former prosecuting attorney. He has published numerous articles on contemporary issues and topics and coauthored several books.

Ian has taught American Jurisprudence at the University of Clermont-Ferrand School of Law in France and lectures regularly on American Law at the prestigious MGIMO in Russia. He has extensive national and international experience in developing, writing, and presenting continuing education programs.

Currently, Ian is the principal in the Redpath Law Offices with offices in Buffalo and New York City where he specializes in criminal and civil litigation. He can be reached at `IanRedpath@redpathlaw.com`.

Dedication

I would like to dedicate this book to my beautiful wife Liz, and children, Eric, Bridget, and Lauren who provide me with love, inspiration, and support.

– Ian Redpath

Authors' Acknowledgments

Our Project Editor Rebecca Senninger kept us moving forward and doing our best work. Thanks Rebecca! We're also most grateful to Amy Fandrei, Acquisitions Editor, for the expert guidance needed to write a techno-legal book that lawyers, managers, information technologists, and judges may use as a reference.

Special thanks to our hard-working copy editors Brian Walls, Virginia Sanders, and Heidi Unger and our technical editor Jake Frazier. We appreciate your feedback and suggestions for improving our chapters.

Publisher's Acknowledgments

We're proud of this book; please send us your comments at http://dummies.custhelp.com. For other comments, please contact our Customer Care Department within the U.S. at 877-762-2974, outside the U.S. at 317-572-3993, or fax 317-572-4002.

Some of the people who helped bring this book to market include the following:

Acquisitions and Editorial

Project Editor: Rebecca Senninger

Acquisitions Editor: Amy Fandrei

Copy Editor: Brian Walls

Technical Editor: Jake Frazier

Editorial Manager: Leah Cameron

Editorial Assistant: Amanda Graham

Sr. Editorial Assistant: Cherie Case

Cartoons: Rich Tennant
(www.the5thwave.com)

Composition Services

Project Coordinator: Sheree Montgomery

Layout and Graphics: Joyce Haughey, Mark Pinto

Proofreaders: Laura Albert, ConText Editorial Services, Inc.

Indexer: Sherry Massey

Special Help: Virginia Sanders, Heidi Unger

Publishing and Editorial for Technology Dummies

Richard Swadley, Vice President and Executive Group Publisher

Andy Cummings, Vice President and Publisher

Mary Bednarek, Executive Acquisitions Director

Mary C. Corder, Editorial Director

Publishing for Consumer Dummies

Kathleen Nebenhaus, Vice President and Executive Publisher

Composition Services

Debbie Stailey, Director of Composition Services

Table of Contents

Introduction *1*

Who Should Read This Book? 1
About This Book 2
What You're Not to Read 2
Foolish Assumptions 2
How This Book Is Organized 3
    Part I: Examining e-Discovery and ESI Essentials 3
    Part II: Guidelines for e-Discovery and
        Professional Competence 3
    Part III: Identifying, Preserving, and Collecting ESI 4
    Part IV: Processing, Protecting, and Producing ESI 4
    Part V: Getting Litigation Ready 4
    Part VI: Strategizing for e-Discovery Success 5
    Part VII: The Part of Tens 5
    Glossary 5
Icons Used in This Book 5
Where to Go from Here 6

Part 1: Examining e-Discovery and ESI Essentials *7*

Chapter 1: Knowing Why e-Discovery Is a Burning Issue 9
Getting Thrust into the Biggest Change in the Litigation 10
    New rules put electronic documents under a microscope 11
    New rules and case law expand professional responsibilities 12
Distinguishing Electronic Documents from Paper Documents 14
    ESI has more volume 15
    ESI is more complex 15
    ESI is more fragile 16
    ESI is harder to delete 17
    ESI is more software and hardware dependent 18
Viewing the Litigation Process from 1,000 Feet 18
Examining e-Discovery Processes 20
    Creating and retaining electronic records 20
    Identifying, preserving, and collecting data relevant
        to a legal matter 21
    Processing and filtering to remove the excess 22
    Reviewing and analyzing for privilege 22
    Producing what's required 23
    Clawing back what sneaked out 23
    Presenting at trial 24

**Chapter 2: Taking a Close Look at Electronically
Stored Information (ESI)** **25**

Spotting the ESI in the Game Plan 26
Viewing the Life of Electronic Information.. 27
    Accounting for age.. 27
    Tracking the rise and fall of an e-mail 29
    Understanding Zubulake I.. 30
    Taking the two-tier test... 34
Preserving the Digital Landscape... 36
Facing Sticker Shock: What ESI Costs 37
    Estimating hard and hidden costs.. 39
    Looking at the costs of being surprised by a request.................... 40

**Chapter 3: Building e-Discovery Best Practices
into Your Company** **43**

Setting Up a Reasonable Defensive Strategy... 44
    Heeding judicial advice 45
    Keeping ESI intact and in-reach 46
Braking for Litigation Holds 48
    Insuring a stronghold 48
    Getting others to buy-in 49
    Holding on tight to your ESI 50
Putting Best Practices into Place.. 51
Forming Response Teams 54
Putting Project Management into Practice 55
    Tackling the triple constraints.. 56
    Managing the critical path 57
Maintaining Ethical Conduct and Credibility... 57

**Part II: Guidelines for e-Discovery and
Professional Competence** **59**

Chapter 4: The Playbook: Federal Rules and Advisory Guidelines. . .61

Knowing the Rules You Must Play By 62
Deciphering the FRCP 63
    FRCP 1 63
    FRCP 16 63
    FRCP 26 65
    FRCP 33 and 34 66
Applying the Rules to Criminal Cases 66
    F.R. Crim. P. Rule 41.. 71
    F. R. Crim. P. Rule 16... 71
    F. R. Crim. P. Rule 17 and 17.1 71
Learning about Admissibility.. 71
Lessening the Need for Judicial Intervention by Cooperation 73
Limiting e-Discovery... 74

Finding Out About Sanctions 75
Rulings on Metadata... 77
Getting Guidance but Not Authority from Sedona Think Tanks 79
Collecting the Wisdom of the Chief Justices and
    National Law Conference 79
        Minding the e-Discovery Reference Model........................... 80
        Following the Federal Rules Advisory Committee.......................... 81

Chapter 5: Judging Professional Competence and Conduct 83
Making Sure Your Attorney Gives a Diligent Effort...................... 84
    Looking at what constitutes a diligent effort 84
    Searching for evidence.. 85
    Producing ESI 86
    Providing a certification... 86
Avoiding Being Sanctioned... 87
    FRCP sanctions... 87
    Inherent power sanctions... 89
Knowing the Risks Introduced by Legal Counsel 91
    Acting bad: Attorney e-discovery misconduct................... 91
    Relying on the American Bar Association and
        state rules of professional conduct 93
Learning from Those Who Gambled Their Cases and Lost 94
Policing e-Discovery in Criminal Cases....................................... 96

Part III: Identifying, Preserving, and Collecting ESI 99

Chapter 6: Identifying Potentially Relevant ESI 101
Calling an e-Discovery Team into Action.................................... 102
Clarifying the Scope of e-Discovery 104
Reducing the Burden with the Proportionality Principle...................... 107
    Proportionality of scale... 107
    Negotiating with proportionality.................................... 108
Mapping the Information Architecture.. 108
    Creating a data map.. 108
    Overlooking ESI.. 111
    Describing data retention policies and procedures................. 112
    Proving the reasonable accessibility of ESI sources............... 113
Taking Lessons from the Mythical Member................................ 113

**Chapter 7: Complying with ESI Preservation and
a Litigation Hold 115**
Distinguishing Duty to Preserve from Preservation 116
Following The Sedona Conference.. 116
    The Sedona Conference WG1 guidelines 117
    Seeing the rules in the WG1 decision tree 119

Recognizing a Litigation Hold Order and Obligation 119
    Knowing what triggers a litigation hold 120
    Knowing when to issue a litigation hold 120
    Knowing when a hold delay makes you eligible for sanctions 122
    Accounting for downsizing and departing employees 122
Throwing a Wrench into Digital Recycling 123
    Suspending destructive processes 123
    Where do you put a terabyte? 124
Implementing the Litigation Hold 125
    Documenting that custodians are in compliance 127
    Rounding up what needs to be collected 127
    Judging whether a forensics-level preservation is needed 130

Chapter 8: Managing e-Discovery Conferences and Protocols 133
Complying with the Meet-and-Confer Session 133
Preparing for the Meet-and-Confer Session 136
    Preservation of evidence 136
    Form of production 137
    Privileged or protected ESI 138
    Any other issues regarding ESI 139
Agreeing on a Timetable 139
Selecting a Rule 30(b)(6) Witness 140
Finding Out You and the Opposing Party
    May Have Mutual Interests 141

Part 1V: Processing, Protecting, and Producing ESI 143

Chapter 9: Processing, Filtering, and Reviewing ESI 145
Planning, Tagging, and Bagging 146
    Taking a finely tuned approach 147
    Finding exactly what you need 147
    Stop and identify yourself 149
    Two wrongs and a right 150
Learning through Trial and Error 151
Doing Early Case Assessment 152
    Vetting vendors 153
Breaking Out the ESI 154
Crafting the Hunt 156
    Deciding on filters 156
    Keyword or phrase searching 157
    Deduping 157
    Concept searching 158
    Heeding the Grimm roadmap 158
Sampling to Validate 159
    Testing the validity of the search 159
    Documenting sampling efforts 160

Doing the Review 161
    Choosing a review platform.................................... 161
    How to perform a review 163

Chapter 10: Protecting Privilege, Privacy, and Work Product......165

Facing the Rising Tide of Electronic Information 166
Respecting the Rules of the e-Discovery Game 166
    Targeting relevant information 167
    Seeing where relevance and privilege intersect 168
    Managing e-discovery of confidential information 170
    Listening to the Masters 172
Getting or Avoiding a Waiver 172
    Asserting a claim... 173
    Preparing a privilege log 173
    Responding to ESI disclosure.................................. 175
    Applying FRE 502 to disclosure................................ 175
Leveling the Playing Field through Agreement........................ 177
    Checking out the types of agreements...................... 177
    Shoring up your agreements by court order.............. 178

Chapter 11: Producing and Releasing Responsive ESI 181

Producing Data Sets 182
    Packing bytes 183
    Staging production 184
    Being alert to native production motions.................. 185
    Redacting prior to disclosure.................................. 187
Providing Detailed Documentation 190
Showing an Unbroken Chain of Custody 192
Keeping Metadata Intact.. 193

Part V: Getting Litigation Ready 199

Chapter 12: Dealing with Evidentiary Issues and Challenges......201

Looking at the Roles of the Judge and Jury 202
Qualifying an Expert.. 202
Getting Through the Five Hurdles of Admissibility.................. 204
Admitting Relevant ESI... 204
Authenticating ESI 205
    Self-authenticating ESI... 206
    Following the chain of custody 206
    Authenticating specific types of ESI 207
Analyzing the Hearsay Rule.. 208
Providing the Best Evidence 210
Probing the Value of the ESI... 210

Chapter 13: Bringing In Special Forces: Computer Forensics 211

Powering Up Computer Forensics...212
    Knowing when to hire an expert..212
    Knowing what to expect from an expert...214
    Judging an expert like judges do...214
Doing a Scientific Forensic Search 215
Testing, Sampling, and Refining Searches for ESI..216
Applying C-Forensics to e-Discovery 218
    Following procedure...219
    Preparing for an investigation...220
    Acquiring and preserving the image 222
    Authenticating with hash...223
    Recovering deleted ESI..224
    Analyzing to broaden or limit..225
    Expressing in Boolean...226
    Producing and documenting in detail..228
Reinforcing E-Discovery..229
    Fighting against forensic fishing attempts....................................229
    Fighting with forensics on your team...230
Defending In-Depth...231

Part VI: Strategizing for e-Discovery Success.............. 233

Chapter 14: Managing and Archiving Business Records 235

Ratcheting Up IT's Role in Prelitigation...236
    Laying the cornerstone of ERM...236
    Pitching your tent before the storm...237
Telling Documents and Business Records Apart 238
Designing a Defensible ERM Program...240
    Designing by committee...240
    Starting with the basics...240
    Getting management on board with your ERM program.............242
    Crafting a risk-reducing policy..244
    Punching up your e-mail policy 245
Building an ERM Program...246
    Kicking the keep-it-all habit 248
    Doing what you say you are 248
Getting an A+ in Compliance..249

Chapter 15: Viewing e-Discovery Law from the Bench 251

Examining Unsettled and Unsettling Issues 252
    Applying a reasonableness standard 252
    Forcing cooperation 253
    Looking at what's reasonably accessible 254
    Determining who committed misconduct.....................................254

Exploring the Role of the Judge..258
Actively participating...258
Scheduling conferences 259
Appointing experts 259
Determining the scope of costs...262

Chapter 16: e-Discovery for Large-Scale and Complex Litigation.... 263

Preparing for Complex Litigation 263
Ensuring quality control 265
Getting a project management process in place 266
Proving the merits of a case by using ESI...........................266
Educating the Court about Your ESI 267
Using summary judgment and other tools 268
Employing an identification system 268
Form of production..269
Creating document depositories 269
Avoiding Judicial Resolution..270
Determining the Scope of Accessibility....................................271
Doing a good-cause inquiry 272
Cost-shifting...273
Getting Help...274
Partnering with vendors or service providers.................274
Selecting experts or consulting companies......................274

Chapter 17: e-Discovery for Small Cases.......................277

Defining Small Cases that Can Benefit from e-Discovery.......278
Theft of proprietary data and breaches of contract 278
Marital matters...278
Defamation and Internet defamation.................................279
Characterizing Small Matters...280
Keeping ESI out of evidence 280
Shared characteristics with large cases 281
Unique characteristics and dynamics................................282
Proceeding in Small Cases...283
Curbing e-Discovery with Proportionality 286
Sleuthing Personal Correspondence and Files 286

Part VII: The Part of Tens................................. 289

Chapter 18: Ten Most Important e-Discovery Rules 291

FRCP 26(b)(2)(B) Specific Limitations on ESI.........................291
FRCP 26(b)(5)(B) Protecting Trial-Preparation
Materials and Clawback...292
FRCP 26(a)(1)(C) Time for Pretrial Disclosures; Objections.................293
FRCP 26(f) Conference of the Parties; Planning for Discovery.............294

FRCP 26(g) Signing Disclosures and Discovery Requests,
Responses, and Objections 294
FRCP 30(b)(6) Designation of a Witness..295
FRCP 34(b) Form of Production..296
FRCP 37(e) Safe Harbor from Sanctions for Loss of ESI 297
Federal Rules of Evidence 502(b) Inadvertent Disclosure 298
Federal Rule of Evidence 901 Requirement
of Authentication or Identification 298

**Chapter 19: Ten Ways to Keep an Edge on Your
e-Discovery Expertise 301**
The Sedona Conference and Working Group Series 302
Discovery Resources...303
Law Technology News 303
Electronic Discovery Law 304
E-Discovery Team Blog 304
LexisNexis Applied Discovery Online Law Library 305
American Bar Association Journal 305
Legal Technology's Electronic Data Discovery 306
Supreme Court of the United States..306
Cornell Law School Legal Information Institute and Wex 307

Chapter 20: Ten e-Discovery Cases with Really Good Lessons 309
Zubulake v. UBS Warburg, 2003–2005;
Employment Discrimination...309
Qualcomm v. Broadcom, 2008; Patent Dispute 310
Victor Stanley, Inc. v. Creative Pipe, Inc., 2008;
Copyright Infringement...311
Doe v. Norwalk Community College, 2007; the Safe Harbor
of FRCP Rule 37(e) 312
United States v. O'Keefe, 2008; Criminal Case
Involving e-Discovery 313
Lorraine v. Markel American Insurance Co., 2007;
Insurance Dispute 314
Mancia v. Mayflower Textile Services Co., et al., 2008;
the Duty of Cooperate and FRCP Rule 26(g)...315
Mikron Industries Inc. v. Hurd Windows & Doors Inc., 2008;
Duty to Confer 316
Gross Construction Associates, Inc., v. American Mfrs.
Mutual Ins. Co., 2009; Keyword Searches 317
Gutman v. Klein, 2008; Termination Sanction and Spoliation...............318

Glossary *321*

Index *333*

Introduction

● ●

*E*lectronic discovery gone wrong is kryptonite to a legal action, as many have learned since the amended Federal Rules of Civil Procedure (FRCP) took effect in December 2006. Now you may urgently want to learn about e-discovery (short for *electronic discovery*) but don't know who to call, or even better, what to read. *e-Discovery For Dummies* is an end-to-end reference and tutorial written for litigators and jurists, corporate counsel and paralegals, information technology (IT) and human resources (HR) managers, executives and record librarians, and anyone who might file a lawsuit or be the recipient of one. For those not engaged in e-discovery now, the time is fast approaching when having a commanding knowledge of it is going to be vital to your career.

Who Should Read This Book?

e-Discovery For Dummies is for everyone needing an understanding of the e-discovery rules of procedure and the protections they provide, and how to position your case to be covered by those protections. IT, HR, records managers, and others who might be responsible for e-litigation readiness or electronic records management should start reading this book as soon as possible.

CPAs who provide forensic information and damage calculations for clients need to be aware of e-discovery issues, particularly the liability implications of metadata contained in client files. Inadvertent disclosure of metadata in client files could remove legal protections. For example, if a client's metadata is disclosed accidentally, then it may enable opponents to use that metadata against the client's interests.

Insurance companies are enormously concerned and interested in e-discovery. Insurers are like the father of the bride — even though no one pays much attention to him at the event, he pays much of the bill. So insurance companies have one of the largest stakes in e-discovery.

If you know nothing about e-discovery or want to sharpen your litigation strategy, this book's for you.

About This Book

e-Discovery For Dummies is an introduction to the hottest legal issue. The e-discovery rules expand the definition of what's discoverable to include electronically stored information (ESI), require parties to discuss ESI during initial meet-and-confer conferences, may provide a safe harbor against sanctions for routine deletion of ESI, and may protect against a privilege waiver for inadvertent disclosure.

The rulings and opinions of various judges provide invaluable lessons that you and your lawyers can learn from this book, much cheaper than learning through experience. We cover the Advisory Guidelines to better prepare you to understand the process of obtaining, protecting, and presenting ESI. You learn how Federal Rule of Evidence 502, enacted in 2008, provides relief for inadvertent disclosure of items privileged under the attorney-client relationship or protected as work product.

Every company and agency needs to be litigation-ready and know how to proceed when requesting or responding to e-discovery agreements. Preparing for litigation implies that all of these new data repositories must be included in a data and records retention policy and program. Security executives involved in litigation could be called upon to describe their company's records retention policy and be knowledgeable of the systems used to manage their department's data. Lacking a credible program or failing to adhere to the policy is indefensible in court and might expose your company to legal risk.

It's an honest presentation of the issues and challenges, strengths and weaknesses of e-discovery.

What You're Not to Read

Depending on your background in law, criminal justice, investigative methods, or technology, you can skip the stuff you already know. If you're the victim, the accused, the plaintiff, or the defendant, feel free to skip sections that don't relate directly to your case or predicament.

Foolish Assumptions

We make a few conservative assumptions, even though we're serious about issues and advice we offer. We assume that:

> ✔ You need to understand e-discovery.
>
> ✔ You use and have a basic understanding of e-mail, the Internet, and digital devices.
>
> ✔ You have an interest in learning from the experience of others.
>
> ✔ You are considering expanding your career to include e-discovery.
>
> ✔ You realize that this book is not legal advice.

How This Book Is Organized

This book is organized into seven parts. They take you through the basics of e-discovery, ESI, rules, advisories, and litigation readiness. They cover the phases from preservation through production. Specialty issues, such as e-discovery in large cases and small cases and computer forensics, are covered. For a more detailed overview of topics, check out the following sections.

Part I: Examining e-Discovery and ESI Essentials

The book starts by introducing you to the e-discovery laws that have changed the responsibilities of legal and information technology (IT) professionals. You read why every lawsuit and most civil cases can and will involve e-discovery and the accessibility of ESI (as well as ESI that's not reasonably accessible).

You learn that most cases are settled as a result of e-discovery because that's when both sides learn the strengths and weaknesses of their position relative to that of their opposition.

Part II: Guidelines for e-Discovery and Professional Competence

This part gives you an in-depth understanding of the e-discovery amendments, The Sedona Conference advisory guidelines often used by the bench in settling disputes, and the expected standards of legal competence and conduct. Although the Federal Rules and advisories guide e-discovery, the competency of counsel turns them into a winning edge. We present the Electronic Discovery Reference Model (EDRM) as it relates to processes of preserving, collecting, processing, reviewing, and producing ESI.

Part III: Identifying, Preserving, and Collecting ESI

In this part, we cover the first phases of e-discovery, namely the identification, preservation, and collection of ESI. These are the steps to take when a lawsuit is filed. You learn what to do when faced with an e-discovery request and the countdown to the meet and confer with opposing counsel within 99 days.

We discuss the meet-and-confer conference in detail. Being prepared to negotiate during this conference can make the difference between a quick settlement and a prolonged battle. There are no re-negotiations or bailouts for bad agreements.

Part IV: Processing, Protecting, and Producing ESI

In the fourth part, we cover the next set of phases from processing of ESI through review, filtering, and the production of responsive, nonprivileged, redacted ESI. You read many examples of motions, mistakes, and monetary sanctions that could have been avoided.

All ESI issues might arise during these phases, including metadata, privilege, work product, keyword searches, and filtering by keyword, concept, and custodian. This part details the review process, which is the most expensive phase in e-discovery.

Part V: Getting Litigation Ready

In this fifth part, we examine the admissibility and relevance rule of electronic evidence, and forensics methods to recover and preserve it. Rules of evidence are subject to judgment, as are the federal rules of civil procedure. This part also covers advanced e-discovery strategies and issues, some of which are the use of experts, sanctions, depositions, and cost-shifting. We explain methods to authenticate evidence in civil trials. One indisputable duty is to keep the chain of custody intact because you can't repair tainted electronic evidence.

Part VI: Strategizing for e-Discovery Success

In the sixth part, you learn about archiving electronic records, which differs from data backups. We discuss electronic records management (ERM) that's necessary to be ready to respond to a request for ESI. The focus shifts from internal to external. We discuss e-discovery from the perspective of the judges and their powers to encourage parties to practice good faith and dissuade gamesmanship.

For large-scale, high-stakes, or unusual cases, you learn the value of partnering with vendors or litigation services companies to augment your expertise. For small cases, ESI may be the most convincing witness.

Part VII: The Part of Tens

Every *For Dummies* book has The Part of Tens, and we give you three of them. The first one covers the must-know rules. The second focuses on keeping you up-to-date. The third one focuses on the courts and career-advancing lessons.

Glossary

We include an e-discovery dictionary of legal and technical terms used throughout this book.

Icons Used in This Book

Useful clues represented by icons highlight especially significant issues in this book. The following paragraphs (with their representative icons) give you an idea of what to expect when you see these icons.

Time is money, and mistakes waste even more. Save yourself time, effort, and the pain of explaining to the court why you did or did not do something that you should or should not have done. These icons flag paragraphs that can be gold mines of information or land mines to sidestep.

Litigation that spans several years and involves many motions are not amenable to short summaries. The same is true of judges' opinions in cases where litigants or their lawyers made more than a fair share of mistakes. These icons provide an in-depth look at real-world cases and issues — both good and bad.

Sanctions ahead! We flag the land mines with this icon to draw your attention to what the rules mandate and what judges expect you to do correctly.

A heads-up and FYI icon on concepts to keep in mind.

Where to Go from Here

In this book, you find the basics of e-discovery rules, procedures, case law, and litigation readiness, but this is an exploding topic. You can use this book as a reference, how-to guide, and path to lifelong learning. Electronic discovery is not a passing phase. Electronic discovery case law is evolving. Litigants are sliding down the learning curve, which may significantly reduce time, costs, errors, and sanctions. When you know the basics and tactics, you have the foundation to expand your knowledge.

If you're looking for a handy reference to the e-discovery steps or the Federal Rules of Civil Procedure and Federal Rules of Evidence, check out the cheat sheet at www.dummies.com/cheatsheet/ediscovery.

Part I

Examining e-Discovery and ESI Essentials

The 5th Wave

By Rich Tennant

"I'm trying to organize the IT guy's documents, and apparently his file system was informed heavily by the Da Vinci Code."

In this part . . .

This part presents e-discovery in digestible chunks so you understand the essentials of e-discovery at its simplest level. We explain e-discovery laws that have re-written the responsibilities of legal and information technology (IT) professions in Chapter 1. Legal and IT — two groups most unlikely to speak a common language or operate at the same tempo — are most responsible for e-discovery success. Also in Chapter 1, you learn that all electronic content that we create, send, post, search, download, or store has a legal name: electronically stored information, or ESI. We cover why this ESI universe is subject to discovery and cite cases where failing to preserve and produce ESI cost litigants serious amounts of money and essentially gutted their cases.

In Chapter 2, you learn why working with ESI is messy even under the best circumstances. You're introduced to the relationship between the age of ESI and the ability to reach out and retrieve it from its storage media. ESI can be online, offline, gone, or somewhere in between. The ability to reach and retrieve ESI determines its accessibility, which in turn influences its discovery status from the perspective of judges (or *the bench*). You find out why it's best to resolve your ESI disputes with the opposing side rather than turn those disputes over to the bench. Also in Chapter 2, we foreshadow the fate of enterprises unprepared for e-discovery. You start to understand that investing in ESI retention and management tools to get into litigation-ready shape is much less risky than whining about why it's too burdensome to respond to an ESI request. Chapter 3 continues these lessons.

Prelitigation best practices get you into a strong defensive position, as you read in Chapter 3. You learn one of the most crucial lessons — that most cases are settled as a result of e-discovery because it's only then that both sides learn the strengths and weaknesses of the other's case. You don't go all in with no chance of winning, at least not more than once. When you do e-discovery right, you have a powerful offensive or defensive weapon.

"We used to say there's e-discovery as if it was a subset of all discovery. But now there's no other discovery."

—Judge Shira A. Scheindlin (2009),
e-discovery rock-star judge

Chapter 1

Knowing Why e-Discovery Is a Burning Issue

In This Chapter

▶ Diving into e-discovery

▶ Seeing electronic information in 3D

▶ Getting the layout of the litigation process

▶ Understanding the steps in the e-discovery process

*B*eginning in 1938, Federal Rules of Civil Procedure (FRCP) have governed the discovery of evidence in lawsuits and other civil cases. *Discovery* is the investigative phase of a legal case when opponents size up what evidence is, or might be, available. During discovery, the parties in a dispute — the *plaintiff* (party bringing suit) and the *defendant* (the party being sued) — have the right to request any information in any format relevant to the case from their opponent. Each party has to respond with either the information or a really good reason why the information cannot be presented.

Despite several updates, FRCP remained largely limited to paper until 2006. Evidence, on the other hand, had gone electronic and onto hard drives of computers and handheld devices. To synchronize the legal system to the realities of the digital age when almost everything is e-mailed or viewed on an Internet-enabled device, electronic discovery (e-discovery) amendments to the FRCP were enacted on December 1, 2006. Put simply, changes to the FRCP mean that almost all discovery now involves e-discovery.

In this chapter, you discover how e-discovery rules rocked the legal landscape by making *electrically stored information* (ESI) discoverable. You read why you must start thinking about e-discovery long before you're involved in a legal action. Electronic discovery is an inescapable obligation (like paying taxes); you must be able to produce all relevant ESI on demand. To produce data and documents, you have to save them in such a way that you can find, open, and read them. You and your lawyers can expect consequences when stuff goes missing. Armed with this information, you then get familiar with the basic stages in the e-discovery process.

Getting Thrust into the Biggest Change in the Litigation

In April 2006, the United States Supreme Court approved sweeping changes to the Federal Rules of Civil Procedure (FRCP). After getting Congress's approval, the amended FRCP became law on December 1, 2006. These amended rules are aimed at one issue — the discovery of *electronically stored information* (ESI). ESI used as evidence is electronic evidence, or e-evidence. Despite their differences, the terms *ESI* and *e-evidence* are often used interchangeably.

As you can guess from the title, the discovery of anything electronic is called *e-discovery*. With most or all decisive evidence being electronic, you need to understand both the legal and technological dimensions of e-discovery — and depending on your job, you may just be competent in one or the other. We talk about the legal side in Chapter 4, which details the new FRCP. Many U.S. state laws are based on federal laws so there's no escaping e-discovery rules. For a description of the federal rulemaking process, visit uscourts. gov/rules/newrules3.html.

You can download a copy of the 166-page FRCP describing its 86 rules from the U.S. Courts' Web site at www.uscourts.gov/rules/CV2008.pdf. If you're new to the rules, you might hold off reading them until you've read Chapter 4 in this book.

Why did e-discovery rules, in effect, steamroll the litigation landscape? The short answer is that lawyers and litigants were unprepared to comply with this type and volume of discovery and all its complexities. Two reasons account for most of this lack of preparedness.

- ✔ **Lawyers are not IT people.** The huge majority of lawyers never had a course in IT (information technology) or e-discovery in their law schools. Electronic evidence lives in many places and forms that are tough to find, collect, store, and interpret without technical skills.

- ✔ **Electronic discovery must be addressed when a lawsuit is filed.** When litigation initiates, so does the e-discovery clock. Comparing Figure 1-1 to Figure 1-2, you see how the discovery phase of litigation has changed. Prior to December 2006, discovery was an afterthought. Most litigation doesn't go to trial, so cases ended before discovery got started. Not anymore.

No matter the size of your case, you need to make sure your lawyer has a clear understanding of the technologies involved and knowledge of the e-discovery rules to meet and manage his e-discovery duties correctly. If your lawyer lacks the tech expertise and the experience to make e-discovery more efficient, you risk e-discovery going wrong; resulting in you getting sanctioned by the judge or maybe even losing your case.

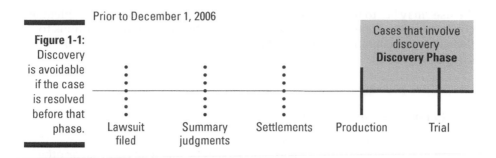

Figure 1-1:
Discovery
is avoidable
if the case
is resolved
before that
phase.

Prior to December 1, 2006

| Lawsuit filed | Summary judgments | Settlements | Production | Trial |

Cases that involve discovery
Discovery Phase

The FRCP applies to every type of litigation. Class action lawsuits, complex corporate fraud, and employment cases (for example, discrimination, wrongful termination, and harassment) involve e-discovery. Government investigations of fraud or improper conduct invariably dig into e-mail, instant messages, contact lists, and appointment calendars. In instances where a marriage is eroding, spouses might want to know and use what the other spouse is searching for on the Internet or texting.

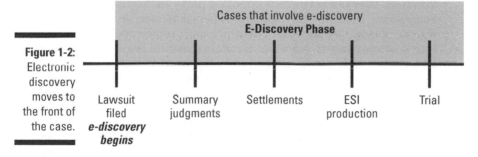

After December 1, 2006

Cases that involve e-discovery
E-Discovery Phase

Figure 1-2:
Electronic
discovery
moves to
the front of
the case.

| Lawsuit filed *e-discovery begins* | Summary judgments | Settlements | ESI production | Trial |

New rules put electronic documents under a microscope

All computer systems, digital devices, and anything with a flash drive used by businesses, government agencies, health care and education institutions, and individuals that store electronic documents (word processing, spreadsheets, calendars, and presentations) are forms of ESI. Everything from terabyte-sized databases to text messages (even Twitter messages, or tweets) may be *discoverable* (subject to discovery) and, therefore, reviewable by others. Contact lists on an iPhone, legacy data on backup tapes, instant messages on a BlackBerry, posts on MySpace, and GPS and EZ-Pass records may be part of the ESI universe.

We use "may be" to temper our statements because privileged and confidential content *may* create exceptions to the rules. You find out about exceptions to the rules, and conditions that cancel (legally, *waive*) those exceptions, in Chapters 4 and 10.

Here's how you should go about finding ESI prior to a trial.

1. **Conduct an initial search.**

   Search data stores, often asking for help from data owners or IT experts, to identify documents, e-mails, spreadsheets, financial records, or other ESI that have been requested. Full-text searching is one of the basic tools used to find documents. Full-text and keyword searching are discussed in Chapter 9. You'll store all documents in a database.

2. **Perform a pre-production review.**

   Review all documents by hand, through a computer review, or most likely using both methods to verify their relevance and to exclude duplicate, privileged, confidential, and irrelevant content. Best practices and pitfalls of pre-production review are covered in Chapter 9.

3. **Perform a post-production review.**

   You hand over the ESI to your opposing party so they can review it. In some cases, the court may appoint a Special Master, or you and your opponent may agree to have a neutral expert review the ES, or you may hire your own expert. A *Special Master* is a neutral lawyer with technical expertise or an IT expert appointed by the court to manage and resolve e-discovery disputes in such areas as forms of production, keywords, and protocols.

During 2009, e-discovery costs amounted to 90 percent of a litigation budget with a majority of the costs associated with the review of ESI. You can take a big bite out of ESI costs by sticking to a disciplined approach to electronic records management in order to reduce the volume of ESI to review. For example, by requiring users to delete personal e-mail and disposing of electronic records that no longer need to be retained, there's a lot less ESI to collect, review, and produce.

New rules and case law expand professional responsibilities

Federal rules and case law pertaining to both e-discovery and e-evidence have added technological competence and ESI management to professional responsibilities. *Case law* is the body of law or precedents created by judges' written opinions and decisions. Rules are interpreted in case law. That is, what the rules are interpreted to mean are determined by judges' opinions, which create case law.

For example, case law on how effectively your keyword search methodology has met its discovery obligations were created by the opinions of judges in three cases: *USA v. O'Keefe* (D.D.C. Feb. 18, 2008), *Equity Analytics v. Lundin* (D.D.C. Mar. 7, 2008), and *Victor Stanley, Inc. v. Creative Pipe, Inc.* (D. Md. May 29, 2008). The case law warns that a lawyer's failure to search an e-discovery database competently will lead to a bad outcome. Subsequent cases involving disputes over keyword or text searching often refer to those decisions.

You can find the text of significant e-discovery opinions using the federal court system's PACER (Public Access to Court Electronic Records) at http://pacer.psc.uscourts.gov. There's a small fee for accessing certain records.

Groundbreaking e-discovery case law stemmed from five opinions in *Zubulake v. U.B.S. Warburg*. *Zubulake* was an employment discrimination case in the Southern District of New York that resulted in opinions that are still referred to as the gold standard in e-discovery. You find out about the Zubulake opinions in Chapter 4.

FRCP requires you to quickly find ESI when required by the court. Waiting until you're facing an e-discovery request (actually, it's a *demand*) to start preparing for one can lead to severe sanctions.

Imagine waiting until a fire has started to install a sprinkler system, develop evacuation plans, or conduct fire drills. Inarguably, the new rules and case law have expanded the job descriptions of managers, lawyers, paralegals, litigation supporters, IT administrators, and data custodians.

Your attorneys and paralegals need to be IT proficient. Your attorneys need to know what ESI to request and to be able to defend their requests when vigorously challenged by the opposition. Attorneys also need to understand your IT infrastructure in order to comply with the request, prevent the destruction of evidentiary ESI (see the nearby sidebar about AMD and Intel), and keep a record of searches that you've conducted to validate the effectiveness of your searches. Your entire IT department must cooperate with your legal team. You must be able to identify, preserve, and collect ESI. With so much information potentially subject to an e-discovery order, your entire legal team — IT professionals and lawyers — must understand both IT and the law so you inadvertently or deliberately don't delete ESI that you're required to preserve.

Biggest e-discovery case catches Intel unprepared

In 2005, Advanced Micro Devices (AMD) brought a lawsuit against its archrival Intel for alleged anticompetitive practices in the chipmaker market. Both parties recognized that they faced the largest e-discovery ever. Estimates of production were roughly "a pile 137 miles high."

The Special Master appointed by the court to hear evidence from both AMD and Intel recommended that Intel be compelled to produce documents that it had declined to submit. In March 2007, Judge Joseph A. Farnan, Jr. gave Intel 30 days to recover more than 1,000 e-mails that it should have but did not preserve.

Intel faced several problems. Its e-mail system running on Microsoft Exchange servers automatically purged employee e-mail every 35 days and senior executives' e-mail every 60 days. Intel used nonindexed backup tapes designed for disaster recovery that were not suited for e-discovery. Trying to find all of the requested e-mail messages that contained specific keywords took a staggering amount of time because each backup tape had to be mounted to restore the contents in order to get them into shape to be searched and reviewed.

In a March 5, 2007 letter to Judge Farnan, Intel's lawyer advised the court and AMD of its extensive and expensive remediation efforts to find and recover lost e-mails. For e-mails sent by employees that hadn't been preserved as they should have, Intel planned to locate them from the e-mail in-boxes of employees who'd received them. The letter also stated:

"the overall scope of the e-mails and documents Intel will be producing is sweeping in breadth and magnitude — and will encompass the equivalent of tens of millions of pages of material from many hundreds of employees with overlapping involvement in communications, both internal and external."

The court scheduled the *AMD v. Intel* case for trial in February 2010.

Being unprepared is expensive. An unprepared manufacturing company spent $800,000 filtering its unmanaged e-mail system in response to an e-discovery request. Roughly 88 percent of their e-mails were irrelevant to the litigation and weren't produced.

Distinguishing Electronic Documents from Paper Documents

When you think of new technology (such as electronic documents) in terms of older technology (circa paper), you don't appreciate its distinctive qualities and capabilities. Legend has it that when electricity was invented and electrical lights replaced gas lamps in 1879, people would change their light bulbs quickly so electricity wouldn't leak out of the socket. Warning signs were posted that read "This room is equipped with Edison Electric Light. Do not attempt to light with match. Simply turn key on wall by the door." In fine print at the bottom of the signs read "The use of electricity for lighting is in no way harmful to health, nor does it affect the soundness of sleep."

The key point is that a technological understanding of electronic documents, devices, and how they are managed is important — so that you don't take a match to them out of ignorance. A helpful approach is to start by comparing and contrasting characteristics of ESI and paper, which we do in the following sections.

Research firm Gartner found that nearly 90 percent of U.S. companies with revenue exceeding $1 billion are facing an average of 147 lawsuits at any given time, and that the average cost to defend a corporate lawsuit exceeds $1.5 million per case.

ESI has more volume

The amount of ESI created per person is measured in megabytes (MB) — roughly 800MB per year. One MB equals 1,048,576 (or 2^{20}) bytes, which would hold the content of a medium-sized novel. A Fortune 1000 pharmaceutical company with more than 70,000 employees archives 35 terabytes (TB) of new e-mail data every year. One TB is roughly 1.1 trillion bytes. The trivia question is, "How many pages of data equal one terabyte?" The answer is 75 million pages. Of the 60 billion e-mails sent worldwide on a daily basis, 25 billion are business-related.

Clearly, the volume of ESI is tough to fathom. Unlike paper, the volume of ESI multiplies because ESI *replicates itself.* When you send e-mail, a copy goes into your sent mail folder and another arrives in each of the receivers' inboxes, which might get stored on e-mail servers or archived. With paper documents, creating multiple copies requires more time and effort.

ESI is more complex

Electronic documents provide more recordkeeping information than a paper copy because metadata are embedded within it. *Metadata* is essentially the history of a document written with invisible ink. Every comment, edit, iteration of a document is hidden within that document, chronicling its life. There is also embedded data frequently stored with an ESI document, such as formulas in spreadsheets. Microsoft Office automatically embeds many different types of metadata in word processing, spreadsheet, and other applications. Examples of metadata are

- ✓ Title, subject, and author
- ✓ Location where the file is saved

✔ Dates and precise times when the document was created, accessed, modified, and printed

✔ Comments, revision number, total editing time, and the template used to create it

Metadata is discoverable when needed or relevant to a matter at hand. For example, you can use this information when there's a question of when a document was created or downloaded, whether it was modified, or backdated. Metadata may help authenticate a document, or establish facts material to a dispute, such as when a file was created or accessed, or when an e-mail message was sent.

Seeking out and viewing metadata embedded in a document is *mining* the document. Many e-discovery disputes are caused by, or because of, metadata. Those disputes are so significant they've led to case law.

Williams v. Sprint is a landmark case concerning metadata. It established the standard that the producing party should produce electronic documents with their metadata intact.

By mining a document, your attorney can view revisions made to the document, comments added by other users who reviewed the document, and whether it was drafted from a template. The disclosure of metadata can lead to the disclosure of client confidences and secrets, litigation strategy, editorial comments, legal issues raised by the client, and other confidential information. See Chapter 10 for explanations of these issues.

ESI is more fragile

Electronic documents are much easier to alter than paper documents without leaving a visible sign of the alteration. The sender of e-mail messages can spoof, or fake, the sender's identity — a spammer's tool of the trade. Data and files can be modified deliberately in numerous ways that may be detectable only with computer forensic techniques. We discuss recovering deleted data in Chapter 2. (For more computer forensics techniques, check out *Computer Forensics For Dummies,* by Linda Volonino and Reynaldo Anzaldua.)

Files can become corrupted. Hard drives crash. Users accidentally or deliberately can overwrite a file by saving a new file with the same filename as an existing one. Backup tapes get re-used, lost, stolen, or may break or get corrupted. Auto-delete policies may delete e-mails after a certain amount of time, even without an intentional action to delete them.

Figure 1-3 contrasts how paper and ESI are destroyed or altered and how they are preserved. Because ESI exists only on some storage media and that media may be overwritten, corrupted, or otherwise be unreadable, you should take affirmative steps to preserve it. Absent deliberate action to preserve the ESI, the expectation is that it will be destroyed or altered. The courts understand this principle. So must you.

Figure 1-3:
Differences
in how
paper and
ESI are
destroyed
and
preserved.

	Affirmative Steps	**Passivity**
Paper	Destroy, alter	Preserve
ESI	Preserve	Destroy, alter

ESI is harder to delete

Electronic documents are much more difficult to dispose of than paper documents even though they're fragile. The fragility/persistence paradox causes a lot of confusion. Jeff Rothenberg, a senior computer scientist at RAND, captured the paradox by pointing out humorously that "digital information lasts forever, or five years — whichever comes first." RAND (www.rand.org) is a nonprofit institution whose mission is to conduct research and analysis to help improve policy and decision-making.

For example, changing the data or formula in a cell of an Excel spreadsheet could be a *destructive change* (no traces of the change) if there are no other copies of that file or tracking changes is turned off. A destructive change or update is one that destroys the prior contents beyond recovery or detection. If you instead delete the Excel file from a hard drive and take the extra step of deleting it from your Recycle Bin, the entire file will remain intact in the same position on the drive unless it is overwritten. You read more about what happens when a file is deleted in Chapter 2. Computer forensics software could recover that file along with information about when it was deleted.

Deleting documents is futile if they were saved to a server, backed up, or e-mailed. Misunderstanding persistence may lead to the discovery of information that was never intended to be retained or that no one knew existed.

There's also the auto-recover or auto-save feature found in software programs that prevents data loss by automatically creating a backup copy of any currently open document every few minutes or other time interval. This so-called *replicant data* is stored on the hard drive as separate documents. Because they may not be deleted when the application program (such as Word) closes, they persist as copies of documents long since changed or deleted.

ESI is more software and hardware dependent

Data is unreadable or meaningless when separated from its original or native software environment. You need software to open and view a file correctly.

If you have five-and-a-quarter inch floppy disks and no computer with that drive, you cannot get at those files. If you don't have the correct software version, you can't open the file. Files stored on floppy disks, Zip drives, or other outdated media can't be accessed without hardware that can read them. If information has been transferred to backup tape, it may be difficult to restore the information because of technology upgrades or deterioration of the tape. When you change accounting software applications, for instance, you may not be able to access legacy (old) data years afterward.

Viewing the Litigation Process from 1,000 Feet

When you get involved in the litigation process, some milestones you can be involved with are shown in Figure 1-4. Notice the rather tight timeline and the two deadlines, which are specified by the amended FRCP. Total elapsed time from when the complaint is served (or lawsuit filed) until your lawyer submits your e-discovery plan to the court is only 120 days. The trial may be scheduled far into the future, which happened with *AMD v. Intel*. AMD filed the complaint in 2005; the trial is scheduled for 2010.

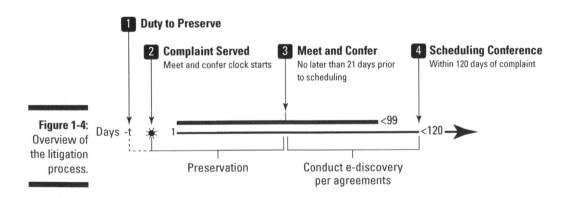

Figure 1-4: Overview of the litigation process.

Although the purpose of the new rules is to provide early structure, uniformity, and predictability to the litigation process, the reality is that right from Day 1 of a lawsuit, you must be ready to start evaluating with your IT team and legal counsel where you stand in terms of your ESI.

Here are the deadlines you need to observe:

✔ **Time minus zero:** Duty to preserve. You need to take affirmative action — active and timely measures — to prevent the destruction or alteration of what might be relevant e-evidence. This duty generally begins when you reasonably anticipate a legal action. That's a tough duty to comply with. Clairvoyance would be helpful because the scope of what needs to be preserved and when are not clear.

Accept that it's difficult under the best of circumstances to know when your duty to preserve has triggered or what you need to preserve. Consult with your in-house counsel on when your duty to preserve ESI kicks in.

✔ **Day 1:** Complaint served. You're on solid ground here because there's no mistaking that a lawsuit is in play. This action starts a clock that counts off days.

✔ **By Day 99:** Meet-and-confer session. You must participate in a meet-and-confer session during which you cooperate with your opponent to negotiate an e-discovery plan. This type of cooperation is new and also a bit of a shock to the legal system that's used to being adversarial. The list of topics to negotiate includes the following:

• Any issues relating to preserving discoverable ESI

• Any issues relating to search, disclosure, or discovery of ESI

• Format in which ESI should be produced

• Scope of ESI holdings

• Estimated costs in terms of difficulty, risk, time, and money of producing the ESI

✔ **By Day 120:** Scheduling conference. A scheduling conference is a hearing attended by all attorneys — yours and your opponents — and the judge to schedule certain dates and deadlines for the case. This event is generally the first time you come before the court.

By forcing these events early on in a case, by way of the FRCP amendments and case law, you really have no choice but to be ready to move forward with e-discovery at the start of a case.

Examining e-Discovery Processes

When you're involved in the e-discovery process, regardless of the type of case or investigation, you need to perform certain functions and meet requirements. Expect that none of the requirements is easy or cheap (in terms of time or money). On the plus side, performing them correctly saves time, effort, disruption, and stress. You face the following e-discovery functions.

Creating and retaining electronic records

Getting ready for e-discovery requires you being proactive. A standard used to evaluate proactive readiness is *reasonableness*. Your ability to demonstrate reasonableness starts with having established control over data, documents, and other electronic records. The base on which e-discovery is built is electronic records management (ERM). ERM is known by other names, such as records and information management, or RIM.

Here's how to set up an electronics rights management system:

1. **Develop an electronic record retention policy.**

   In light of litigation trends and declining storage costs, you can fall into the trap of believing that it's wise to save generously. Developing a keep-it-all retention policy is not the best approach because it focuses on the wrong factor — storage costs.

   You may think the FRCP requires you to save everything or save all e-mails. Regulated industries or certain types of companies, such as those in the financial, healthcare, and pharmaceutical sectors, have government regulations in place such as save all communications for seven years. But absent such regulation, the Supreme Court has indicated that you can set your own reasonable retention policy.

   Even if storage is cheap, management is costly. Good ERM is expensive because of the management, not the storage. As you read in Chapters 2 and 3, you need to keep your eye on the costs of reviewing electronic records to identify responsive ones. Define what is essential and needed as opposed to saving everything.

   Without an enforceable retention program and a secure, auditable archive and electronic records management solution, the costs associated with e-discovery are daunting, as you read in the *AMD v Intel* case.

2. **Implement the electronic records retention policy.**

   Even your best electronic records retention policy is of little use if employees don't implement it in a correct and uniform manner. Everyone who deals with records — employees, contract workers, interns, and vendors — must receive sufficient and proper training on the policy. You need to document the training in detail.

3. **Monitor compliance with the policy.**

   Most likely, your retention program is partially automated and partially manual because end users need to categorize their records. To verify that retention requirements continue to be met, you have to monitor compliance.

4. **Destroy electronic records at the end of retention periods.**

   When electronic records no longer need to be retained, you need a secure way to destroy them.

5. **Change policies when you reasonably foresee litigation.**

   As soon as you reasonably expect to be involved in litigation, you must immediately set aside your ordinary electronic record retention program and implement a more demanding policy. This litigation-hold policy is critical, as you read in Part III. The litigation-hold policy must comply with the special requirements established at the meet-and-confer session and the scheduling conference.

No "model" electronic records retention program fits all. You should base your retention program on a case-by-case examination of your business, the legal and regulatory requirements of your industry and jurisdiction, and what use your company is likely to make of the documents, both for business and litigation purposes.

Identifying, preserving, and collecting data relevant to a legal matter

Assuming that electronic records are managed properly, the next step when facing litigation is to identify the relevant records, preserve them so they cannot be altered, and collect them for further review.

Methods used to identify relevant ESI may have been agreed to at the meet and confer or scheduling conference — although the duty to identify and preserve did start before this conference, when litigation was reasonably anticipated. If the meet and confer or scheduling conference has already happened, ask your lawyer whether an agreement is in place.

You have to preserve the ESI until it's needed. Preservation takes many forms, as discussed in Chapters 2 and 7. One of your difficulties at this stage is preserving data that is in use by the business. A lot of attention in case law has focused on data that is not reasonably accessible (see Chapters 2 and 3). Equally challenging is preserving live data because you cannot simply hand over a backup tape.

The standard for duty to preserve comes from the opinion of District Court Judge Shira A. Scheindlin, from the Southern District of New York, in *Zubulake v. UBS Warburg LLC*, 220 F.R.D. 212 (S.D.N.Y., Oct. 22, 2003). That case is referred to as *Zubulake IV* because it was the fourth in a series of what are called the *Zubulake decisions*.

Processing and filtering to remove the excess

As with every stage in the e-discovery process, there are strategies and best practices for the processing and filtering of ESI. After preserving and collecting the ESI, you'll confront the costly tasks of processing and reviewing the data for responding to the investigation, claim, or litigation.

Determining what to process is a balancing act of costs and risks. Gartner estimates the cost of reviewing 1GB for e-discovery is $18,750. Clearly, costs are reduced by reducing the volume to be filtered. Risks are increased by reducing the amount of ESI to process because relevant e-evidence might be excluded. Breaching e-discovery obligations can result in sanctions or worse even if processing and filtering were done in good faith. In Chapter 9, we explain this critical stage in detail.

Reviewing and analyzing for privilege

Confidential conversations and communications that are protected by law from being used as evidence or revealed to others are referred to as *privileged*. Examples of privilege are conversations or letters between a person and an attorney (*attorney-client privilege*), therapist, physician, priest, minister, or spouse. Privilege is a major source of argument between opposing lawyers. Unless there's an exception, privileged ESI is not discoverable. There are an almost interminable number of exceptions to privilege.

You must review all ESI to identify what is and is not privileged. This stage may be the most expensive depending on the stakes of the case. ESI that you must review visually is much more costly than a coarser review using software for the same volume of ESI.

We talk more about privilege in Chapter 10.

Producing what's required

You start with the universe of ESI, filter out what's irrelevant, duplicated, or privileged, and then have the pool of ESI to produce. Before producing the ESI, you may need to do additional reviews.

If form of production was not specified by the requesting party at the meet-and-confer session, you might have some options. Producing ESI in native format is common because it's cheaper than having a forensics image created. With native production, if it existed as a .docx file, you produce it as a .docx file. Turn to Chapters 11 and 13 for more info about how to produce ESI.

Complications emerge when you have documents with attachments, for example, e-mail messages with attachments or project management files with attached resource files. Other complications are identified in Chapter 10.

FRCP Rule 34(b)(ii) allows you to produce ESI in a form or forms in which you ordinarily maintain it. Other reasonably usable forms may also be acceptable.

There are pros and cons concerning form of production. When balancing production risks and costs, keep in mind that the form of production most likely must include the metadata.

Clawing back what sneaked out

If ESI is produced that should not have been, a situation known as *inadvertent disclosure,* you can request its return via a clawback agreement. Revealing the content of your privileged communications or documents to your opponent is suboptimal because you can't take back what they've learned about you. Despite this downside, clawbacks are not unusual. When review or processing is not done thoroughly, you'll produce ESI that you shouldn't have. The consequences for not producing on schedule because the review is incomplete may be worse than the risks associated with clawback.

Clawback agreements may be discussed during the meet-and-confer session. Despite any agreements, numerous conditions apply to clawbacks. Courts might have to decide whether the producing party has met those clawback conditions.

We talk more about clawback agreements in Chapter 10.

Presenting at trial

Judges have little to no patience with lawyers who appear before them and don't understand their ESI or the ESI of the opposing side. The same applies to you if you're called upon to testify on behalf of your company's ESI retention policies, storage locations, or other e-discovery issues in court. No one can operate effectively in the courtroom without understanding e-evidence, where ESI is created and stored, how to collect and review it, how to recover it in a forensically sound manner, and how to have it admitted into evidence at trial. Chapter 5 discusses the professional competence and conduct of your lawyer.

You want to make sure that your lawyer and all your company's witnesses are armed with the knowledge to competently and confidently testify in court. Make time for these lessons. When your lawyers asks for information, be sure to prepare reports and diagrams that non-technical people (the judge or members of the jury) can understand.

Chapter 2

Taking a Close Look at Electronically Stored Information (ESI)

In This Chapter

▶ Keeping a step ahead of your opposition

▶ Watching ESI as time goes by

▶ Locking down discoverable ESI

▶ Preparing for shocking costs

*L*itigation is complex, expensive, disruptive, and risky — issues well-known to those in information technology (IT). Litigation costs of the Fortune 500 firms in 2006 — the year that e-discovery amendments to the Federal Rules of Civil Procedure (FRCP) went into effect — were an estimated $210 billion, or a hefty 33 percent of after-tax profits. Losers can be facing a multimillion dollar price tag. As you read in this chapter, being prepared for litigation has its rewards, and cashing in on them requires understanding electronically stored information (ESI). For example, your company may be pressured into settling the case, regardless of its merits, because of the inability to find, or the cost of finding, necessary documents or e-mail messages.

ESI is at the core of e-discovery responsibilities — whether it's understanding your computer systems, collecting or preserving ESI, preparing for depositions, or not getting outsmarted by the opposing party. In this chapter, you get up to speed on ESI language as it's defined by noteworthy court opinions and the rules. A group of judges, through their mini-landmark decisions, have spearheaded efforts to define and interpret ESI standards and terminology.

Knowing how ESI storage affects the ease of its discovery is your starting point when preparing electronic records retention plans and prelitigation readiness strategies. Storage can be active, near active, offline, or archived. If you have an understanding of IT and ESI terminology and the relationship between ESI and litigation, you're ready to negotiate, persuade, request, and defend.

Spotting the ESI in the Game Plan

Think of cases and their investigations as competitions between players on opposing full-contact sports teams. Both sides want to gain access or block access to evidence to help them win. Competition can resemble the fierceness of a Stanley Cup playoff, where the goalie's purpose is to block access to the net while the opposing team fights to gain access to it.

We look at the issues in the fight over the accessibility of ESI. Specifically, in this chapter you find out about these types of technology-related disputes:

✔ Whether ESI is or is not subject to discovery

✔ Whether ESI is reasonably accessible and recoverable

✔ Whether all requested and responsive ESI has been turned over

✔ Who will pay to produce

When your team gets into disputes with your opposing party, everybody's costs increase. Why? If disputes hit an impasse, the dispute may get pushed to the judge for resolution. To avoid having the judge serve as referee, the rules reward cooperation and punish anything less. The key to cooperation and cost-containment is having a thorough understanding the ESI terminology. You can see its importance by looking at what's discussed and debated at the meet-and-confer conference:

✔ What ESI is available

✔ Places where ESI resides

✔ Difficulty producing the ESI

✔ Which formats the ESI will be produced in

✔ Estimated cost of production

Your job is to provide your legal team with this information so that they can negotiate from a position of strength. Raw (unrefined) ESI requests increase e-discovery costs and waste the court's time, and can cast doubt on your lawyer's ESI IQ. A judge may be more willing to negotiate or exercise leniency with e-discovery obligations if you're knowledgeable and honest and don't try to hide or destroy evidence. If a judge believes that you don't understand ESI or don't want to follow e-discovery rules, he may naturally be impatient and more demanding.

Best to resolve disputes before they end up on the bench

Courts don't accept ignorance (such as "the request is too vague") or being unprepared ("I can't find it") as an excuse for not producing ESI relevant to a lawsuit. That would be like telling the Internal Revenue Service (IRS) that you didn't pay your taxes because its directions were too vague or you couldn't find your receipts. There's no good outcome. In *Johnson v. Kraft Foods N. A.*, defendants objected to the terms *databases, record layout,* and *data* *dictionaries,* claiming they were vague and ambiguous, even though the plaintiff had provided definitions of those terms. Not persuaded by their excuses, the judge overruled their objection on the grounds that counsel could and should have known their meanings. Wasting a judge's time with obvious lies about ESI is a sign of bad faith that may easily put you on the bad side of the court, where you might just stay.

Viewing the Life of Electronic Information

Your company's electronic records have a life span. Ideally, you have an electronic records management (ERM) plan in place, which includes keeping all electronic records from the time of creation (or receipt) until their required retention period or their value expires, whichever is later.

You must preserve electronic records relevant to current or reasonably foreseeable litigation regardless of whether its retention period has passed or you feel it's no longer of value. At least, that's what's supposed to happen. You can check out methods to preserve electronic records in Chapters 8, 13, and 14.

Accounting for age

Electronically stored information ages, and it doesn't age well. ESI becomes less accessible as it gets older. As accessibility decreases, the costs of finding, recovering, and getting it into readable shape increase quickly. This predicament is recognized in Federal Rule 26 (see Chapter 4), which provides protection from excessive or expensive e-discovery requests, except when a party doesn't deserve that protection. As an electronic record ages, how and where you store it changes, too. Electronic records are kind of like clothes.

Items you wear often are stored in the easiest-to-reach closets. This quick-reach storage space is at a premium, so it's used only for the most active clothes. Hobby or seasonal items that are worn less often, such as fishing, golfing, snowboarding, or hunting gear, are kept somewhere in your home but not with active clothes. Clothing that's out of style or no longer fits may be packed up and moved to the crawl space in the attic, where it awaits the unlikely event that a retro look becomes popular or a diet plan works. The latter group consists of items you never really expect to wear again, but you're also not ready to get rid of. At the extreme, items may be donated, converted to rags, or thrown out. The same sort of organization that you use for clothing happens with ESI.

Computer data storage, or simply *storage* or *memory*, refers to devices and recording media that retain ESI for some interval of time for retrieval later. Storage systems are inevitable for computing. All computing platforms, from handheld devices to super computers, use storage systems for storing data temporarily or permanently. There are three types of basic storage types and their corresponding degree of accessibility, including the following:

✔ **Online:** *Online* in this context means that you have immediate (direct) access to the files. Files saved to your hard drive are online because when you click a file's icon, the file opens immediately. Even files that you can't find on your laptop (perhaps because you didn't organize them intelligently) still fall under the heading of online.

Online media are random-access media. *Random access,* also known as *direct access,* simply means that you can access a stored file directly regardless of its location on the storage medium, as shown in Figure 2-1. *Sequential access* is the opposite of random access because files are accessed in the order of their storage. Because they're sequential, if you want to read any particular file or block of data stored on tape, you must read the tape from the beginning, as with any type of tape recorder. See Table 2-1 for a comparison of random and sequential storage and access.

Figure 2-1:
Random access compared to sequential access of files.

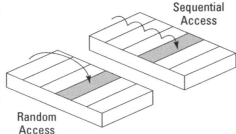

Sequential Access

Random Access

✔ **Near-line:** Near-line is a contraction of *near-online*. *Near-line storage* is removable media, such as DVDs, CDs, or flash drives, that store files randomly. When you use near-line storage, the files are available to you in a short period, such as within a few minutes. ESI is reasonably accessible because you can pop in a DVD or flash drive and quickly get access to its contents. Like online, near-line storage allows for random access to the ESI.

✔ **Offline:** ESI that's offline isn't readily available. With *offline storage*, you typically store files on magnetic tape that requires restoration in order to be read. The tapes themselves are transferred to another location for physical storage. Magnetic tape is a sequential storage medium and is often used as backup for disaster recovery situations.

Table 2-1	Comparison of Random and Sequential File Storage		
Storage Type	**Arrangement of ESI on Media**	**Access**	**Type of Media**
Random	Files are stored in available spaces on the media.	The time to access any of the files is equal because of direct access.	Disk, flash drive, CD, DVD
Sequential	Files are stored in the same order in which they were transferred to the media.	The time to access a file depends on its position on the tape.	Tape

The manner in which files are stored to media determines how you access or retrieve them. Also, the type of media determines how the files are stored. The time it takes to find a specific file depends on whether the storage is sequential or random.

Tracking the rise and fall of an e-mail

To put the idea of the life of ESI into practice, take a look at the life of one of the most popular types: e-mail. As much as 70 percent of all company information is contained in or attached to e-mail. The life of a work-related e-mail from a client may progress as follows:

✔ You receive an e-mail in your inbox. After reading it, you move it into your Client folder. At this point, the message is online, residing on your company's e-mail server.

✔ After 21 days, the e-mail is automatically backed up to less-expensive tape storage, removing traces of its existence from the e-mail server.

✔ After 365 days, the e-mail is marked for destruction according to the company's record retention policy. ESI that's marked, but not overwritten, continues to exist as residual data.

✔ On day 390, the actual destruction of the e-mail occurs when the backup tape is reused, overwriting the information that was marked for destruction.

ESI transitions through several storage media to make room for new and incoming ESI. Your e-mail can be anywhere in its life span when an e-discovery request calls for it. The ease with which you can locate it depends on where it is. Stated another way, the burden associated with locating that e-mail is

✔ Lowest when the e-mail is stored on the e-mail server (a server is a hard drive)

✔ Highest when the e-mail has been moved to backup media that's offline

✔ A moot point when it has been destroyed through the overwrite process

FRCP and Federal Rules of Evidence are general guidelines, not detailed processes. So it's up to the judges to determine whether ESI is reasonably accessible. Judges recognize that e-discovery burdens and costs depend on the ESI's accessibility, which changes as it ages. The accessibility of ESI is one of the reasons why the meet-and-confer conference happens early in the litigation. You want to catch the ESI in its earliest stage and preserve it from destruction — assuming, of course, it hasn't already reached that state.

Courts are becoming increasingly stern with both requesting and producing parties who don't prepare for the meet-and-confer conference and who then must revise agreements they've made. Preparation includes preserving all potentially relevant ESI. If you don't, you might get rebuked by the judge, and when you lose the judge's trust, you won't easily get it back.

Understanding Zubulake 1

One of the earliest e-discovery case laws created a way to approach the accessibility issue that's discussed in the preceding section. The case, *Zubulake v. UBS Warburg LLC* (S.D.N.Y. 2003), is referred to as *Zubulake I.* UBS, the defendant, is a financial advisory and securities business.

The complications that can come up in handling ESI became clear in 2004, when U.S. District Judge Shira A. Scheindlin wrote a series of influential opinions in *Zubulake.* Five separate rulings and hundreds of pages of analysis went into

✔ Figuring out what ESI is discoverable

✔ Determining how the cost of retrieving, copying, and distributing electronic records should be shared by the parties

✔ Deciding whether sanctions should be imposed for failing to produce requested ESI

The case was so influential that it was partially written into the FRCP amendments in 2006. Because of the importance of the first *Zubulake* case, understanding the nature of the e-discovery dispute is helpful.

Zubulake was an employment (gender) discrimination case filed in 2003 by Laura Zubulake, who was an equities trader at UBS. After the lawsuit was filed, UBS objected to Laura's request for responsive e-mails from August 1999 when she was hired through October 2001 when she was fired. She requested all e-mails sent by or between UBS employees concerning her. Archived e-mails existed only on backup tapes and optical drives.

According to Christopher Behny, who was deposed to explain UBS's e-mail retention policies, all e-mails sent or received by UBS employees were stored on backup tapes. UBS's automated backup program created a snapshot of all e-mails on a given server at the time the backup was made. Of the many ESI issues, several of them are pointed out here:

✔ UBS had redundant e-mail backup and preservation protocols. E-mails were backed up on backup tapes and on optical disks.

- A copy of all e-mails that UBS traders sent to or received from external sources was simultaneously written onto optical disks. Optical disks are neither erasable nor rewritable, so they couldn't be overwritten.

- Internal e-mails were stored on the tape backup system but not on the optical system.

- UBS had retained each optical disk used since the system was put into place in mid-1998.

- The optical disks could be searched easily using the Tumbleweed program.

✔ UBS backed up its e-mails at three time intervals. The protocols were as follows:

- E-mails were backed up daily, at the end of each day. Daily backup tapes were kept for 20 working days.

- E-mails were backed up weekly, on Friday nights. Weekly tapes were retained for one year.

- E-mails were backed up monthly, on the last business day of the month. Monthly tapes were retained for three years.

- At the end of the tapes' retention schedule, they were recycled or reused.

Because of the timing of the backups, some e-mails were never backed up. For example, if a user both received and deleted an e-mail on the same day, it wouldn't reside on any backup tape.

✔ The Security and Exchange Commission's (SEC) Rule 17a-4 requires every broker and dealer to

". . . preserve for a period of not less than 3 years, the first two years in an accessible place . . . [o]riginals of all communications received and copies of all communications sent by such member, broker or dealer (including inter-office memoranda and communications) relating to his business as such."

UBS claimed that some of the ESI requested by Laura was inaccessible, in part because of cost. Restoring those e-mails would cost approximately $175,000, excluding the cost of attorney time. Each backup tape would take an estimated five days to restore. Because each tape represents a snapshot of the hard drive of one server in a given month, each server/month had to be restored separately on a hard drive. Then, using the Double Mail program, an individual's e-mail file could be extracted and exported to a Microsoft Outlook data file. After all those preparations to access the e-mail files, they could then be opened in Outlook and searched.

In deciding the issue of accessibility in response to UBS, Judge Scheindlin set precedent. She looked at the type of media on which the ESI is stored and the cost to produce it. Production costs depend on the accessibility of the ESI, which in turn depends on the media on which it is stored. The court identified five sources, or categories, of data used by most companies and listed them in order of decreasing accessibility. Notice the similarities and differences between these legal definitions of data sources and the technical definitions of stored data:

✔ **Active, online data:** The active stage is when the ESI is being created, received, or processed; or when it must be quickly and frequently accessed. Online storage involves magnetic disks, such as hard drives, which provide access within milliseconds.

✔ **Near-line data:** This category involves automated or robotic storage systems. Access speeds range from a few milliseconds up to two minutes. The storage media, such as optical disks, are removable.

Accessible versus inaccessible in federal cases

In the determination of whether ESI is accessible for e-discovery, Judge Scheindlin stated:

"Of these, the first three categories are typically identified as accessible, and the latter two as inaccessible. The difference between the two classes is easy to appreciate. Information deemed 'accessible' is stored in a readily usable format. Although the time it takes to actually access the data ranges from milliseconds to days, the data does not need to be restored or otherwise manipulated to be usable. 'Inaccessible' data, on the other hand, is not readily usable. Backup tapes must be restored using a process similar to that previously described, fragmented data must be de-fragmented, and erased data must be reconstructed, all before the data is usable. That makes such data inaccessible."

✔ **Offline storage and archives:** This category is either magnetic tape or optical disks and is referred to as JBOD, which is short for *just a bunch of disks.* It differs from the preceding two categories in that the storage media are labeled, organized in shelves or racks, and accessed manually. Offline storage is meant for disaster recovery or for archiving records that will probably never be accessed. In either case, the media won't be searchable. If disaster recovery is needed, the entire tape or disk is loaded.

✔ **Backup tapes, commonly using data compression:** Backup tapes are sequential access media. Like ESI stored for disaster recovery, the data is not organized for retrieving individual files. Retrieval typically requires restoring contents of the entire tape. Adding to the challenge and cost is the need to reverse any compression that was used to fit more bytes of data on the disks. The discovery of ESI from disaster recovery backup tapes and other sources that are not reasonably accessible requires proof that their relevance outweighs their retrieval and processing costs. In addition, the court may consider the extent to which their retrieval disrupts business and information management activities.

✔ **Erased, fragmented, or corrupted data:**

- Files that are erased are not necessarily gone unless they've been overwritten by a new file.

- A *fragmented file* is one whose contents were cut up and stored in separate (noncontiguous) areas.

- *Corrupted files* are files that have been damaged by computer viruses, or a hardware or software malfunction. Documents sometimes become corrupted by viruses or as they're e-mailed from one type of e-mail system to another. Only after significant processing can these files be accessed, if they can be accessed at all.

Nothing in the rules — specifically, Rule 34(b) — prevents the court from ordering that paper is a "reasonably usable" form where the only other source for the information is not reasonably accessible.

Taking the two-tier test

The five types of data sources are further grouped into two tiers, which form the basis for two-tier discovery and what is called the *two-tiered test.* Two-tier discovery is defined in Rule 26(b)(2), which you can read more about in Chapter 4. The two-tiered test is a distinction between ESI found on sources that are reasonably accessible and sources that are not reasonably accessible because of undue burden or cost. The mapping of the five sources to the two tiers is as follows:

- ✔ **First-tier:** This tier consists of the first three types of data sources (active, near-line, and offline), which are defined as reasonably accessible sources.

- ✔ **Second-tier:** This tier consists of the latter two data sources (backup tapes and erased, fragmented, or corrupted data), which are defined as not reasonably accessible.

Federal courts have refused to find "good cause" to order discovery from inaccessible sources when potential benefits don't outweigh the burdens and costs.

Although reasonably accessible sources are those available without undue burden or cost, what constitutes *undue* remains a judgment call.

The two-tiered approach is used by courts for two purposes:

- ✔ **Determining the scope of appropriate e-discovery:** That is, to identify what is discoverable.

  - *First-tier sources:* Relevant, nonprivileged, reasonably accessible ESI is considered to be within the scope of discovery. This is, it's discoverable, and you must produce it. A court order isn't needed.

  - *Second-tier sources:* Even when the source of ESI isn't reasonably accessible and is presumed to be outside the scope of discovery, you must still identify the ESI by category or type if it's potentially responsive. Note that this puts you between a rock and a hard place: If the source is not reasonably accessible (because it's on unlabeled or nonindexed backup media, for example), how can you determine whether the ESI is potentially responsive? Tricky, isn't it? Although you need to identify only sources of ESI that are not reasonably accessible, it might end up being discoverable if the requesting party is determined to access it. The requesting party has the option of showing *good cause,* a reason that the ESI is essential to its case, which might persuade the court to order you to produce ESI from second-tier sources.

✔ **Figuring out how to allocate (shift) the cost of producing ESI among the parties:** Figuring out who should pay for production or how to allocate costs to each party is no less of a mess than figuring out what's discoverable. The oversimplified approach is:

- *First tier-sources:* Producing party pays.

- *Second-tier sources:* Costs may be shared by both parties. This is referred to as *cost shifting* because some costs are shifted from the producing party (who typically pays) to the requesting party. If a court orders discovery of second-tier ESI, your lawyer can ask the other party to help pay to produce it.

You can read about cost-shifting rules and related case law in Chapter 4.

Nothing's easy when it comes to e-discovery. An element of mystery always exists because of the judgment calls — literally, the decision calls of judges. Also, ESI doesn't fit neatly into cost categories. For example, active data is the number-one source of discoverable ESI, but it can still be tough and expensive (or, in legal-speak, an undue burden) to produce for litigation. Consider the following situations that complicate accessibility:

✔ **Bankruptcies:** ESI doesn't disappear just because a company files for bankruptcy. The duty to preserve ESI doesn't disappear, either. In a 2006 bankruptcy-related case, *In re Quintus Corp.,* Avaya acquired all the assets of Quintus, which had gone bankrupt. Later, the trustee filed a lawsuit for breach of contract against Avaya. Among other things, the trustee requested ESI, but Avaya failed to produce it. During the trial, the trustee learned that the requested ESI had been destroyed. Unfortunately for Avaya, the court found in favor of Quintus and held that, "Avaya deliberately deleted the debtors' electronic records in order to give itself more computer space . . . [F]urther, Avaya did not merely alter the evidence, it destroyed it. Thus, the court concluded that the most severe sanction of judgment against Avaya [for discovery abuse] was warranted."

ESI is essential in bankruptcy cases and proceedings. Financial records are subject to discovery so they can be analyzed to identify illegal transfers or insider transactions. E-mail and financial records support or refute an actual fraud allegation. As a result, the incentive to destroy incriminating ESI can be irresistible, but this incentive is countered by even more powerful disincentives, such as losing a case.

e-discovery in California overturns Zubulake decision

In July 2009, California overturned the *Zubulake* decision. California's new e-discovery law, known as the Civil Discovery Act, did away with the two tiers specified by *Zubulake*. The act makes discoverable any ESI that's stored for disaster recovery. Any company conducting business in California, therefore, may be required to produce all relevant ESI regardless of whether it's active, archive, backup, or disaster recovery material.

The Civil Discovery Act requires that the ESI be produced as it's kept in the usual course of business, or that it be organized and labeled to correspond with the categories in the request. However, the courts generally don't impose sanctions on a party or its attorney for failing to provide ESI that has been lost, damaged, altered, or overwritten as the result of the routine, good faith operation of an information system.

✔ **Mergers or acquisitions:** When companies merge with or acquire other companies, they often use different types of systems. Because of incompatibility, some electronic records are converted to the prevailing format, leaving certain areas of the old system extremely difficult to access.

✔ **Proprietary systems:** Many businesses have custom-built or customized data systems that were not designed with good search tools. When ESI is produced from these systems, it can't be comprehended.

✔ **Transaction databases:** The contents of these databases are so volatile that they require a lot of manipulation to produce.

Preserving the Digital Landscape

Retrieving content from servers, archives, backup tapes, and other media is just the beginning. You then need to preserve it — in the event that you have to process it and produce it to the requesting party.

Between the processes of identifying ESI as discoverable and then producing it is the none-too-trivial process of preservation. Preservation requires that you maintain ESI in an unaltered state or its native form. This obligation to preserve is referred to as a *litigation hold,* which you find out more about in Part III. Preserving ESI creates lots of anxiety because you can't easily control it. The following list describes some of the many factors affecting your ability to preserve ESI and enforce litigation holds:

✔ ESI can be destroyed by the normal or automated operations of a company's computer systems.

- ✔ Stopping routine or automated computer operations might be impossible without additional hardware or other equipment. ESI may need to be moved to a secure server or archive.

- ✔ Trying to preserve and secure ESI is a juggling act for IT staff whose day jobs don't leave time for them to retool to become e-discovery collection superheroes.

- ✔ Trying to convince employees not to destroy or tamper with files, e-mail, and other information related is tough because of their inclination to do exactly the opposite or their mistakes when preserving it.

- ✔ Preserving and continuing to enforce litigation holds can last for years. All new ESI that meets the litigation hold criteria must be held on to, too.

Computer systems automatically perform numerous functions. They create, change, update, discard, or overwrite data as part of their routine operations, often without anyone's direction or awareness. Computers further complicate preservation and production because ESI might be deleted but can continue to exist in ways that are difficult to locate, retrieve, or review. Or, it might become progressively less accessible over time. Although the rules don't fully define your duty to preserve, it's comforting that the rules recognize the problems you face. But if you don't deliberately preserve ESI, expect no mercy. No matter how bad the e-evidence, it's better to produce it and take your lumps than to destroy it. Why? Because the law has harsh penalties meant to deter the destruction of evidence. One of the harshest takes place when a judge gives an adverse jury instruction. Referring to the *Zubulake* case in which UBS deleted e-mails and said that several computer backup tapes were missing, Judge Schelndlln told jurors they could conclude that the data had been destroyed because it contained damaging information. That instruction played a big part in the $29 million judgment against UBS.

Cherry-picking through ESI to remove risky content is neither legal nor wise. When litigation triggers, it's necessary to prove that the deletion of this content was consistent with a good faith retention policy that you've applied rigorously.

Facing Sticker Shock: What ESI Costs

The first FRCP is a reminder to be fast, fair, and frugal, according to New York Magistrate Judge James C. Francis IV. He states the following:

> "Cases differ in cost and complexity. You have to sit down and figure out things like how much money and resources should be spent for a case that has a maximum award of $250,000. Electronic discovery can easily cost millions of dollars if you don't rein things in."

---

e-discovery thrives in tough times

Litigation is countercyclical: As the U.S. economy melts down, litigation ramps up. The 2008 financial crisis (and the worst bear market since the 1930s) drove up the number of lawsuits. In 2008, investors filed 210 federal securities class-action lawsuits, up 19 percent from 176 lawsuits in 2007, according to the Stanford Law School Securities Class Action Clearinghouse (`http://securities.stanford.edu`). Altogether, plaintiffs claimed that they had been robbed of $856 billion, or 27 percent more than in 2007. These cases involve enormous volumes of ESI from companies with offices that are spread worldwide.

In one case, after a large commodities and financial services firm was caught shifting hundreds of millions in debt off its books (this type of "creative accounting" is illegal), the banks that had underwritten the company's initial public stock offering were sued for securities fraud. The lawyers and the e-discovery vendor Fios, Inc., retained by the banks in this case, faced an e-discovery nightmare: The banks had more than 100 data custodians, widely scattered ESI stored on many types of media, and a large team of reviewers working at different locations across the USA. More than 70 unique ESI productions were made.

Fortunately, judges take proportionality tests into consideration (see Chapter 4). That's nice, but it's sobering to look at costs that others have paid. The proportionality principle might not be obvious when you look at these price tags:

- In 2002, in *Murphy oil v. Fluor Daniel,* Fluor Daniel spent $6.2 million to restore and print e-mail from 93 backup tapes.

- In 2002, in *Rowe Entertainment v. William Morris Agency,* the William Morris Agency spent $9.7 million to restore e-mail from 200 tapes, in addition to hundreds of thousands of dollars to retrieve and review 250,000 e-mail messages.

- In *Bank of America Corp. v. SR Int'l Bus. Ins. Co.* (2006), the restoration and organization of offline e-mail data from 400 backup tapes was an estimated $1.4 million.

When litigation hold mistakes are made, you might be forced to resort to backup tapes to satisfy your discovery obligations. Of course, these are avoidable e-discovery costs. In addition to these costs, there's the financial hit from the disruption caused when your company has to shut down its e-mail server or financial systems as part of a preservation order because you failed to properly enforce a litigation hold.

Electronic discovery is also costly in terms of legal review. Once the content is restored, a legal team reviews it for relevance to the case at an estimated cost of $1,800 to $2,500 per gigabyte (GB). If your company stores 25 terabytes (25,000GB), a discovery review of 25 percent of the information can cost between $11 million and $16 million.

In some cases, you can't locate all ESI within the allotted time. Or, you might not be able to place holds on all potentially responsive ESI. Some of it will be deleted during the lawsuit. Not being able to rope in ESI correctly can lead to stinging sanctions.

Estimating hard and hidden costs

Everyone wants to reduce the costs of e-discovery, and one way to do that is to take control of ESI. The $6 million question, which in this context is not simply a familiar expression, is *how?*

First, you need to break down the costs. The two cost buckets are

- **Hard costs:** *Hard costs* are those expenses that you pay by writing a check. In accounting terms, these are direct costs. Examples are mostly external expenses, such as legal services, third-party e-discovery fees, additional servers for preserving the ESI, and so on. Basically, hard costs are incurred when someone is sending you a bill or invoice to pay. Hard costs can break down further to correspond to the steps in the e-discovery process.

- **Hidden costs:** *Hidden costs* are the costs incorrectly allocated to other budget lines. Hidden costs are also referred to as *soft* or *indirect* costs and tend to be internal. Employees' time spent on e-discovery instead of their regular job duties is a prime example. Business disruption and commotion are also in the hidden cost bucket.

Next, you evaluate which activities provide the best leverage on those costs. Considerations are

- Direct hard dollar costs are easiest to control in the short term. It helps that they're easier to calculate courtesy of the monthly invoice. Of the e-discovery stages, processing and review costs tend to consume the biggest chunk of cash. The cost per labor hour is highest for those activities because they're done by lawyers or paralegals.

- The soft costs of collecting and producing ESI, if done internally, tend to pale in comparison to review costs.

- The potentially biggest cost driver comes from the courts. You can get hit with a sanction or an unfavorable decision for not playing fair.

You get the smallest bang for your buck in the short term by cutting the costs of identification, preservation, and collection Your big payoff comes from working with your e-discovery team — lawyers and IT people alike — in order to focus on cutting costs of ESI processing and review.

One example of the tremendous cost of keeping everything comes from a large chemical company's internal study. To persuade business leaders of the need for effective document retention and disposal policies, the company's legal department conducted an internal cost assessment of a three-year litigation project. Two of its findings were

- ✔ Of the 75 million pages of text they reviewed during the 3-year period, more than 50 percent of the documents were out of date and should have been deleted.
- ✔ The cost of reviewing out-of-date documents amounted to $12 million.

Looking at the costs of being surprised by a request

If you wait until litigation is approaching to figure out what ESI you have, you've waited until it's too late to do anything to control costs. Imagine waiting for a fire to install a sprinkler system. There's no upper bound on costs in that scenario.

When e-discovery requests are made, the meter is ticking. Trying to do just a preliminary estimate of what's discoverable or responsive and what's not, and mapping where that ESI resides can easily take several weeks. You read about data maps in Chapter 6. When you're packing mega-repositories holding ESI that have to be indexed before the meet-and-confer conference, and there's no plan to jump into action, you're wide open to sanctions from the court and power plays by your opposing party.

Five ways to cut costs are

- ✔ **Cut down how much content you keep.** You can minimize the costs of archiving, preserving, restoring, and reviewing ESI, and the risk of sanctions for being out of compliance. Of course, you must take into consideration operational, legal, and regulatory requirements.
- ✔ **Organize ESI for litigation purposes.** Historically, ESI was organized for disaster recovery, which requires a full restore of the data and doesn't require finding and retrieving a few files or e-mails. But when ESI is organized and stored on tape for disaster recovery purposes, it's less accessible for precise search-and-rescue litigation missions. ESI now needs to be organized, indexed, and stored on media that facilitates responding to litigation.

✔ **Send a message from top management.** The rules and courts hold the company and its senior managers responsible for litigation-readiness policies and procedures. In turn, senior managers need to send a clear message to all data custodians and employees that such policies and procedures are important and must be followed. The ability to respond to e-discovery requests is highly dependent on data custodians and employees preserving what's needed and disposing of what isn't. Providing mandatory training sessions, e-mailing reminders of ESI retention policies, and imposing penalties for noncompliance help reinforce the message. This method is based on the "what's important gets done" principle.

✔ **Build a team of e-discovery experts.** This team should include legal, IT, and human resources representatives and senior managers. As in a fire department, when an emergency occurs, trained experts immediately respond. They manage the situation by containing the blaze and minimizing damage. Managing e-discovery also requires people who have specialized skills and know how to respond to demanding activities. Because of tight deadlines and sanctions for missing them, you need a team that's ready to respond intelligently. At the extreme, if your company cannot prepare for the meet-and-confer conference or is unable to respond to e-discovery requests, you've lost.

✔ **Invest in outside help from e-discovery service providers.** For most companies, getting litigation-ready or responding to an e-discovery request requires help from one or more e-discovery service providers. Categories of services include

- Design and offering of training programs

- Data gathering and media restoration

- Computer forensics

- ESI hosting, processing, review, and production

These upfront investments in time, effort, and money, such as the ones you made in reading this book, can pay off in a single case — smart choice.

The courts are saying that there's no plea to ignorance that will not waste money.

Chapter 3

Building e-Discovery Best Practices into Your Company

. . . .

In This Chapter

▶ Preparing the best defense

▶ Teaming up for a win

▶ Following the critical path

▶ Factoring in ethics and credibility

. . . .

*V*ery few cases are settled before discovery (before trial most likely, but not before discovery). They're settled *as a result of discovery* after both sides learn the strengths and weaknesses of the other's case. Decisions about whether to settle, or the terms of settlement, might begin to become clear only during e-discovery. That's the importance of e-discovery and the value of doing the groundwork before facing litigation or a subpoena. Rush-job reactions rarely end well because they can't withstand judicial scrutiny and are very expensive because they usually entail paying "rush" fees to vendors and over-time to employees.

You want to be able to respond quickly and intelligently when you learn that you're about to be a defendant or a non-party to litigation. A non-party, also called a *third party,* is neither a defendant nor plaintiff, but a company that gets swept into the case because it possesses relevant ESI. It's easy to forget that e-discovery isn't just about producing ESI to the other side. Electronic discovery is also about finding e-mail and documents that prove your innocence to shelter you from false claims and companies taking a crack spin at the litigation wheel of fortune.

In this chapter, we discuss best practices in preparation for e-discovery, or *prelitigation best practices,* to help get your company into a rock-solid position while keeping cost and risk under control. Getting prepared before litigation is looming gives you a tactical advantage, which just might be the decisive one. You're better positioned to negotiate with opponents and to justify the reasonableness of your actions to the court. Courts don't demand perfection, but they expect good faith efforts from you.

Setting Up a Reasonable Defensive Strategy

American film director and actor Woody Allen casually observed that in life "80 percent of success is just showing up." A lot of litigation success, like life, is showing up at the meet-and-confer conference prepared for e-discovery. The timeline in Figure 3-1 shows that your prelitigation strategy begins when you can reasonably anticipate litigation. By applying a defensive prelitigation strategy that's monitored actively, you're ready to respond. Risk and cost are directly related to quickly identifying, monitoring, and managing ESI when litigation holds are needed. You can read how litigation holds need to throw a straightjacket around routine data operations to preserve relevant ESI in the section "Braking for Legal Holds" in this chapter. In contrast, if you can't defend your strategy (perhaps because you don't have one), you should be very worried (perhaps even alarmed).

An overview of prelitigation readiness best practices is not complete unless we also point out the worst practices that can bulldoze your credibility or case. Claiming ignorance about the whereabouts of missing documents, even if it's true, or taking a passive or lackadaisical (in legalese, "purposeful sluggishness" or "willful blindness") approach to ESI archiving are worst practices. Any defense that sounds like an excuse coming from Beavis and Butthead is damaging.

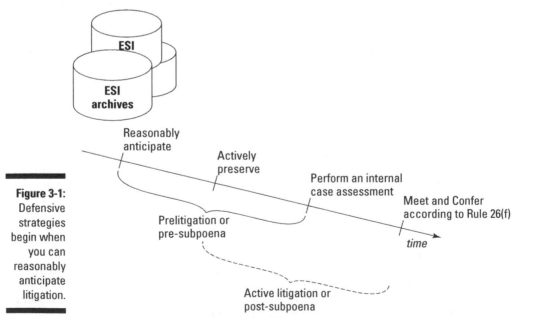

Figure 3-1: Defensive strategies begin when you can reasonably anticipate litigation.

In e-discovery disputes, the outcome comes down to what a judge or magistrate finds is reasonable under the circumstances of each case. The Federal Rules of Civil Procedure (FRCP) provide only a blueprint to follow for e-discovery, but there are still best practices for prelitigation regardless of the court you're in.

Heeding judicial advice

An obvious prelitigation best practice is to follow the advice of judges. Judges have the power, courtesy of Rule 37(f), to impose sanctions if you fail to obey an order to provide or permit discovery. This to-the-point wording recognizes a binary situation: Either you obey or you do not obey. As Yoda had warned Luke Skywalker, "there is no try." Sanctions for not obeying range from monetary fines to *adverse inference instructions*, which entails telling the jury they can assume you've something to hide. The judge could even dismiss your case.

You can improve your strategy by learning from others' experiences. Judges have set precedents that deal with prelitigation readiness. The following lists the lessons learned and the cases they are cited in:

- **Take affirmative steps to preserve ESI:** In *Zubulake v. UBS Warburg* (2004), Judge Shira A. Scheindlin held that it's no longer sufficient merely to issue a passive litigation hold throughout your company. A *litigation hold*, or *legal hold*, is an order to stop destruction and preserve all records, regardless of form, related to a legal action. In other words, you must take *affirmative steps* to hold onto e-evidence.

- **IT must be informed of their duties:** In *Kevin Keithley v. The Home Store. com* (2008), Magistrate Judge Elizabeth D. Laporte ruled that the defendant could not claim its IT personnel were ignorant of the importance of preserving ESI. For being reckless by not taking affirmative steps to safeguard data, defendants paid hundreds of thousands of dollars for plaintiff's attorneys' fees and were hit with an adverse jury instruction.

- **Lawyers must supervise the process:** In *United States v. Philip Morris USA Inc.* (2004), Judge Gladys Kessler held that corporate (in-house) lawyers must "forcefully intervene" to ensure that e-evidence is preserved. The rules require, and case law enforces, that in-house lawyers learn enough to actively manage and participate in proper preservation, collection, review, and production of ESI and not pass off that responsibility to the IT department. It's their responsibility to put litigation hold instructions in writing, distribute them widely, follow up frequently, and confirm that they've been followed religiously.

✔ **Consider electronic evidence and its authenticity from the outset:** In *Lorraine v. Markel Am. Ins. Co.* (2007), Magistrate Judge Paul W. Grimm makes it clear that you need to think about ESI evidentiary issues much earlier than with hardcopy evidentiary materials. ESI becomes inaccessible and may be deleted a lot faster than hard copies. You need to consider how potential e-evidence is handled by records retention programs, and be able to promptly suspend automated processes that could alter or overwrite relevant ESI. You also need to be prepared to deal with ESI authentication challenges. Authentication requires that you keep metadata intact and may require that e-mail or documents be examined by a computer forensic expert, as you find out in Chapter 13. A judge may rule that your e-mail or other documents are inadmissible evidence if there's doubt about their authenticity.

✔ **Your legal counsel is responsible for the litigation hold, but your company is in the line of fire too:** In *Arteria Property Pty Ltd. v. Universal Funding V.T.O., Inc.* (2008), Judge Ronald J. Hedges sanctioned the defendant for failing to preserve the content on its Web site even though a third-party Web designer (intermediary) managed it. Hedges stated the following:

"This Court sees no reason to treat Web sites differently than other electronic files. . . . Despite the inevitable presence of an intermediary when posting content on the Web, the Court finds that Defendants still had the ultimate authority, and thus control, to add, delete, or modify the Web site's content."

To keep current with prelitigation best practices, see Chapter 19. For an in-depth review of seminal cases, see Chapter 20.

Keeping ESI intact and in-reach

Another obvious but often overlooked best practice is keeping ESI that needs to be kept. You may hear this referred to as archiving or preserving, or as a litigation hold, although the meanings of these terms differ depending on the context or timeline. Here's how you might distinguish these concepts:

✔ **Archiving is the retention of ESI in an organized way and with an index.** Archiving is done with a specialized archiving system that enables you to centrally manage the archive. The index makes the content searchable. The index is comparable to an index in a book that you use to find a word in the book.

Archives differ from backup copies in that backups can be unsearchable data dumps. Archiving begins when ESI must be retained for business, compliance, regulatory, or audit purposes. During this stage, companies operate their businesses normally, continually producing ESI and using it to do business.

✔ **Preserving is archiving with intent.** The term *preservation* implies something mandatory, or a greater sense of urgency, because of the matter at hand. There's a duty to preserve ESI according to business, regulatory, and litigation requirements, but no duty to archive.

Depending on the case and ESI, preservation (like authentication) may also require the forensic imaging of a hard drive, which you can read about in Chapter 13.

✔ **A litigation hold is both a red alert and a lockdown.** A litigation hold is written notice from in-house counsel and management to data custodians, IT staff, and those who are likely to have relevant ESI.

It's also a lockdown on data repositories to protect them from being altered, deleted, or lost either accidentally or deliberately. For example, files can be locked down by changing the file's permission from unrestricted (allowing full access and edit permission) to restricted (providing permission to read, but not to edit).

Being a non-party puts you under the rules

Even if you're not a party to litigation, your ESI may become subject to e-discovery. A court can order you to produce relevant ESI even if you're a non-party. Consider the experience of the audit firm PricewaterhouseCoopers (PwC). PwC was a non-party in an e-discovery dispute, *United States ex rel. Parikh v. Premera Blue Cross* (2007). Defendant Premera Blue Cross had hired PwC to audit the Medicare payments it had received. In November 2006, PwC received a subpoena ordering it to produce all its e-mails with Premera. PwC produced only some of the requested e-mails arguing that the cost of retrieving the archived e-mails was too burdensome. Note that PwC objected on the grounds that the *retrieval* was too expensive, but didn't identify the standard it used to calculate the expense. The court, in its response to PwC's objection, focused on the production costs and not the retrieval costs. The court's response was, in part, as follows:

"We understand that PwC has and will produce e-mails that are not archived and are otherwise available and we infer that the cost of retrieving archived e-mails would be considerable. Nevertheless, if PwC . . . 'is preparing to produce some ... e-mails,' the implication is that it has retrieved all e-mails. Taking PwC at its word then, the cost of retrieval has already been assumed and the argument is over the cost of production. In this Court's opinion, the cost of production is minimal."

PwC was ordered to produce the disputed 6,500 e-mails and bill to Plaintiff's counsel for the reasonable cost of production.

Braking for Litigation Holds

Courts have uniformly held that the FRCP and case law impose on you and your attorneys a joint obligation to preserve all ESI and other evidence that's relevant to issues in the lawsuit, or that could lead to the discovery of relevant evidence. There's no escaping this duty. Compliance with the litigation hold process in a timely manner is critical. Not doing so can result in painful court-ordered monetary sanctions; adverse inference jury instructions; or, worst case, a default judgment against your company.

The first part of your strategy should be to put a litigation hold on anything that might be subject to discovery. Litigation holds don't take care of themselves. For a genuine litigation hold, you have to actively implement steps that you can trust will slam on the brakes on inappropriate ESI disposal immediately. Direct all questions and concerns to your in-house lawyers to whom you report. You may be responsible to implementing the hold, but legal counsel must review your company's litigation hold process and procedures, ensuring that they're defendable to the court.

Assign the management of litigation holds only to those people who you can trust to perform that duty. Relying on *custodians* (employees) to preserve ESI is not sufficient evidence of a good faith litigation hold effort.

Insuring a stronghold

Here are steps that you together with legal counsel can take when a litigation hold starts:

1. **Identify what ESI needs to be preserved, where it is, and who has a copy of it.**

   Before a litigation hold notice is even drafted, you and your attorney must work together to determine what documents are relevant based on what dates and time periods are relevant to the elements of the case, the location of every device storing it, and the data custodians who control those documents.

2. **Designate someone to be in charge of the litigation hold.**

   You need someone who has the authority, time, and expertise to manage the hold process on a daily basis until that duty is released. Appoint someone with technical skills because holds disrupt computing operations. This is also the go-to person for technical questions and problems from data custodians, end users, and even legal counsel.

   The litigation hold can span several years so appointing a successor can help with the continuity.

This role may expand to that of designated corporate witness, also referred to the *30(b)(6) witness,* who testifies in a *deposition* (testimony under oath outside of court). Chapter 7 goes into more detail about how to pick an ideal 30(b)(6) witness.

3. **Notify everyone potentially involved in the litigation hold.**

You need to tell data custodians, IT staff, and those within the scope of the hold the specific actions they need to take and the actions they must not take. Like all policies that you might have to defend later, the language and directions need to be clear and doable.

Finding out about a litigation hold is like spotting a radar detector while you're driving on a highway. If you're speeding, you automatically hit the brakes. And if you're not speeding, you still automatically hit the brakes. That is, your reaction may be exactly the same (pent-up guilt, maybe). If you learned that your e-mails might be exhibit A in a lawsuit, would you be tempted to delete them, litigation hold or not? If yes, you realize that you need to prevent others from doing the same thing.

4. **Actively verify compliance and document your efforts.**

Compliance with the litigation hold policy has to be monitored so people know that the policy isn't just for show. You'll need to provide evidence that the policy was proactively monitored, so document your efforts and any remediation you made to bring the hold up to standards.

Keeping a complete record in order to assure, and if necessary to prove, reasonable efforts to meet the duty to preserve is worth the tedious effort. Litigation hold notices are useless unless they're enforced and it's verified that you're in compliance. Your company and your attorneys are jointly responsible.

5. **Release the hold.**

When the coast is clear, release the hold and thank people for their cooperation. Being nice now might help you during the next litigation hold.

Getting others to buy-in

Not everyone will take you or the litigation hold seriously. Here are some tips for getting others to follow through on the hold:

- ✓ **Communicate directly with all key producers, users, and owners of potentially relevant ESI to learn or confirm what they possess.** You want to directly contact these people in order to minimize the chance of ESI that you didn't know existed materials later.

- ✓ **Explain to employees their role and responsibilities throughout the litigation hold and the reason for the extra work or disruption.** To motivate, be clear that their compliance will be monitored.

✔ **Monitor and follow-up with key personnel to verify their compliance with litigation holds.** You can safely assume that people will ignore your written notices about litigation holds unless they know that their compliance is being monitored.

✔ **Inform managers and IT staff to keep all ESI from accounts of departing employees until they're told that the hold is over.** Develop procedures for preserving ESI when custodians leave the company and their duties are reassigned, especially in prospective litigation holds.

✔ **Notify IT staff to suspend the routine wiping of hard drives, which may be done when computers are reassigned, or servers.** In *Padgett v. City of Monte Sereno* (2007), the defendant was sanctioned when an employee, who had no knowledge of pending litigation, reformatted a co-worker's hard drive that stored relevant ESI. The court held that the defendant failed to take adequate precautions to preserve the co-worker's computer equipment.

✔ **Examine litigation hold procedures on a regular basis to verify that they continue to function as needed.** Again, being as proactive as possible always looks good with the court.

✔ **Keep information secure.** Protect ESI from cyber-nastiness while it's in hold with intrusion detection systems, anti-malware and spyware software, and firewalls.

✔ **Act in good faith (always a best practice) and document that you did so.** You'll want to back up your actions just in case you have to justify them in court.

Claiming ignorance about missing documents, even if it's true, and being passive about protecting ESI are not acceptable defenses.

Check out Chapter 7 to find out how to design, implement, and preserve a litigation hold.

Holding on tight to your ESI

Billions of e-mails, documents, and spreadsheets are created by companies every day — and a huge number are destroyed each day in the normal course of business. Users make their own deletion decisions and companies have automated e-mail deletion software and their own document retention and destruction policies. Doing a litigation hold in under these chaotic conditions is not going to be easy. No matter how difficult, you cannot transfer litigation hold obligations to employees.

Phillip M. Adams and Associates v. Dell, Fujitsu, Sony, ASUS Computer International, et al (2009) illustrates this point. The case involved several major computer manufacturers charged with illegally using Dr. Phillip Adams's patented software. The court singled out ASUS, one of the defendants, because of its response to the e-discovery request. ASUS produced very few documents, and claimed that it had not destroyed any relevant documents. Because of their suspiciously poor response, the plaintiff asked the court for sanctions alleging that ASUS had deliberately destroyed e-mail evidence. Deliberate destruction of evidence is called *spoliation*.

To defend against spoliation charges, ASUS explained that

- ✔ Employees were responsible for preserving e-mails by downloading them to their individual computers because its e-mail servers were incapable of archiving.

- ✔ Employees themselves decided which e-mails to preserve.

- ✔ Employees' computers were routinely replaced, and individual employees were responsible for determining which information should be transferred to a new computer. Information the individual employee did not save was erased.

The Court rejected ASUS's argument that it had made employees responsible for managing and retaining e-mail. The court found that ASUS violated its duty to preserve the information and that the loss of ESI wasn't due to the "routine, good faith operation of electronic information systems." The court's response included the following explanation:

> "An organization should have reasonable policies and procedures for managing its information and records. . . . The absence of a coherent document retention policy is a pertinent factor to consider when evaluating sanctions. . . . It is clear that ASUS' lack of a retention policy and irresponsible data retention practices are responsible for the loss of significant data."

This case illustrates why e-mail retention policies and procedures, as well as archiving technology, are invaluable best practices. Having electronic records management (ERM) programs that include ESI retention policies are key to a spoliation defense. (We discuss setting up an ERM in Chapter 14.) Conversely, relying on your employees' judgment for managing and retaining e-mail or other documents is a worst practice.

Putting Best Practices into Place

Stored ESI spans everything from network drives and computer hard drives to iPods and cellphones. But that's not all. Potential ESI exists on social networks, social media sites, and collaboration platforms. (Social networks and media are collectively known as Web 2.0, which is pronounced Web-2-O, like H-2-O.) This section explains these three potential sources for ESI and also their discoverability.

Common characteristics of Web 2.0 are that the content is user-generated, edited, and deleted; and the content changes constantly. Users may mistakenly believe that what they do or say is private, short-lived, or really deleted.

User activity on social networking sites like Twitter, LinkedIn, Facebook, and MySpace is serious concern for companies because it's discoverable and may fall within a litigation hold. Content from Web 2.0 may be discoverable for several reasons:

- ✔ Much of the content gets archived for indefinite lengths of time.

- ✔ Employees may be using various forms within the scope of their jobs.

- ✔ Posts and files relevant to litigation may reside only in the Web 2.0 space.

- ✔ Web 2.0 storage solutions, like landfills, are growing rapidly and are bound to catch the attention of litigants. There was a time when e-mail and text messages weren't central to e-discovery.

Best practices for social media, at this point, are to treat Web 2.0 content as much like other ESI as possible. Recognize that trying to get a handle on Web 2.0 is like herding cats. For prelitigation purposes, the main preparations to undertake are

- ✔ **Create an inventory log.** Note which media and networks are being used by your company, divisions, departments, other units, and employees. Log names, types, dates, and reasons for use.

- ✔ **Document where the info goes.** Find out who stores the content, what their data destruction policies are, and how to obtain authenticated copies of the content.

In *Biegel v. Norberg* (filed February 2008 in the Superior Court, County of San Francisco), a chiropractor sued a former patient for defamation and invasion of privacy based on the patient's critical postings on Yelp. Norberg, the former patient and defendant, tried to spin his defense into a freedom of speech cause. Visit Citizen Media Law at `www.citimedialaw.org` for cases on defamation, copyright infringement, and free speech on Web 2.0 media.

Social networks

Social networks are Web-based services that allow individuals or companies to build a public or semi-public profile within a bounded system. Time spent on social networks surpassed that for e-mail for the first time in February 2009. Social networking technologies include

- ✔ **Blogs:** A blog is a Web site that's used for self-publishing. The term *blog* is short for Web log.

- ✔ **Podcasts:** Audio or video content that is downloaded for viewing or listening offline. Any device that can play MP3 audio files can be used to play podcasts.

✔ **RSS:** RSS stands for Really Simple Syndication. RSS feeds send updated information automatically to a digital device. Users control which RSS gets fed to their devices.

✔ **Wikis:** A wiki is a Web site used as a collaboration tool. Pages can be changed and published immediately using only a Web browser. Pages are automatically created and linked to each other. A successful global wiki is Wikipedia, which can be found at `www.wikipedia.com`.

Social media sites and platforms

Social media refers to the content created and published on a social Web site by anyone who wants to. Social media is made up of personal and commercial conversations and connections enabled across channels of mass impact and scale. Social media are more easily discoverable than just about any other form of user-generated content for as long as it remains online. Most content is archived and retained. Social media service providers retain content regardless of users' expectations of privacy. For example, the full text of a string of personal e-mail messages sent between two Facebook members can be subject to discovery or subpoena years later. Of course, there are more than a few elected officials who have found their personal messages the news feature on Fox or CNN.

A few of the many very popular social media sites are

✔ **YouTube (`http://youtube.com`):** A video sharing Web site where users can create, upload, view, and share video clips.

✔ **Facebook (`http://facebook.com`):** A site that started out as a service for university students but which has evolved to the point where one-third of its global audience is aged 35 to 49 years, and one-quarter is over 50 years old.

✔ **MySpace (`http://myspace.com`):** MySpace is one of the world's largest social networks.

✔ **LinkedIn (`www.linkedin.com`):** A service for building a network of professional contacts.

✔ **Yelp (`www.yelp.com`):** Members can post local reviews for the purpose of creating a local online community.

✔ **Twitter (`http://twitter.com`):** A microblogging platform for sending and receiving short text messages called *tweets*.

Increasingly, companies are using enterprise social media platforms such as Jive or SocialText that enable internal blogs and wikis. If your company uses social media networks or platforms, you must take steps during a litigation hold to ensure that the data can be preserved, retrieved, and produced if requested. For example, if your company uses Twitter to reach its customers, you need to be prepared to preserve and produce those postings if relevant to a litigation. Even though this data is not in the custody or control of your company, it does not excuse the duty to be able to preserve and collect it.

Collaboration platforms

Collaboration platforms are Web-based technologies used primarily for accessing, viewing, and sharing documents. With these platforms, you're dealing with the Web instead of the hard drive for file storage. The two most widely used Web-based collaboration tools are

- ✔ **Google Docs:** A free Web-based application offered by Google used to work together on word processed documents, spreadsheets, and pre-sentations. With Google Docs, you can easily and collaboratively create, edit, and upload Microsoft Word documents or Excel spreadsheets.
- ✔ **Microsoft Office Live Workspace:** A Web-accessible technology that allows Microsoft Office users to collaborate easily on documents.

With either Google Docs or Office Live, specific documents or entire work-spaces can be shared with other people of your choosing.

Forming Response Teams

Electronic discovery is not just for IT or legal experts. Consider what e-discovery touches:

- ✔ Electronic records management
- ✔ Risk management
- ✔ Litigation holds
- ✔ ESI storage, disruption of computing operations, disaster recovery
- ✔ Data preservation, authentication, and recovery of deleted or corrupted data
- ✔ Human relations, if employee misconduct is involved
- ✔ Accounting, if fraud is involved
- ✔ Public relations or damage control

As with any incident response situation, you want to assemble an e-discovery response team to help take care of your ESI preservation duties. The e-discovery response team should be composed of senior management (the data owners), corporate (in-house) counsel, IT staff, outside counsel, human relations managers, accounting managers, and possibly an e-discovery ser-vice provider or vendor. Electronic discovery vendors are invaluable (mean-ing that they're worth the expense) if you have no experience or expertise.

The chances are not in your favor that the team will work in harmony when in crisis. Someone with clout, patience, and a coaching personality is a good candidate for being in charge. If no such person exists, select someone who understands the e-discovery FRCP, which you can find out more about in Chapter 4. Electronic discovery is about the rules and case law, not about IT.

IT and legal professionals sometimes differ on how to respond to e-discovery requests. Lawyers don't understand the intricacies of ESI and storage devices. IT experts don't understand rules of evidence or depositions. This leaves a knowledge gap among team members. Misunderstanding of specialized terminology coupled with bad group dynamics can neutralize even a brilliant legal strategy for winning a case.

Putting Project Management into Practice

Electronic discovery fits the definition of a project. A *project* is a collection of activities that need to be completed to achieve an outcome. Characteristics of a project that also are characteristics of prelitigation and e-discovery are

- ✔ Has an identifiable beginning, end, schedule, and approach, which is determined for the most part by the rules, court order, or other authority outside of your control.
- ✔ Has milestones marking completion of a series of tasks, such as the review of a specific volume of ESI.
- ✔ Has multiple activities that might occur sequentially or concurrently. If e-discovery activities are not done concurrently, you can expect to miss many milestones and scheduled deadlines.
- ✔ Uses resources (people, equipment, and money, for example) specifically allocated to the tasks that need to be completed. You are one of those resources.
- ✔ Recognizes that your resources are also your constraints, due to limited resources or deadlines. If when laying out the project and doing the math on work-hours needed and availability of workers, you estimate a shortage, that's the time to fix that deficiency.
- ✔ Has end results with specific goals — typically time, cost, performance, or quality. Your e-discovery request pretty much clarifies the end results.
- ✔ Involves a team of people, which is the e-discovery team.

Two of the factors driving the management of the e-discovery project are

- ✔ What's at stake with the case
- ✔ How savvy the opponent is

Tackling the triple constraints

When you're involved in prelitigation, you're challenged to simultaneously manage what project managers call the triple constraint (see Figure 3-2):

- ✔ **Time or schedule,** which includes many time-critical events such as the meet-and-confer session and scheduling conference
- ✔ **Scope,** which notoriously morphs as the project progresses
- ✔ **Budget or cost,** which is rarely sufficient from the outset

Figure 3-2:
The triple constraint of project management.

The earlier you identify the constraints, the better your chances of intelligently prioritizing and deciding on trade-offs. You may need to make trade-offs to balance time, scope, and costs so as not to compromise quality of the work (see Figure 3-3). Production is useless if done on time, but privilege is produced.

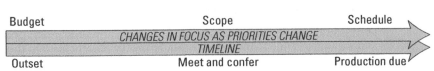

Figure 3-3:
As the schedule moves along, your priorities change.

If you're struggling with dealing with all three, check out *Project Management For Dummies* by Teresa Luckey and Joseph Phillips (Wiley).

The successful project manager in e-discovery has to play many roles: part manager and technical expert, part litigator and paralegal, and part coach and problem fixer. Taking the time to define constraints and critical tasks early on reduces your stress level and panic.

Managing the critical path

Tasks must be completed in a specific order to get the job done. In e-discovery, you identify before your preserve and collect; and you preserve and collect before you process, review, and analyze until you're able to produce the responsive ESI. Certain tasks make up what is called the *critical path,* which is an important principle of project management. Smartly, those tasks are called *critical tasks*. The critical path consists of activities or tasks that must start and finish on schedule or else the project completion will be delayed — unless action is taken to expedite one or more critical tasks There are many non-critical paths composed of tasks that may or may not be critical. The critical path may change throughout a project so you need to monitor and manage the critical and non-critical paths.

The purpose of the critical path method (CPM) is to recognize which activities are on the critical path so that you know where to focus your efforts. You use critical tasks to identify or prioritize trade-offs.

Maintaining Ethical Conduct and Credibility

Companies involved in e-discovery have duties, like the duty to preserve ESI relevant to the litigation, duties to meet deadlines, and many more that you read about throughout this book. Failure to maintain your ethical conduct and credibility creates risks of sanctions. In brief, taking those risks is not worthwhile. Failure to exercise prelitigation best practices, resulting in the destruction of e-evidence, is illegal. Chances of getting caught destroying e-evidence are increasing as judges and opponents become more aware of the technology side of e-discovery.

The biggest risk with the severest sanctions is a charge of spoliation. Spoliation is the dreaded "you're guilty of destroying evidence," which is an obstruction of justice.

You can read about spoliation and its consequences in Chapter 4.

Part II

Guidelines for e-Discovery and Professional Competence

The 5th Wave   By Rich Tennant

"I've been an expert computer witness for over 20 years. I've testified about fraudulent whatnots, failed doohickies, missing thingys, you name it."

In this part . . .

This second part gives you an up-close look at the e-discovery amendments to the Federal Rules of Civil Procedure, the advisory guidelines that are taken seriously by the bench, and the generally expected standards of legal competence and conduct. As a lawyer practicing in the e-discovery arena, an IT person drafted into an e-discovery team, or someone wanting to know what to look for in their legal counsel, you get valuable advice in Chapters 4 and 5.

In Chapter 4, you get better acquainted with e-discovery rules, the concepts of proportionality, and the importance of balancing the cost of a case with its importance. You're introduced to the new Federal Rule of Evidence 502 and other evidence rules that apply to the admissibility of ESI. We discuss the industry-standard Electronic Discovery Reference Model (EDRM) and the guidelines of The Sedona Conference, a non-partisan think tank on law and policy. With this foundation, you're better prepared to understand the process of preserving, collecting, processing, reviewing, and producing ESI.

Also in Chapter 4, you read how the e-discovery rules introduce new obligations and expand lawyers' role in handling cases involving ESI, both civil and criminal cases. Legal competence now includes technological competence. You see that lawyers are expressly advised to become familiar with their client's computer technologies and ESI-management policies before the Rule 16 Pretrial Conference.

Courts can be critical of lawyers who don't acquire this familiarity, which we cover in Chapter 5. You find out why relying on the American Bar Association's (ABA) Model Rules of Professional Conduct can be a career-saver, and the downside of straying from these rules. You recognize when calling upon the court for clarification or for complex litigation is the wise thing to do.

"If you can't explain what you're doing in simple English, you're probably doing something wrong."

—Alfred Kazin, American critic and author

Chapter 4

The Playbook: Federal Rules and Advisory Guidelines

In This Chapter

▶ Playing by the rules

▶ Seeing the criminal side of the rules

▶ Questioning admissibility

▶ Listening to Sedona

▶ Keeping up with the judges

▶ Paying attention to the e-discovery model

▶ Knowing what the Advisory Committee meant

*T*o win a legal action you must be able to prove your case. How you con-vince the court that your side of the story is true is controlled by various federal rules of procedure and evidence, or state equivalents. ESI is the ideal witness because of its perfect memory and persuasiveness, but only if it's considered relevant according to federal rules, state rules, or by some other authority. Both parties and non-parties to litigation need to understand and follow the rules. Imagine a hockey game played without rules. How would you know who wins or when the game is over if you don't know how the game is played? That's why there's a rulebook.

Fortunately, you have rulebooks to follow with e-discovery, too. In fed-eral civil matters, e-discovery is controlled by the Federal Rules of Civil Procedure (FRCP). In criminal cases, e-discovery is controlled by the Federal Rules of Criminal Procedure (FRCrimP). Throughout the process of e-discovery is the paramount concern of getting evidence you can use in court to prove your case. Rules of e-discovery are set forth in the Federal Rules of Evidence (FRE). In state court matters, e-discovery is covered by the equivalent rules of the state.

In this chapter, you find out about e-discovery and evidence rules applicable to ESI. You can be involved as a party or a third party who's holding ESI that another party wants. The basic structure we present helps you understand the process of obtaining, protecting, and presenting ESI.

Knowing the Rules You Must Play By

The courts amended the FRCP (see Chapter 1) when they realized they were futilely trying to text message with rotary phones. The FRCP is now in the new millennium filled with iPhones and ESI.

If the FRCP is the global positioning system for e-discovery, then the road-map was drawn in *Zubulake v. UBS Warburg*. There were five *Zubulake* opinions oddly enough, called *Zubulake* I, II, III, IV, and V. Four of those were groundbreaking opinions in the area of ESI (see Chapter 2). Judge Scheindlin laid the foundation for much of the e-discovery rules now in effect. You see these cases come up throughout this book.

Although you have a lot of guidance and structure in civil matters, the same cannot be said of criminal law. As a result, courts have been applying the concepts of the civil rules to deal with e-discovery in criminal matters. Even in federal court, a special local rule may apply to e-discovery. Although the FRCP is the overriding rule, local courts may have slight modifications. Care must be taken to make sure that the local rule is followed.

You can't assume that federal law will govern your case. State cases will be handled under state rules of e-discovery. Many states have adopted rules similar to the FRCP but not uniformly. When in doubt, ask your attorney.

Throughout the entire e-discovery process, you should consider how ESI could affect the outcome of your case. Just because you have it, doesn't mean you can use it. You may be right, but can you prove it? What is admissible in court is determined by the rules of evidence. In federal cases, that is the Federal Rules of Evidence (FRE). Each state has its own rules of evidence. In most situations, they are similar to the federal rules but not exact. It is important that your attorney is familiar with the applicable evidentiary rules. The case can be won or lost here. Table 4-1 compares the applicable rules for various types of cases.

Table 4-1		Comparison of Applicable Rules for e-Discovery				
Type of Case	*Apply FRCP*	*Apply F.R. Crim. P.*	*Apply State Rules of Proce-dure*	*Apply Any Local Rules of Proce-dure*	*Apply FRE*	*Apply State Rules of Evidence*
Federal Civil	Yes	No	No	Yes	Yes	No
Federal Criminal	Reference Only	Yes	No	Yes	Yes	No

Type of Case	Apply FRCP	Apply F.R. Crim. P.	Apply State Rules of Procedure	Apply Any Local Rules of Procedure	Apply FRE	Apply State Rules of Evidence
State Civil	Reference Only	No	Yes	Yes	No	Yes
State Criminal	Reference Only	No	Yes	Yes	No	Yes

Deciphering the FRCP

The FRCP sets out a path to manage a lawsuit from the filing of a complaint to its conclusion. The filing of a complaint by a plaintiff commences a civil case. The party sued is the defendant. The failure to follow the FRCP properly can result in everything from sanctions to actually losing the case. Don't rely on the forgiveness of a judge; strict adherence to the rules is always your best policy.

In Federal Court, all federal rules apply to a lawsuit. Thus, in any case, all the FRCP must be considered and reviewed.

FRCP 1

The first rule of the FRCP is often overlooked because of its simplicity. However, it sets forth a clear purpose for the rules: To secure the just, speedy, and inexpensive determination of every action. Remember this when establishing your plan of discovery and possible cost. You can reduce cost by applying best practices (Chapter 3), proper planning (Chapters 6 and 8), or possibly shifting some of the cost to your opponent (Chapter 12).

FRCP 16

The courts manage e-discovery through Rule 16. The court's scheduling order sets the time to complete discovery and may provide for the following:

- ✔ Limits on the extent of discovery.
- ✔ Provisions on disclosure or discovery of ESI.

✔ Any agreements of the parties asserting claims of privilege or protection after production, such as clawback or quick-peek agreements. (See a complete discussion in Chapter 10.)

✔ The dates of future conferences or the trial.

✔ Any other matter appropriate to the court to include.

Request an incorporation of agreements into the scheduling order. If your opponent fails to comply with the agreement, then they have violated a court order. See Chapter 9.

The scheduling and planning conference takes place after the court has received your meet-and-confer report (see the next section). This conference cannot be later than 120 days after the complaint was *served* (not *filed*) on the defendant. Hopefully, you and your opponent can reach agreements to reduce e-discovery cost.

The court may issue a preservation order under Rule 16(c) or a protective order:

✔ **Preservation:** A preservation order clearly defines what ESI you and your opponent need to preserve. Having specific directions of what to preserve is significant to avoid possible sanctions if you happen to lose discoverable ESI due to a lack of understanding of what you should have preserved.

A preservation order allows you to get your hands around the ESI that you need to preserve early in the process. Preservations issues are discussed in greater detail in Chapter 7.

✔ **Protective:** A protective order provides that certain ESI is not subject to discovery. You generally ask the court for a protective order when the other party is seeking to discover privileged or protected ESI that is not subject to disclosure. This is discussed in Chapter 10.

Always be prepared. Rule 16(f) gives the court broad authority to inflict pain (sanction) on you or your attorney for failing to obey a scheduling order or pre-trial order.

Being unprepared or failing to participate effectively in an order puts you at risk of being sanctioned. Judges have great latitude in sanctions, including the expenses incurred by the other side because of your actions. These cost penalties may be in addition to the sanctions related to Rule 37. (Rule 37 provides the court with great latitude in crafting sanctions against you if you fail to properly participate in e-discovery. This is discussed in detail in Chapter 5.) The ultimate sanction is losing your case.

The bottom line is that your lawyers and IT professionals have a 120-day window to learn your ESI issues and to learn about e-discovery.

FRCP 26

Knowing is half the battle. In e-discovery, knowing Rule 26 may be most of the war. Rule 26 is essential in discovering your opponent's ESI. One of the most important aspects of discovery is the meet-and-confer session. Rule 26(f) requires that you meet with your opposing party at least 21 days before the scheduling conference (called the *meet and confer*). This can be a make-it-or-break-it moment for your case. All discovery issues are addressed at the meet-and-confer session. You must be prepared and come with a plan. See Chapters 8 and 10 for more details.

Local court rules may limit the date for the meet-and-confer session to expedite cases. Consult with your attorney to make sure you know when your meet and confer is.

If you're a party to litigation, Rule 26(a) requires that you either provide a copy or a categorical description and location of any ESI that may be used to support your claims or defenses. The other side does the same thing, and it can help reduce the cost of e-discovery. The disclosure must be in writing and made at or within 14 days of the meet-and-confer session. Don't panic; you don't need to know everything at that time. Just disclose what you know and tell the rest later. Disclosure is an ongoing requirement. All pre-trial disclosures are due within 30 days of the trial date, and the other party has 14 days to object. Failure to object could result in a waiver of objections for trial purposes. These time limitations illustrate the need to be litigation ready as discussed in Chapter 3.

Generally, under Rule 26(b)(1), you can discover any nonprivileged matter relevant or likely to lead to evidence relevant to your claim or defense. However, there are some limitations. If you can demonstrate that the ESI is not reasonably accessible because of undue burden or cost, you may not have to produce the ESI. (Chapter 6 discusses what is deemed not reasonably accessible.) The court can still order you to produce it if, for example, the benefit from production outweighs the cost. The court may make also your opponent pay for the ESI production. (See Chapter 12 on how to shift e-discovery cost to the other party.)

An important aspect of e-discovery is that you may be able to withhold ESI if it is privileged or protected. See Chapter 10 for more info.

You must be familiar with the rules applicable to properly protecting ESI. A large volume of ESI makes it difficult to avoid an inadvertent disclosure of privileged or protected ESI, but you have ways to undo what you just did — sometimes, no harm no foul. Chapter 10 discusses this significant topic.

Requesting properly

A proper request can reduce cost and obtain relevant ESI more efficiently. Make sure your request is what you want and how you want it. In *Autotech Techs Ltd. P'ship v. Automationdirect. com* (2008), the plaintiff produced ESI requested by the defendant. There was no request for the metadata. Sometime later, the defendant decided they wanted the metadata. Judge D'Onofrio was not sympathetic. The judge noted that the plaintiff had complied with production of the ESI and the defendant could have requested the metadata earlier. Therefore, the defendant "must be satisfied with what it asked for."

FRCP 33 and 34

You may request a party to answer written questions, or *interrogatories*. Rule 33(d) allows the responding party to specify the records to be reviewed and the location of the records as well as a reasonable opportunity to examine, audit, and make copies of the records. This applies only when the answer to the question may be determined from the records and the burden of getting the answer is the same for either party.

Rule 34(b) allows you to request the form of the ESI to be produced. You may also "inspect, copy, test, or sample the other parties' ESI." If you are the responding party, you may object to the request and state the form of ESI you intend to use. You must translate ESI into a reasonably useable form. If no form of ESI is requested, you then produce ESI in the following manner:

✔ The form in which the ESI is ordinarily maintained

✔ A form that is reasonably useable

Applying the Rules to Criminal Cases

ESI is becoming increasingly more important in criminal cases. From Enron to Bernie Madoff, the need to discover, review, and analyze ESI is essential in criminal investigations and prosecutions. Because more than 90 percent of documents today are generated in electronic format, ESI is taking a paramount role.

Although the rules and case law on e-discovery in the civil arena have been developing at a rapid pace, the same cannot be said in criminal law. Issues include Fourth and Fifth Amendment constitutional arguments and state constitutional concerns. The procedural rules are set forth in the Federal Rules of Criminal Procedure (FRCrimP) as well as the states' versions of criminal procedure codes.

The Fourth Amendment has a general prohibition against searches and seizures without a warrant. Some exceptions include

- ✔ **Search incident to an arrest:** Law enforcement has the right to search an area within the suspect's immediate control when they arrest someone. This is generally for law enforcement's protection and may not give them the right to seize ESI — say a computer — unless it poses a threat.

- ✔ **Protective sweep:** Law enforcement may search an immediate area if they have reason to believe another suspect is nearby.

- ✔ **Plain view:** Law enforcement does not need a warrant for contraband in plain sight. This would probably not apply to any ESI.

- ✔ **Consent search:** A person may give law enforcement the right to search. The consent must be voluntarily given with full understanding of the person's rights.

In *United States v. O'Keefe* (2008), Judge Facciola said, "It is foolish to disregard them (the FRCP) merely because this is a criminal case, particularly where, as is the case here, it is far better to use these rules than to reinvent the wheel when the production of documents in criminal and civil cases raises the same problems."

The FRCP will be looked at for guidance while the FRCrimP evolves on these issues.

If the government wants what you have, it requests a search and seizure warrant by filing an application or affidavit. The procedure is in Rule 41. The application identifies the location of the property to be searched and seized, and includes facts that support why the government needs (and should get) the property.

Figure 4-1 shows an application for a federal search warrant. States have similar applications or affidavits. Note that the application is sworn before a judge.

Figure 4-2 shows a federal search and seizure warrant that a judge issues from the application. Note that unless the judge authorizes delayed notice, a copy of the warrant and a receipt for the property taken must be given to the person or left at the premises. Law enforcement then conducts the authorized search and seizes the property per the warrant. They will be required to provide the court with an inventory of what was seized.

Figure 4-3 shows a copy of a federal return, which lists property taken. For ESI, the return needs to list only the property seized that stores the ESI.

At this stage, your attorney usually challenges the warrant and the application for it, generally on constitutional grounds.

AO 106 (Rev. 01/09) Application for a Search Warrant

United States District Court

for the

In the Matter of the Search of)
(Briefly describe the property to be searched)
or identify the person by name and address))   Case No.
)
)
)

APPLICATION FOR A SEARCH WARRANT

I, a federal law enforcement officer or an attorney for the government, request a search warrant and state under penalty of perjury that I have reason to believe that there is now concealed on the following person or property located in the _____ District of _____ *(identify the person or describe property to be searched and give its location)*:

The person or property to be searched, described above, is believed to conceal *(identify the person or describe the property to be seized)*:

The basis for the search under Fed. R. Crim. P. 41(c) is *(check one or more)*:

☐ evidence of a crime;

☐ contraband, fruits of crime, or other items illegally possessed;

☐ property designed for use, intended for use, or used in committing a crime;

☐ a person to be arrested or a person who is unlawfully restrained.

The search is related to a violation of _____ U.S.C. § _____ , and the application is based on these facts:

☐ Continued on the attached sheet.

☐ Delayed notice of ____ days (give exact ending date if more than 30 days: _____) is requested under 18 U.S.C. § 3103a, the basis of which is set forth on the attached sheet.

_____
Applicant's signature

_____
Printed name and title

Sworn to before me and signed in my presence.

Date: _____

_____
Judge's signature

City and state: _____

_____
Printed name and title

Figure 4-1:
Application for a federal search warrant.

AO 93 (Rev. 01/09) Search and Seizure Warrant

UNITED STATES DISTRICT COURT
for the

In the Matter of the Search of) *(Briefly describe the property to be searched* *or identify the person by name and address)*)	
)	Case No.
)	
)	
)	

SEARCH AND SEIZURE WARRANT

To: Any authorized law enforcement officer

An application by a federal law enforcement officer or an attorney for the government requests the search of the following person or property located in the _____ District of _____ *(identify the person or describe the property to be searched and give its location)*:

The person or property to be searched, described above, is believed to conceal *(identify the person or describe the property to be seized)*:

I find that the affidavit(s), or any recorded testimony, establish probable cause to search and seize the person or property.

YOU ARE COMMANDED to execute this warrant on or before _____

(not to exceed 10 days)

❏ in the daytime 6:00 a.m. to 10 p.m.   ❏ at any time in the day or night as I find reasonable cause has been established.

Unless delayed notice is authorized below, you must give a copy of the warrant and a receipt for the property taken to the person from whom, or from whose premises, the property was taken, or leave the copy and receipt at the place where the property was taken.

The officer executing this warrant, or an officer present during the execution of the warrant, must prepare an inventory as required by law and promptly return this warrant and inventory to United States Magistrate Judge

_____

(name)

❏ I find that immediate notification may have an adverse result listed in 18 U.S.C. § 2705 (except for delay of trial), and authorize the officer executing this warrant to delay notice to the person who, or whose property, will be searched or seized *(check the appropriate box)* ❏for _____ days *(not to exceed 30)*.

❏until, the facts justifying, the later specific date of _____ .

Date and time issued: _____   _____

Judge's signature

City and state: _____   _____

Printed name and title

Figure 4-2:
Federal
search and
seizure
warrant.

AO 93 (Rev. 01/09) Search and Seizure Warrant (Page 2)

Return		
Case No.:	Date and time warrant executed:	Copy of warrant and inventory left with:
Inventory made in the presence of :		
Inventory of the property taken and name of any person(s) seized:		

Certification

I declare under penalty of perjury that this inventory is correct and was returned along with the original warrant to the designated judge.

Date: _____

_____
Executing officer's signature

_____
Printed name and title

Figure 4-3:
Federal
search and
seizure
return.

Your attorney may also seek to have the court determine that the evidence seized cannot be used in court. For example, by arguing that what was seized was beyond the warrant. The application must establish *probable cause* (a reasonable belief that a crime has been committed and evidence of such may be at the site).

F.R. Crim. P. Rule 41

Effective December 1, 2009, F.R. Crim. P. Rule 41 will be amended to address some ESI issues. It establishes a two-step process when ESI is involved. The first step is the seizure and then a subsequent review of the ESI. That review must be consistent with the warrant. Anything else can be challenged by your attorney and possibly be inadmissible. There is no time frame established for this review because it can take a substantial amount of time. This is especially true with hidden traps or encryptions. The government gives you an inventory return form, which describes the physical storage media seized or copied (for example, a laptop is described; not the data contained on it).

F. R. Crim. P. Rule 16

F. R. Crim. P. Rule 16 allows you to discover any ESI that the government has in its possession that:

- Is material to your case
- The government intends to use at trial against you
- Was taken from or belongs to you

F. R. Crim. P. Rule 17 and 17.1

Rule 17.1 provides for pre-trial conferences to promote a fair and expeditious trial. Under Rule 17, the court may issue a subpoena for a third party to produce records at trial or at another time and place. The court may allow you to inspect all or part of the ESI. For practical purposes, with more and more ESI and possible third-party ESI that could assist in the defense, it is likely there will be future changes to mirror the civil rules. The government will usually get its ESI by consent or warrant.

Learning about Admissibility

ESI may be discoverable but not necessarily admissible in court. In court, the judge determines what evidence is allowed to be presented. In a jury trial, the jury only hears what the judge allows them to hear. The rules are contained in the Federal Rules of Evidence (FRE). Throughout the entire discovery process, you must give some thought to whether something will be admitted as evidence.

The first two rules of evidence for you to remember are

- *Only* relevant evidence is admissible.
- *All* relevant evidence is admissible *unless* there's some *other rule* that says it isn't.

Ponder for a moment the second rule. If you think the rule is saying that evidence is admissible unless it's not admissible, you're right! The FRE is full of rules with multiple exceptions. Even the exceptions have exceptions. However, with a few basics, you can make sense out of the general rules.

We also discuss admissibility issues in Chapter 12.

The first rule of evidence law splits all the ESI in a legal action into two parts: *relevant* and *irrelevant*. That sounds simple, but it isn't. With the many variants on the road to getting something admitted, you come across some roadblocks:

- ***Exclusions*** are anti-rules. Evidence that is under an exclusion reverses the rule. Say one rule allows that an e-mail message be used as evidence. Any exclusion to that rule reverses it. Then that e-mail message would not be allowed as evidence. Some evidence may be excluded because it is privileged or protected (see Chapter 10).

- ***Exceptions*** are rules that are anti-exclusions. If an exception is found to the exclusion, then the exclusion is ignored. An e-mail message that had been ruled inadmissible would become admissible again. Some evidence that is privileged or protected can still be admitted with a waiver exception. Evidence of someone saying something against his or her interest can be deemed relevant with an exception.

Two issues often complicate whether ESI is relevant or irrelevant:

- **Authentication:** Authentication means that the ESI is what you say it is. If you can't authenticate your evidence, it isn't allowed in the court.

- **Best evidence:** Rule 1002 requires that you must use an original to prove the contents. An original is any printout or other output readable by sight, shown to reflect the data accurately. Rule 1003 allows you to submit a copy unless there's a debate about its authenticity, and then the court won't allow the copy.

Figure 4-4 illustrates the basic steps in determining what e-evidence is admissible. Judges have the authority to decide that evidence is not admissible in the trial.

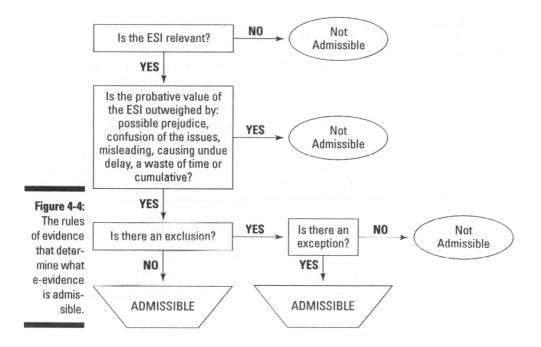

Figure 4-4:
The rules
of evidence
that deter-
mine what
e-evidence
is admis-
sible.

Lessening the Need for Judicial Intervention by Cooperation

Playing nice is the best way to avoid involving the judge in the e-discovery process. The FRCP gives great latitude to both you and your opposing party in dealing with e-discovery. If you are a requesting party, know what ESI you want. If you are the responding party, know what you have and how to access it. If you have privileged or protected ESI, know how to find it to avoid inadvertent disclosure. Judges would prefer that you work out a plan of discovery without the need for unnecessary, time-consuming, and costly motions.

Your entire e-discovery team — lawyers and IT people alike — must work together from the onset of anticipated litigation. Because of the accelerated time frames, a lack of knowledge could lead to a critical error. You must be aware of what you have and what form you have it in. Know the systems, legal and technical. The best practice is to have protocols and procedures in advance. Use of best practices (see Chapter 3) and planning (see Chapter 6) decreases the need to involve the judge. The meet-and-confer session provides a means of limiting the involvement of the court.

The judge in *William A. Gross Const. Assoc., Inc. v. Am. Mfg. Mutual Ins. Co.* (2009), chastised the parties for forcing the court into the "uncomfortable position" of having to craft a keyword search methodology. Judge Peck said it best when he said, "Electronic discovery requires cooperation between opposing counsel and transparency in all aspects of preservation of [ESI]."

The Sedona Conference Cooperation Proclamation recognizes the importance of cooperation in the process of e-discovery to meet the goals of FRCP Rule 1 for a just, speedy, and inexpensive determination of a case. The Proclamation makes it clear that cooperation by attorneys is consistent with the duty to be a zealous advocate for the client. This is implicit in the FRCP, which requires a level of cooperation to avoid sanctions. The proclamation calls for a "paradigm shift for the discovery process."

Things to consider to accomplish this cooperation include:

- ✔ Utilize an internal ESI discovery "point person" to assist counsel. This may also be helpful in later use of expert testimony if needed.

- ✔ Exchange information on relevant data sources, including those not being searched.

- ✔ Provide early disclosures on ESI.

- ✔ Jointly develop automated methodologies for search and retrieval of relevant ESI.

- ✔ Promote early identification of forms of production.

- ✔ Consider court-appointed experts, mediators, or other alternate means to resolve disputes that may arise without resort to the court.

Rule 53 provides a unique opportunity for you to avoid situations like those in *Gross*. You can agree to ask the court to appoint a Special Master to assist in the e-discovery process, resolve disputes, and reduce cost. A Special Master is a person, generally a forensic person or attorney, appointed by the court to assist in the discovery process. The Master may be used to provide assistance to the court, to you and your opponent, or both on a wide variety of e-discovery issues. See Chapter 10 for more on the Masters.

Limiting e-Discovery

Just because you want a certain piece of evidence, doesn't mean you can get it from your opponent. Only ESI that is relevant or is expected to lead to relevant evidence is subject to discovery. If the ESI is privileged or protected, it generally isn't part of discovery. This is discussed in Chapter 10. Courts are not sympathetic if you attempt to impose settlements on the other party by running up the cost of e-discovery. Nor are the courts patient if you use e-discovery as a fishing expedition.

The FRCP provides the courts with the power to place boundaries on the conduct of e-discovery. Rule 26(b)(2)(C) allows the court to limit discovery if:

✔ The discovery sought is unreasonably cumulative

✔ The discovery unreasonably duplicates other discovery

✔ The ESI can be obtained from other more convenient, less burdensome, or less costly sources

✔ The requesting party has had plenty of time to obtain the ESI

✔ The likely benefit of discovery is outweighed by the burden or expense of the discovery

You may also seek a protective order limiting or denying discovery. The court may issue a protective order for good cause to protect against the following:

✔ Annoyance

✔ Embarrassment

✔ Oppression

✔ Undue burden

If you want a protective order, you must certify to the court that you made a good faith effort to resolve the dispute before involving the court. Protective orders may be used for privileged and protected ESI. They are also effective to limit fishing expeditions from overly broad requests. For example, a request for "all e-mails" is overly broad. A request for "all e-mails from Manager A to Manager B from the period May 1, 20XX and June 2, 20XX" generally are enforced.

If you are a non-party, you can move to quash or modify the subpoena. You may also seek a Rule 26 protective order the same way any party can.

Another method that is employed by the courts is cost shifting. This can be used when the cost of compliance is out of proportion to the likely benefit or when the ESI is not reasonably accessible. Sometimes you have to pay the piper if you want to hear the music. Cost shifting is analyzed in Chapter 12.

Finding Out About Sanctions

You can avoid the wrath of the courts if you're prepared, knowledgeable, and play nice. The court has wide latitude in sanctioning you if you fail to cooperate or comply in e-discovery (Rule 37). Cooperation doesn't mean giving in; it means working with FRCP Rule 1 in mind.

You may request sanctions on the other party or the court may do so. The court may order you to comply with any type of discovery, not just ESI-related discovery. Non-parties may be held in contempt of court (Rule 45).

If the court has an order that you've not complied with, you may be considered to be in contempt of court. (For example, not following the discovery plan incorporated into a scheduling order or a pre-trial order.) The court has many options including:

- ✓ Treating the matters relating to the unproduced ESI as proven by your opponent. This is *adverse inference*.
- ✓ Prohibiting you from relying on the unproduced ESI in your claim or defense.
- ✓ Eliminating a claim or defense.
- ✓ Postponing your case until compliance.
- ✓ Dismissing your case completely or partly.

The rules are clear that these sanctions can be cumulative. Additionally, you may be forced to pay your opponent's expenses caused by the failure to obey the order.

If there is not an order but a failure to produce, the same sanctions can apply. The rules provide safe harbor for certain ESI.

Rule 37(e) provides that the court cannot impose sanctions for failing to produce ESI that you've lost from routine, good-faith operation of the system.

Good faith is crucial. When litigation is anticipated, you have a duty to hold the ESI and preserve it. At that point, steps must be taken to avoid any destruction of the ESI, even if by routine operation.

If the ESI is not available, the courts look to determine whether you've destroyed it by routine operation. It is important that you have a data retention policy and show compliance with it. This is beyond the duty to preserve. Chapters 6 and 7 look into this further.

In *Doe v. Norwalk Community College (2007),* the court refused to apply the safe harbor as the defendants had not followed their document retention policy. The defendants did not have a policy that was consistently followed, and the court would not acknowledge what they had was a retention policy. Having a policy but not following it is the same as not having it.

As a sanction, the court can take an adverse inference, meaning that the reason it is unavailable is that it would be adverse to the party not producing it. An adverse inference in the situation before the court requires the following factors:

- ✔ There is a duty to preserve.
- ✔ The lose or destruction of the ESI was intentional.
- ✔ The ESI is relevant.

If your opponent does not participate in the meet-and-confer session in good faith, the court can make them pay your costs, including attorney fees, because of their actions.

If you request sanctions, you must provide a certification that you attempted to confer to resolve the issues. You must have done so in good faith.

Rulings on Metadata

Generally, when you hand over your ESI to your opponent, it's in its native format. The phrase *native format* means that the ESI has its metadata intact. *Metadata* is the information about who created a file; when it was created, accessed, or modified; and other documentation.

Rules 26(b) and 34(a) and (b) make it clear that metadata is subject to e-discovery. Working backward, that means that you must manage metadata so that it's preservable, searchable, and producible. Any attempt at deleting metadata puts you on a collision course with legal disaster. Sloppy or ad hoc handling of metadata (legally known as *improper handling*) won't be a career-building move. Rule 37(f) provides a safe harbor if you manage metadata as part of normal business practices according to reasonable policies, including automated metadata management and accidentally losing metadata.

You won't find a specific rule that you can turn to and learn everything that applies to metadata issues. Those issues are co-mingled with a variety of rules and notes, shown in Table 4-2.

Metadata is not an expense item when it comes to litigation readiness. Metadata helps you organize, identify, and review your ESI to reduce time and cost.

Table 4-2	Metadata Rules and Notes	
Rule	*Key Issues*	*Right Things to Do*
16(b) and 26(f)	Requires understanding ESI issues.	Implement reasonable and defensible plans and procedures for dealing with ESI that would satisfy the court's standard of reasonableness. Prepare to deal with metadata early and in every case.
26(b)(2)	Metadata may not be considered *not reasonably accessible*.	Design, implement, and monitor policies, procedures and systems for preserving and handling metadata in ESI. Prepare to produce metadata in every case.
34(A)	Metadata is discoverable.	Include metadata in your strategy for litigation holds.
34(B)	Requesting party can specify the format in which ESI is produced, including native file format with metadata intact.	Prepare to produce in native file format because scanned or printed ESI may not satisfy the duty to preserve. Implement systems and policies to preserve and produce ESI in native file formats.
37(e)	You have a safe harbor from sanctions if metadata is deleted in the course of routine, good faith operations of your information systems.	Manage metadata like all other ESI knowing that the outcome of all cases may depend on it. Design and implement policies and procedures that can be automated to create consistent metadata handling.
Advisory Committee Notes to Rule 34	If ESI is maintained or stored in a form that's electronically searchable, then the format used to produce that ESI cannot significantly degrade its electronic searchability.	Purge unnecessary metadata, such as records of changes to documents or stray comments by users.

Getting Guidance but Not Authority from Sedona Think Tanks

The Sedona Conference is a non-partisan think tank on law and policy. A number of working groups address various issues of ESI from assessing what is inaccessible to Rule 45 subpoenas. The working groups consist of lawyers, jurists, and consultants that work to provide best practices and commentary on e-discovery issues. Lawyers, judges, and parties look to the Sedona Conference for guidance in the area of ESI retention and production.

The Sedona Guidelines Principles, Second Edition, Best Practices Recommendations and Principles for Addressing Electronic Document Production is required reading for anyone dealing with ESI. Whether you're a lawyer, judge, or IT person, this is a powerful tool when confronted with e-discovery. There are 14 principles related to e-discovery. This and other working papers may be downloaded from www.sedonaconference.org.

Implementing the Sedona Principles and related commentaries does not mean automatic success. They are only guidelines and recommendations without the force of law. However, the courts do look to them and cite them frequently.

Disagreeing with Sedona does not mean you are wrong but should give you a reason to look again. Ultimately, you must defend what you do and how you do it. Sedona is helpful but not the final determination.

Collecting the Wisdom of the Chief Justices and National Law Conference

The mission of the Conference of Chief Justices is to improve the administration of justice within the states, commonwealths, and territories of the United States. Its working group on e-discovery has promulgated a set of guidelines for e-discovery. If you have a matter in state court, you should consult these as possible guidelines in interpreting the state's e-discovery rules.

The guidelines are meant to help reduce uncertainty in dealing with state level e-discovery issues. The guidelines make it clear that they are not meant to be model rules, but only guidances to be used with other resources cited in the guidelines, including the FRCP. The guidelines may be downloaded at www.ncsconline.org/images/EDiscCCJGuidelinesFinal.pdf.

American Bar Association's Civil Discovery Standards

The American Bar Association (ABA) has specific standards relating to e-discovery, including a list of factors the court should consider in deciding how to allocate cost. The ABA standards are not law but provide guidance for interpretation. They may be downloaded at www.abanet.org/litigation/discoverystandards. Failing to abide by the ABA standards may create an ethics issue in e-discovery, as discussed in Chapter 5.

Do not confuse the Chief Justices and National Law Conference with the National Conference of Commissioners on Uniform State Laws. They are also a nonpartisan think tank on various issues of state law. They have issued a set of Model Rules for e-discovery. Although the goal is to have states adopt a uniform set of laws and rules, these Model Rules are simply the Conference's recommendations without force of law. This reference tool for your arsenal can be downloaded at www.nccusl.org/Update/Docs/Finals_NC/URRDOESI_Final_Oct07_NC.doc.

Minding the e-Discovery Reference Model

The Electronic Discovery Reference Model (EDRM) Project was put together to address problems that were identified in e-discovery. The model is meant to provide a flexible framework for e-discovery as shown in Figure 4-5. The EDRM is a reference — not law — and is available for download at www.edrm.net.

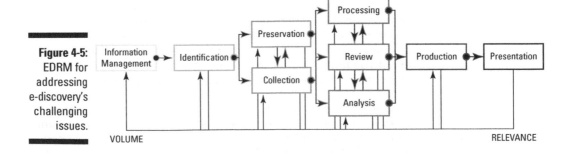

Figure 4-5: EDRM for addressing e-discovery's challenging issues.

Following the Federal Rules Advisory Committee

When in the process of federal rulemaking, the Federal Rules Advisory Committee provides guidance on what the proposed rule intends. The process is as follows:

- ✔ Initial review by the Advisory Committee
- ✔ Publication of the proposed rule for public comment
- ✔ Final approval of the proposal or revised proposal by the Advisory Committee
- ✔ Approval by the Standing Committee
- ✔ Judicial Conference approval
- ✔ Supreme Court approval
- ✔ Congressional review and approval

One of the best tools of interpretation in your e-discovery toolbox is the Advisory Committee Notes that accompany the rules. Considered very persuasive, the notes give insight into how to interpret the rule and the intent of the committee.

Chapter 5

Judging Professional Competence and Conduct

In This Chapter

▶ Diligently seeking ESI

▶ Providing penalties for e-discovery misconduct

▶ Assessing problems with legal counsel

▶ Following attorney rules of professional conduct

▶ Gaining insight from others

▶ Applying sanctions cases

The world of ESI provides dramatic new challenges for both you and your lawyers. The complex world of e-discovery can make you more reliant on your attorneys and any outside vendors your attorneys hire. Selecting the wrong legal counsel can result in you losing your case. In this chapter, we cover how you can make sure your lawyer is doing the best job for you.

To give you a fighting chance in court, various Rules of Professional Responsibility govern attorneys. From the American Bar Association (ABA) Model Rules of Professional Conduct to the various state rules, they establish the ethical responsibilities of an attorney in the representation of a client. We cover those rules as well in this chapter so that you know when your attorney may not be acting in your best interests.

Ultimately, you can be held responsible for your attorney's conduct, meaning you can be sanctioned by the court and you can even lose your case. But with the help of this chapter, you can avoid any type of sanctions.

Making Sure Your Attorney Gives a Diligent Effort

Your attorney must give your case his best diligent effort. In the following sections, we talk about the due diligence your lawyer owes you.

You bear the ultimate responsibility in e-discovery; your due diligence must be used during the entire process. You must exercise diligence in hiring competent counsel and/or third-party vendors. Diligence must also be applied to the working relationship with those third parties.

If you're thinking of representing yourself because you think you can get away with less than due diligence, you need to think twice. Clients who represent themselves may find that the court does not show them any additional consideration. In *United States v. Two Bank Accounts,* the court did not show leniency to the self-represented party in relation to discovery.

Attorneys have an additional due diligence burden imposed by the professional ethics while representing you. We discuss these rules later in this chapter.

Looking at what constitutes a diligent effort

The nature of the legal profession is that attorneys are zealous advocates for their clients. This is both a legal and ethical obligation. To effectively exercise this obligation, the attorney must make a diligent effort, which is often called *due diligence*. A diligent effort means that your attorney is representing you in all aspects of the case in a professional manner and doing what a competent attorney would do under the same circumstances. It applies both the legal obligations imposed under the law and relevant rules as well as the applicable ethical standards. Failing to exercise due diligence exposes the lawyer to a malpractice suit.

Unfortunately, you can't always know if your attorney is doing a good job. Generally, only the judge and your opponent's attorney can accurately evaluate your attorney's performance. If your attorney isn't doing the following things, you should consider whether he's doing his due diligence for you:

- ✔ **Keeps you in the loop at all levels of the case.** This includes copies of correspondence. You can often judge from a reading of the various correspondence if something seems wrong.

- ✔ **Gives you a proper amount of time.** If your attorney is regularly asking for things at the last minute, it's an indication of a lack of appropriate planning and preparation of your case.

- ✔ **Files a lot of motions.** Another possible flag is an abundance of motions before the court. This may show that there is a lack of cooperation.

- ✔ **Discusses with you the litigation plan.** A seasoned attorney has a good idea how the litigation will proceed from a procedural basis and you can set benchmarks. This will be reviewed and revised as the case progresses. The key is communication.

You're the client and are paying for representation. You should not be shy about questioning anything your attorney does or proposes to do. You have a right to know why something needs to be done and if there is a better more cost effective way of doing it. Your attorney may have a good explanation and in fact it may be the other attorney that is causing problems. You should feel free to question the progress of your case at any time.

Searching for evidence

When a case has been filed, your attorney starts a search for the piece of evidence that can help your side win the case, the *smoking gun*.

If you hear your attorneys talking about a smoking gun, they haven't started channeling Clint Eastwood. Sometimes the smoking gun does exist. In *Ernst v. Merck & Co., Inc.*, e-mails showing that Merck scientists had concerns over a drug were introduced in the case, which resulted in the plaintiff being awarded more than $253 million dollars.

In most cases, there isn't one smoking gun. Your attorney must build a case by voluminous circumstantial (indirect) evidence that proves your position to be correct. This is the heart and soul of e-discovery: to find as much everything possible to build a compelling case.

FRCP 26(a)(1) establishes an obligation on you to provide your opponent with a copy or a description by category and location of all documents, ESI, and tangible things within its possession and control that it may use to support its claim. Your lawyer has to hand over everything as long as it's relevant and not privileged or protected, even if not admissible in court. With one exception: FRCP 26(b)(2) permits your lawyer to withhold ESI that is no longer reasonably accessible because of undue burden or cost (see Chapter 6).

By the time of the meet-and-confer session, your lawyer must have a comprehensive knowledge of your computer technology, the architecture of your ESI storage system, the location of any ESI, and the native formats and metadata that the ESI is in. Additionally, he should be conversant enough in technology to understand your opponents' technology issues. Close communication is essential among everyone on your side so your attorney doesn't give away anything that may be harmful to your case and that your attorney knows what to ask for from the other side.

Producing ESI

The FRCP also imposes an affirmative duty on you and your attorney to make a diligent effort to produce ESI as long as it's not privileged or protected. The stakes are high and the potential sanctions significant. Most of the problems that could be encountered can be avoided by hiring knowledgeable legal counsel from the onset of the litigation or earlier.

When served with a subpoena, non-parties have the same obligation to produce ESI, although courts tend to be more sympathetic to protecting non-parties from incurring significant expenses in responding to a subpoena.

Your attorney must be conversant in the issues inherent in producing ESI. Subtle nuances in the technology and issues surround the preservation, collecting, reviewing, and producing of ESI. Ignorance is not a defense. In *Garcia v. Berkshire Life Ins. Co. of America,* the court rejected the attorney's assertion of technical incompetence. If the attorney was technically ignorant, then the attorney should have sought assistance from someone with technical competence.

When the duty to preserve relevant ESI is established, your attorney must make a diligent effort to identify, protect, and preserve potentially relevant ESI. Judge Scheindlin explained in *Zubulake* that your lawyer must continue her diligent effort throughout the case and not just at the beginning. From the litigation hold (see Chapter 7) to taking ongoing, regular affirmative steps to ensure that all relevant, nonprivileged, or protected ESI (or sources of ESI) are discovered, preserved, and produced. It is not sufficient for your lawyer be proactive only in establishing the litigation hold and preservation. There is a professional obligation on your lawyer conduct all e-discovery in a diligent and candid manner.

Providing a certification

Every disclosure and every request, response, or objection must be signed by you or your attorney. FRCP 26(g) requires this certification that to the best of the person's knowledge, information, and belief, after making a reasonable inquiry:

✔ A disclosure is complete and correct as of the time made.

✔ A discovery request, response, or objection is

- Consistent with the rules and the law or by a nonfrivolous argument to extend or modify the law.

- Not for any improper purpose, such as to harass, cause unnecessary delay, or needlessly increase the cost of litigation.

> • Neither unreasonable nor unduly burdensome or expensive considering the needs of the case, prior discovery, the amount in controversy, and the importance of the issues.

Avoiding Being Sanctioned

The courts have wide latitude in sanctioning participants — including you — in the e-discovery process. There are two ways: pursuant to the FRCP or by the court's inherent power. We discuss both ways in the following sections.

The ultimate sanction is losing your case because of bad conduct rather than the case's merits.

FRCP sanctions

Here are some ways a judge can sanction you or your attorneys according to the Federal Rules of Civil Procedure (FRCP):

- **Limitless scope of discovery:** FRCP 26 contains some provisions that allow judges to punish discovery misconduct. The courts may, if the judge deems it appropriate, award expenses to your opponent. For example, in the case of a motion for a protective order, the court may provide the prevailing party with costs. Although not a sanction, the court may also limit the scope of any discovery if it is duplicative or the burden or cost outweighs its likely benefit.

- **An improper certificate under FRCP 26(g):** Section 3 states that the court must impose an appropriate sanction on the signer, you if your attorney signed it, or both. The sanction may include paying your opponent's reasonable expenses, including attorney fees, as a result of the violation. (See the previous section to find out what a proper certificate contains.)

- **Failure to obey a discovery order or to provide a person required for examination:** The court has many potential sanctions under Rule 37(b)(2)(A). They include:

    - Directing that the matters in the order or other facts be considered established or proven.

    - Prohibiting you from supporting or opposing certain claims or defenses or introducing certain related matters into evidence in court.

    - Striking any of your claims or defenses in whole or part.

    - Delaying the proceedings until you've obeyed the order.

- Dismissing your action in whole or part.

- Giving a default judgment for or against you. This means that if the court found the other side has engaged in egregious misconduct it could decide the case in your favor without a trial.

- Treating your failure to obey as a contempt of court.

- Instead of or in addition to any of the preceding, order you to pay the reasonable expenses, including attorney fees, caused by the failure to obey. If you can prove your failure was substantially justified or other circumstances, the judge molt likely won't award expenses.

✓ **Failure to disclose or supplement previously disclosed information when new information is discovered, as required by Rule 26:** Under FRCP 37(c) the court may order that the information or witness may not be used in court. This will not apply if you can justify your failure or your failure doesn't prejudice your opponent. In addition to or in place of this sanction, the court may:

- Order you to pay reasonable expenses for your opponent.

- Inform the jury of your failure to comply.

- Impose other appropriate sanctions including those for failure to obey an order.

✓ **Failure to appear for a deposition or to respond to interrogatories:** Your opponent may motion the court for sanctions. To request this, the motion must be accompanied by a certification that they've conferred in good faith or attempted to confer with you to resolve the issue. The sanction may include costs but also may include any of the sanctions in FRCP Rule 37(b)(2) (A)(i)-(vi).

✓ **Failure to provide ESI lost as a result of the routine, good-faith operation of an electronic system:** FRCP Rule 37(e) may give you a safe harbor that, absent exceptional circumstances, a court may not impose sanctions.

✓ **Failure to participate in good faith in the meet-and-confer session:** Rule 37(f) provides a broad sanction for the assessment of costs, including attorney fees incurred by the failure to participate. This means that your attorneys must be knowledgeable about your ESI issues by the time the meet-and-confer session occurs.

Using a third-party vendor doesn't relieve you of liability for e-discovery misconduct. You bear the ultimate responsibility. The court will consider who was at fault in determining the type of sanction. For example, if your third-party vendor causes you to regularly miss deadlines or respond less than fully to a request for ESI, the court is not likely to dismiss your case — even the first time. *In re Seroquel Products Liability Litigation,* the court held that a party is responsible for the errors of its vendors. Blaming a failure on someone else is not a defense.

Inherent power sanctions

In addition to the sanctions in the FRCP, the courts have broad authority to sanction under their inherent power to control the conduct of a case. The inherent power is not established by specific rule. *Inherent power* dictates the court is responsible and has the power to oversee the conduct of all cases that are brought before it.

This includes the ability to sanction for misconduct without a specific rule if the court believes you or your attorney's conduct is wrongful. The available sanctions range from monetary sanctions, to adverse inferences (for example, a judge can tell a jury it may assume you destroyed ESI because it wouldn't have been in your favor), to dismissal of your case or claim. (These essentially parallel Rule 37 sanctions in the FRCP we discuss in the previous section.)

But many courts consider sanctions for these behaviors as well:

- **Simple negligence** is established if you have a legal duty, such as to preserve certain ESI, but failed to take the steps a reasonable person would have done to preserve that ESI and as a result some relevant ESI was destroyed. Negligence is without intent. For example, you may have failed to take all steps necessary to identify the relevant ESI at the inception of the litigation hold.

- **Reckless conduct** is beyond simple negligence but may not be intentional. However, it may be so reckless that the court treats the conduct as if it were intentional. For example, if a company had a duty to preserve ESI, but took only minimal steps to identify and preserve it without considering whether relevant ESI being destroyed. This could be the result of bad faith or just incompetence.

- **Bad faith** is the result of reckless misconduct or an intentional act. To be intentional, you must have intended either the act or the result. For example failing to properly institute a litigation hold knowing that relevant ESI will be destroyed.

Although bad faith or reckless conduct is not necessary for Rule 37 sanctions, they are relevant to the type of sanction the court may give. The court may provide a lower level of Rule 37 sanction, like costs without finding culpability, dismissal of your case, or an adverse inference. If the court gives an adverse inference, it's saying that you didn't produce evidence because it wouldn't have been in your best interests.

In *Coleman (Parent) Holdings, Inc. v. Morgan Stanley & Co.*, the court had ordered Morgan Stanley to search the oldest full backup tape for its employees involved in a transaction to produce all nonprivileged, relevant e-mails and to certify compliance. After certifying compliance, they uncovered thousands of backup tapes that had not been searched because of errors in their search techniques. However, they failed to immediately notify the court. The actions of both Morgan Stanley and their counsel upset the judge who noted, "Lack of candor has frustrated the court and opposing counsel's ability to be fully and timely informed." With sanctions, the court shifted the burden of proof on the fraud issue to Morgan Stanley. The court instructed the jury that it could consider that certain portions of the plaintiff's complaint true for the purposes of the case, read a statement to the jury concerning spoliation by Morgan Stanley, and instructed that the jury may consider this when awarding any damages. The result was a jury verdict of $1.45 billion dollars (yes, with a B) that included $850 million in punitive damages.

Various sanctions by courts

In *Keithley et al. v. The Home Store.Com, Inc.*, the court noted that an adverse inference may be under either its inherent power or Rule 37. It adopted the approach that to give an adverse inference in the situation before the court, there must be

- A duty to preserve the evidence

- The records were not preserved with a culpable state of mind

- The destroyed evidence was relevant to the case

In *Nursing Home Pension Fund v. Oracle Corp.*, the defendant's former CEO willfully destroyed e-mails and other relevant evidence in a class action suit against Oracle. As a sanction, the court instructed the jury that it could infer that the missing evidence was unfavorable to the defendants. The court chose not to impose the ultimate sanction of finding for the plaintiff because it determined that public policy favors determining cases on their merits; the adverse inference meets that goal and still does not allow any benefit from the misconduct.

Judge Wake in *Atlantic Recoding Corp. v. Howell* stated, "Imposition of a default judgment is therefore the only appropriate sanction, both for its deterrent effect and to remedy the prejudice inflicted on the recording companies and on the court." Judge Wake found that default was appropriate under both Rule 37(b) and the inherent powers because of the tireless efforts of the defendant to remove relevant ESI from his computer. Defendant also failed to cooperate with plaintiff's attempts to have a forensic examination of his computer.

The court in *Phoenix Four, Inc. v. Strategic Red. Corp.* found that the attorney was grossly negligent in not performing a diligent search for sources of ESI. The court imposed a sanction on the attorney of more than $30,000. Attorneys may also wish to review the 2009 case of *Bray & Gillespie Mgmt. v Lexington. and Lexington Insurance Company.* In that case, as a result of misconduct the Federal District Court Judge ordered the attorneys to pay costs of the other party incurred as a result of their misconduct.

Knowing the Risks Introduced by Legal Counsel

Discovery is the province of the attorneys. Competent counsel can save you money by working with you to develop a less time-consuming, and more productive, document search and review. Your attorney may also cause sanctions to be imposed on you for discovery misconduct. The very nature of discovery requires that attorneys operate with honesty and integrity in the process. Failing to comply with discovery responsibilities (say, by failing to make reasonable inquires or by outright dishonesty) may result in a variety of sanctions.

You extend your risk if your attorneys hire other e-discovery vendors. Third parties may be used for such things as data forensics, collection, processing, data hosting, consulting, and review. This may include lawyers and non-lawyers. Further, a third party may be needed to provide specialized expertise. For example, to collect data from an outdated native format. We discuss outside vendors in Chapters 13, 16, and 17.

If your lawyer hired a third-party vendor, you and your lawyer are not relieved of your e-discovery obligations. If a vendor is part of your team, make sure you do the following to ensure that he can meet the needs of the e-discovery:

- **Review the economic stature of the vendor.** A vendor going into bankruptcy could result in missed deadlines, lost documents, additional costs, and possible sanctions.

- **Communicate.** Constant and open communication is imperative. In today's realm of ESI, the attorney probably hasn't seen all of the ESI. In order to make a certification, your attorney must coordinate and oversee the e-discovery process and take independent steps to verify the completeness of the ESI production.

Acting bad: Attorney e-discovery misconduct

The misconduct of the attorney may result in sanctions to the attorney, you, or both. In addition to the sanctions under the FRCP and the inherent power of the court, the attorney is subject to applicable rules of professional conduct.

In determining the professional competence and conduct of your lawyer, there are a number of different rules. Table 5-1 covers the applicability of various rules.

Table 5-1	Rules Applicable to Attorney Conduct	
Rule	**Binding**	**Remedy**
FRCP	Binding on both parties and lawyers	Sanctions by the court
Case law/Inherent power	Binding on both parties and lawyers	Sanctions by the court
ABA Model Rules of Professional Conduct	Guidance for lawyers	None
Code of professional conduct per state	Binding on lawyers	Sanctions by state's bar association including possible disbarment (in some states it is the state Supreme Court)

In *Qualcomm Inc. v. Broadcom, Inc.,* the defendant wanted information from Qualcomm. During trial preparation, the attorneys for Qualcomm learned of 21 relevant e-mails but did not produce them to the court. When a witness testified to their existence, Qualcomm lost the case. Qualcomm pointed fingers at its outside legal counsel, but the court noted that Qualcomm had an extensive in-house legal staff and the ability to do what was required in discovery. The court noted that Qualcomm just lacked the desire to do so. As a sanction for the misconduct, the court ordered Qualcomm to pay Broadcom in excess of $8.5 million in Broadcom legal fees and referred the matter of the lawyers to the State Bar of California for possible disciplinary action.

If you're looking to hire legal counsel in cases where ESI may be an issue, here are ten questions you need to ask the attorney:

 ✔ How many attorneys in the firm handle ESI related matters? A sole proprietor can provide competent and effective representation to the same degree as a larger firm.

 ✔ What is the background and experience of those attorneys handling ESI and e-discovery? The main attorney, often a partner, retains the obligation to supervise the work of associates.

 ✔ Does your firm outsource any aspect of e-discovery? You want to make sure that there is experience in ESI issues and if outsourcing is used that there is a strong level of oversight and control exercised by your attorney.

 ✔ If you outsource, how do you select the vendor? Your costs may be significantly affected by the software used or available to the attorney.

 ✔ Is there any relationship between the firm (or any principal in the firm) and the outsourced vendors?

 ✔ What is your supervisory protocol for assuring the quality of the vendor's work?

✔ Who will be the person in the firm responsible for my case? You want a person in the firm that serves as your direct contact. Someone you can call if you have a question.

✔ How will I be billed for this engagement? It is important to know how your attorney is going to bill for services rendered and at what rates. Most large firms have a sliding rate scale based upon the level of the person performing the services. Partners charge more than staff associates. You will want to how the attorney's time is calculated. Is it on the quarter hour or the tenth of an hour? How much do they charge for a phone call?

✔ How will I be billed for vendors' services? Your attorney may use outside vendors and should be able to explain why and how that will be cost effective for you.

There is no one right answer to these questions. If the attorney doesn't know what she might do, it should be taken as a negative. The bottom line is that you must have a level of comfort and communication to move forward.

After you solicit responses, you'll be in a better position to select your attorney.

Relying on the American Bar Association and state rules of professional conduct

The American Bar Association (ABA) Model Rules of Professional Conduct serve as guidance for lawyers and as a foundation for most state rules. Lawyers must follow the guidelines of conduct in the jurisdiction in which they are licensed. When there isn't a state rule, there are Model Rules or best practices (such as the Sedona Principles).

The goal of the rules is to provide ethical standards for the practice of law. In handling lawsuits, including e-discovery, there are a number of applicable rules of ethics. Here are the most important rules:

✔ **Your lawyer must provide competent representation (Model Rule 1.1).** This requires that your lawyer demonstrate the legal knowledge, skill, thoroughness, and preparation necessary for the representation. Ethically, your lawyer must be knowledgeable about e-discovery issues or bring in someone who is. Yes, lawyers need to be competent in technology to practice in e-discovery.

✔ **Your lawyer must act with reasonable diligence and promptness (Model Rule 1.3).** We talk more about this in the earlier section, "Making Sure Your Attorney Gives a Diligent Effort."

✔ **Your lawyer must make a reasonable effort to expedite the litigation (Model Rule 3.2).** This coincides with the FRCP Rule 1, which we discuss in Chapter 4. Communication between you and your lawyer are essential, and Model Rule 1.4 requires that your lawyer promptly and reasonably consults and communicates with you on the matters of representation.

✔ **Your lawyer must not obstruct another party's access to evidence or unlawfully alter, destroy, or conceal a document or other material having potential evidentiary value (Model Rule 3.4).** Nor may a lawyer counsel or assist another person to do so. This duty starts with the duty to preserve (Chapter 7) and extends throughout the process. The court in *Bratka v. Anheuser-Busch Co.* noted the obligation of the lawyer to exercise some degree of oversight over their client's employees to ensure compliance.

✔ **Your lawyer has a duty to correct any false statement previously made and not to offer any evidence the lawyer believes to be false (Model Rule 3-3).**

✔ **Your lawyer can't knowingly reveal information concerning your representation or any of your confidences or secrets (Model Rule 1.6).** The large amount of potential ESI makes it more likely that such information may be inadvertently disclosed. If your lawyer inadvertently discloses privileged information, check out Chapter 10.

✔ **If your lawyer receives a document that is privileged or protected, he must promptly notify the other side if it reasonably appears the disclosure was inadvertent (Model Rule 4.4).** Even though FRE 502 provides that inadvertent disclosure in federal cases doesn't constitute a waiver, the information is out there. For example, it may lead to other admissible evidence or may potentially be admissible to other purposes such as to refute an assertion made by a witness (impeachment). FRE 502 is a federal rule and states may approach its use differently. Whether your attorney can use it or not is up for debate.

Learning from Those Who Gambled Their Cases and Lost

Throughout this chapter, we refer to cases where the courts have sanctioned parties or attorneys. Just in case we didn't make the point clear, the following is a brief listing of some additional cases:

✔ An adverse inference in *Zubalake* contributed to a $29.2 million dollar verdict.

✔ The SEC imposed a $10 million fine on Bank of America Securities after they repeatedly failed to furnish requested ESI.

- For spoliation, the court in *United States v. Philip Morris* precluded the use of any defense witness who failed to follow the preservation order, awarded $2.75 million in monetary sanctions ($250,000 for each corporate manager who failed to comply with the order), and payment of plaintiffs costs incurred in the spoliation.

- In *Ajaxo, Inc., et al. v. Bank of America Technology and Operations, Inc., et al.*, the court sanctioned the plaintiffs and their counsel for failure to obey a court order and produce the ESI in a searchable format.

To use or not to use privileged documents

The Model Rules do not address whether your attorney can use privileged evidence accidentally received from the other side in court. State rules are split on how to handle it. Here are a few things to think about:

- In *Rico v. Mitsubishi Motor Corp.,* the trial court judge disqualified the attorney from the case for using privileged documents to try to discredit the opposing party's expert witness. The California Supreme Court upheld the decision.

- In *Mira Inc. v. O'Brien,* a Massachusetts court allowed a privileged communication to be used to impeach a witness whose testimony was not consistent with the letter.

- The New York County Lawyers Association has a formal opinion (No. 730) that a lawyer refrain from reviewing inadvertently disclosed information that is subject to privilege or protection.

- There is an ethical controversy on the ability of counsel to mine another party's documents for hidden information. This is especially sensitive if there is metadata or if the form requested allows for mining of information. A lawyer must be aware of the potential while negotiating a discovery plan and the form of production.

- The American Bar Association's standing committee on ethics in Formal Opinion 06-442 stated that reviewing and using embedded data in ESI is not unethical for an attorney. It also found a duty on the disclosing attorney to avoid inadvertent disclosure. For example, scrubbing the metadata, or at a minimum, entering into a clawback agreement as discussed in Chapter 10. This position has not been uniformly adopted by all the states.

- In New York, the ethics committee in Opinion 749 held that attorneys should not use available technology to examine and trace e-mail and other electronic documents. To do so is a violation of the New York rules of conduct.

- Other states vary in what can be done. Colorado provides that an attorney may mine the data unless the attorney has been notified that it was inadvertently sent. Maryland allows its use. Pennsylvania takes an intermediate approach by putting the decision on the attorney judgment in light of all the facts. There is some consistency in providing that there is an ethical obligation on the sending attorney to assure that privilege or protected ESI is not disclosed, including metadata.

We can't say it enough — you're ultimately responsible for how your case goes. You can be sanctioned for your lawyer misconduct and you can even lose your case.

Figure 5-1 provides an ethical decision-making flow chart for actions or inactions in e-discovery.

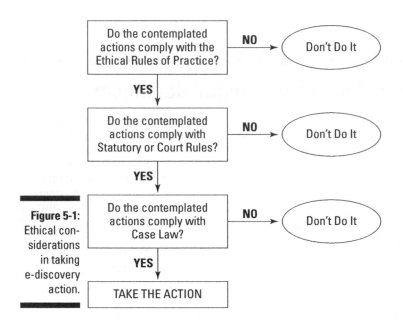

Figure 5-1:
Ethical considerations in taking e-discovery action.

Policing e-Discovery in Criminal Cases

The Federal Rules of Criminal Procedure (FRCrimP), as discussed in Chapter 4, establish certain discovery requirements. These are both on the prosecutors and defendants. In the high profile case of Senator Stevens, the United States Attorney General moved to dismiss the case against Senator Stevens. One of the main reasons was the failure of the government to turn over the defense's potentially exculpatory evidence. It also resulted in the judge issuing a contempt citation against a number of government lawyers.

Destroying evidence, including ESI, in a criminal matter can be considered an obstruction of justice under 18 USC 1503. This is a criminal offense for anyone involved and has been extended to include concealing, attempting to conceal, altering, or distorting a document. This applies to judicial proceedings once it is known that a proceeding has commenced.

For hearings before Congress or an agency of the government, the same rules apply under Section 1505. This applies when notice of an investigation is about to begin. The determination of when notice is made and the duty to preserve begins is a question of fact for the court to determine on a case-by-case basis.

There is a broader provision in Section 1510 that makes it illegal to obstruct the giving of information on a crime to federal investigators even without an actual case or agency action.

In addition to these specific crimes, there are general crimes that may be charged, such as conspiracy or concealment of a crime. Also you can be charged with criminal contempt of court for failing to obey a court order or subpoena.

Part III

Identifying, Preserving, and Collecting ESI

The 5th Wave

By Rich Tennant

"Don't laugh. It's faster than our current recovery system. Besides, the judge doesn't need to know how we found the file, does he?"

In this part . . .

In this part, we cover the steps to take when a lawsuit has been served. You learn what to do when you're facing an e-discovery request, marking that day as day-zero (t_0) on the countdown to the meet and confer with opposing counsel within 99 days (t_{99}).

You need to mobilize a team that keeps the e-discovery processes flowing smoothly, but simply flowing may be the best you can get, as you read in Chapter 6. Your objective is to identify what ESI is potentially relevant and accessible, figure out which data custodians are within the scope of the request, and use legally-defensible means to limit the burden of e-discovery. And you thought that identifying ESI was going to be tough!

Preserving ESI, like catching lightning, has challenges that you learn in Chapter 7. You learn why simply telling users "don't touch" will motivate them to delete their e-mails (within scope) at warp speed. You start to understand how to play the high-stakes game of ESI-Hold'em.

In Chapter 8, you see real action with the opposition in the meet-and-confer session. Your take-away from this negotiation in an e-discovery plan must be presented to the court 21 days later. As you read, you have to comply with this plan so arriving armed with ESI-intel makes you dangerous to your opponent. Total elapsed time is 120 days after the lawsuit is served. If you mess up the negotiation, don't expect to re-negotiate or get any other type of bailout.

"The skillful strategist defeats the enemy without doing battle."

—Sun-Tzu, 6th century BC military commander

Chapter 6

Identifying Potentially Relevant ESI

In This Chapter

▶ Rallying the task force

▶ Assessing the scope

▶ Taking costs down a notch

▶ Preparing an ESI data map

▶ Understanding that more people don't always make the task easier

*T*he legal system is built on the parties — and not the courts — developing the evidence for the case. During the first e-discovery stage, *identification,* that's exactly what you're doing. Many critical and combative activities go on during identification, such as identifying the type and location of all the ESI that you may need to preserve or negotiating the scope of e-discovery with your opponent.

If you've received an e-discovery request or anticipate one, your top priority is to identify potentially relevant ESI. You begin by figuring out the appropriate search criteria, such as the names of people who might have the ESI, the devices where the ESI is stored, the date ranges when it was created, the key words that it contains, and other protocols that are specified in the e-discovery request. Armed with the search criteria, you find the right digital haystacks to search and then search them to find the location of the data, files, and attachments.

In this chapter, you find out more about identifying ESI of potential relevance to the legal action according to a formal response plan. You read how to negotiate the scope of e-discovery to arrive at an agreement with the opposing side. These agreements, done right, greatly reduce the risk of evidence spoliation motions. Expect the opposing side to take heavy swings at your search protocols and results. Litigation is full of fiery disputes over whether your efforts to identify responsive documents (no matter how incriminating) were made in good faith. Your defense, as always, is the detailed documentation showing your reliable and reasonable data mining efforts. Regardless of the disruption to your work and the routine operations of the IT department, you do perform your e-discovery duties thoroughly and in good faith.

Calling an e-Discovery Team into Action

This is not a computer simulation. You're now in an active legal action and need to learn what ESI to preserve and the locations where they're stored. In this chapter, we focus on assembling a team to identify what needs to be preserved and what doesn't. We cover how to preserve the ESI in Chapter 7.

Identification is a team effort. The first step is to assemble an e-discovery team (or task force, if you prefer) of capable and reliable people. Following a project management approach, as you read in Chapter 3, helps ensure that deadlines are met and resources are not overallocated.

A dead giveaway that you've overallocated resources is that someone needs to be in two or more places at the same time or work 60 hours per week for several months.

Team size varies because you need enough members to cover the workload and areas of expertise. As you'd expect, team size depends on the type and magnitude of the case. Too many people on a team lead to team members deflecting their responsibility to others or assuming that someone else was taking care of it. You can read about other problems caused by overstuffed teams in the section "Taking Lessons from the Mythical Member" later in this chapter. When there are too few people, deadlines get missed and stress builds.

A cross-functional e-discovery team has the following representatives and skills:

- ✔ **General counsel (GC):** General counsels are your company's legal advisors who are under the gun to identify ESI and storage locations with the help of IT. They are held accountable for monitoring the litigation hold (see Chapter 7) and ensuring compliance with it. They're also referred to as *in-house counsel* or *corporate counsel*.

- ✔ **External counsel:** These are the litigators. They're the lawyers who specialize in lawsuits and the court system. Also called *trial lawyers*, they're retained by your company. They have the most extensive knowledge of the rules of procedure, rules of evidence, and recent case law. External counsel also have their own staff of paralegals and litigation supporters who you may be working with closely throughout e-discovery.

- ✔ **IT personnel:** There's a wide range of IT personnel whose expertise you need, including the chief information officer (CIO), database administrator, and network administrator. If someone manages the e-mail server and accounts, that person may play a starring role.

- ✓ **Records managers or data librarians:** Your company may not be large enough to have someone dedicated to this job function, but if it is, you need their expertise. Even if no one has this job title, someone must perform these roles.

- ✓ **Human resources (HR) personnel:** HR serves a legal function, and for employment lawsuits or issues involving departing employees, it's needed.

- ✓ **Accounting personnel:** If the case involves a spectacular accounting breakthrough or financial meltdown, such as those of Madoff, Enron, or Lehman Brothers, or if it impacts the bottom line, you need an accountant. Select an accountant who is familiar with the IRS, Securities and Exchange Commission (SEC) regulations, and disclosure requirements of other regulatory agencies.

- ✓ **Information security (infosec) or disaster recovery personnel:** Infosec staff know your company's IT infrastructure and data archiving policy and programs, both the formal (written) ones and the informal ones. While you're preserving ESI and protecting it from contamination by malware, IT operations may get disrupted, which requires their support. For cases involving intrusions into users' accounts, their expertise is crucial.

  People in the company may have a burning desire to access files and e-mails to delete incriminating content. Infosec personnel guard against such electronic whiteout.

- ✓ **An e-discovery expert or vendor:** You may need expertise that you can't find in your company. Partnering with a vendor can help you with forensically preserving ESI (if needed), ensuring chain of custody, searching and *deduping* (removing duplicates) ESI, meeting review and production deadlines, or any of the many steps in e-discovery. Preparing in advance of litigation by selecting a set of preferred vendors or partnering with vendors reduces time, stress, and risks.

The e-discovery team needs to know about your data retention and business processes. Schedule an initial meeting during which you can make sure roles, responsibilities, timelines, and what's at stake are clear. IT leads the technical requirements while lawyers make sure that the rules are followed and deadlines are met. Your team leader will most likely be a legal person.

Create a list of the names of team members, their job titles, and contact information. You want job titles because e-discovery can last for a year or longer, and people may change jobs within the company or leave it. As you lose members, you replace them with new people with similar job titles.

Clarifying the Scope of e-Discovery

You'll probably have some trouble nailing down the scope of e-discovery for your case. Even when you think you've captured all ESI in the scope, the other side may file a motion that makes you go dig through ESI again. Or someone finds a stash of DVDs, flash drives, or tapes with responsive ESI. Or the judge may issue decisions that change the scope — by ruling on the date ranges, data custodians, or search terms. Accept surprises and disruptions as part of your job or you'll be driven crazy putting out fires.

Scope of e-discovery has three dimensions. Defining the three dimensions is not a linear process, but a process of many revisions. Think of all ESI as fitting into a cube (see Figure 6-1), and you need to identify only those chunks that fall within the scope. The scope of relevant ESI, which custodians are within the scope, and the data ranges all can change throughout the case up to and including the trial. There are consequences for not being prepared, such as sanctions or not being able to use ESI to prove your case, because companies are obligated to be prepared.

An unexpected dramatic expansion of the scope of e-discovery is not unusual. Have contingency plans to be able to scale up. One method is to partner with a vendor who can bring in the needed resources on short notice.

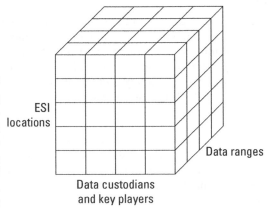

Figure 6-1: A three-dimensional cube view of the scope of e-discovery.

ESI locations

Data ranges

Data custodians and key players

During the identification process, you generally assess these three scopes:

✔ **Data custodians and key players:** Interview individual holders, or custodians. Data custodians are those who know how ESI is kept, where it's kept, and how accessible it is. Key players are those who are somehow associated with the elements or ESI of the case. Business clients, customers, and others outside your company may be key players. Those who might be witnesses should be interviewed in person or via some other live method, such as video conference or phone call. Interviews can also be done using surveys or forms via the Internet or paper.

✔ **Responsive ESI and locations:** This is the content that's reasonably or potentially relevant to the case and may include texts, address books, and calendars from handheld devices. You need to identify the location of potentially responsive ESI, its availability or accessibility, and its format.

✔ **Date ranges or time frames:** These are the start dates and end dates that define the time range of interest in the investigation.

You're identifying not only what's within scope, but also the limiting factors that exclude them from the scope. Limiting the scope is covered in the section "Reducing Burden with the Proportionality Principle" in this chapter.

Follow these steps to perform all your duties related to the three scopes:

1. **Make an initial or early case assessment of the data custodians and holders of hot docs and other responsive ESI.**

   Based on the elements of the case, you have a general idea of who might have control or custody of the ESI most likely to be responsive. You may be identifying key people by job function, project worked on, department, office, geographical location, or some other combination of criteria. Or you may have enough information to identify people by name. Early case assessments often change because the party filing the lawsuit may re-file it with additional demands or one or more charges may get dropped from the suit.

   Ask your attorney whether the lawsuit includes names. Then there's no mystery about who the key players are, at least at the outset.

   Often a few data custodians have the bulk of responsive ESI even when there are more than 100 custodians. As a general guideline, 5 to 10 data custodians have as much as 80 percent of the documents. If there are many data custodians, group them into two buckets:

   • *Major data custodians:* Those who have a high percentage of the responsive ESI.

   • *Minor data custodians:* Those who may have a small percentage of responsive ESI.

2. **Make a broad initial assessment of which ESI is responsive and where it's located.**

   Consider all types of ESI that pertain to the case, which could be performance and financial records, contracts and drafts of contracts, purchase orders, text messages, and e-mail. Think in terms of buckets into which you put content to sort out more completely later. Useful ESI buckets are

- *Definitely falls within the scope:* ESI that's within the time range and obviously related to the elements of the case goes into this bucket. For example, in employment cases, you have a good idea of whose e-mail messages are within scope. For fraud cases, you know that financial statements, reconciliations, and adjusting entries will be key evidence. Dealing with dates can get complex if you've upgraded your company's information technology applications and database (for example, by migrating from legacy systems to SAP or Oracle enterprise systems). Verify that the dates are accurate so that you don't collect, review, and produce ESI that you didn't need to be produced — and that you produce what's relevant.

  If the modified, accessed, and created/change of status (MAC) times of files must be verified, then you need the help of a computer forensics expert. MAC times can be hours off, and MAC dates can be off by several years. This creates a loophole that the opposing side may use to challenge the admissibility of your ESI, or the judge may refuse to allow it into evidence.

- *Might fall within the scope:* This is like a temporary folder for ESI. Put ESI into this bucket if there's a chance (that is, it is within the time range or is from a person of interest) you might need to produce it. If you don't know for sure, err on the side of caution. The scope of the case itself may expand or contract, and the ESI in this bucket can move to one of the other two buckets.

- *Outside the scope:* What gets tossed into this bucket, either deliberately or by default (if it no longer falls into the scope of the other buckets), is ESI that you may later have to defend as not being reasonably anticipated to be relevant. This ESI would not be subject to a legal hold, as you find out more about in Chapter 7.

Be realistic or pessimistic in your early case assessment. Keep in mind that you're brainstorming, and attempts at precision may increase time and costs, but not much else. As the case progresses and the fog of uncertainty lifts, you can update these buckets. Some cases come down to only a few documents or messages. Most likely, you're not going to find only those few hot docs (these are like smoking guns) at this time. Other cases involve loads of documents. Your determinations help prepare for the meet-and-confer session. After the meet-and-confer session, you can refine your buckets.

3. **Verify or correlate the time frames to events.**

   The specific start or end dates may not be specified. Instead, the dates may be references to events. Even if dates are listed, you want to verify their validity. It's quite possible that people will make mistakes or typos, and they could stretch the truth.

Be sure everyone on the team knows when the final product is due, as well as the interim deadlines along the way.

Reducing the Burden with the Proportionality Principle

External counsel uses information from your e-discovery team to determine — and then negotiate or argue — the cost or burden of producing certain ESI versus the benefits. Proportionality is a negotiating weapon that you can use only if you can actually show or explain the proportions.

If you understand what ESI is not reasonably accessible but potentially relevant early in the litigation, even before e-discovery is conducted, you can give your lawyer the necessary info to limit the scope of discovery during the meet-and-confer session. He can negotiate any information that is reasonably accessible to you, including the burden or cost of retrieving and reviewing the information.

Proportionality of scale

Proportionality of scale, according to Rule 26(b)(2)(C), is meant to balance the value of the case with the cost of producing different kinds of ESI. The rule states in part:

> "A party need not provide discovery of electronically stored information from sources that the party identifies as not reasonably accessible because of undue burden or cost."

Proportionality is ultimately determined by the disputed issues, the law (the rules), and the courts (judges). Beginning with the scheduling meeting, judges are involved in the case. Judges resolve conflicts, balance competing interests, and settle any motions to compel production or attempts to resist production. A *motion to compel production* is a request to the court to force the opponent to produce ESI. To counter the motion, the opposing party may attempt to convince the judge not to grant the motion.

The scope of ESI is broad and not limited to what may be used at trial. Federal courts and many state courts allow you to discover any ESI relevant to the claim. Whether it's admissible is another issue for the lawyers to fight over.

Negotiating with proportionality

After you identify the sources of ESI that are potentially responsive but not reasonably accessible, use that intelligence to negotiate a better position: One that's lower risk, lower cost, or lower burden. Here are some of them:

- ✔ You can ask for a temporary reprieve or pardon from having to produce the tough stuff.

- ✔ You can ask for a reprieve from any sanctions for not producing it until the court demands that you turn it over.

- ✔ Ask your opponent to show good cause for you producing the ESI. At a minimum, this buys you some time. If the opposing side can't show good cause or you can defeat their attempt, you're spared. Be careful of this trap if you're the requesting party.

- ✔ You can ask the court to shift the cost of producing the not reasonably accessible ESI to the requesting party — away from you.

By classifying ESI as accessible or not reasonably accessible, you're in position to ask to have that ESI excluded under Rule 26(b) or shift some of the costs under Rule 26(c).

Mapping the Information Architecture

The FRCP requires that you know your IT architecture and that you can describe it at a *granular* level — a level that's detailed enough to identify the scope of e-discovery. You'll most likely convey this information with a data map. Data maps make it easier to implement litigation holds as well as the collection, review and production of ESI and the identification of key witnesses. Developing a data map is your first step in understanding the flow of ESI, which is critical to in-house counsel in litigation. The detailed information in a data map can include facts that outside counsel can use to convince opposition or the court that certain forms of ESI are too tough or costly to access.

The data map is designed to provide the information needed to create the proposed e-discovery plan for the meet-and-confer session.

Creating a data map

Preparing a data map is smart preparation. A data map is like a catalog that lists your company's records and describes them by business unit, if appropriate, and the types of storage media on which they're maintained. Each business unit in your company identifies its own retention policies and explains the reasons for any differences from the company's written policies that may exist.

The completed data map gives you a full picture of the nature, type, and location of all records and retention policies within your company. The map serves as the base for educating outside counsel your e-discovery team.

A data map shows ESI at a granular level by identifying the following information for each ESI type or electronic record (e-record) in use. You and the team build the data map by function, department, or division, while you research and answer these questions:

- **Who are the data custodians?** Identify and interview custodians to learn about their responsibilities and practices. Find out who's responsible for maintaining each department or division's business records. Verify the extent to which they actually comply with the electronic records retention procedures. Don't ignore anyone's deviations in practice from existing records retention policies. Write them all down. These custodians may be called upon to elaborate on each e-record type and retention. Be aware that data custodians may be called to testify in depositions or court.

- **Where are your computers, laptops, handheld devices, and data servers, and who uses them?** Identify your computer equipment and key users. Users may become witnesses, too. Data maps list the data stores, including file and e-mail servers, desktop and notebook computers, portable drives and optical media, and handhelds.

- **What format is the ESI in?** The default format is *native* format, the format in which the ESI was originally created. But check with your lawyer about whether the requesting party has specified a format.

- **What are the data retention schedules and policies, disposal policies, backup policies, and archiving rules?** Identify onsite and offsite data storage locations, portable storage media, and possibly the personal storage locations of key players. The FRCP has specific requirements for the storage and production of different types of metadata. You may be required to produce ESI in their native formats.

  Explain how these policies are monitored or enforced (or how you believe they're enforced). Routine destruction of old ESI may be acceptable, as long as a consistent and good faith policy is in place. To support your defense about data that's not readily accessible, this analysis should also document the costs associated with accessing ESI from backups, restoring ESI from backups, and any hardware or software needed to access and restore the ESI.

If ESI has been deleted, particularly from laptops and computers, you can likely recover it using computer forensics tools. Don't make the mistake of claiming that the e-mail messages are gone when they're in covert condition.

Figure 6-2 shows an example of a data map.

B. *Master Inventory, Tier 1*

Quick Index

Category	Commercial Name	Page
Applications		
Accounting	QuickBooks	7
Backup	BRMS	8
	BackupExec	9
	EMC Retrospect	10
	IBM Tivoli Storage Manager	11
Business Intelligence	SAS Institute	12
	OutlookSoft	13
Collaboration, E-mail, and	IBM Lotus Notes/Domino	14
Instant Messaging	IBM Lotus QuickPlace/Quickr	15
	IBM Lotus SameTime	16

Applications, Business Intelligence

System-application Description of system-application IT Contact	When was this system-application first deployed by Acme?	Where is the data stored (not OS, system files)?	What type of data (native file format) is associated with this system (database, unstructured text, semi-structured, XML, etc.)	Has there been any system-application wide purging or deletion (either on a systematic or one-time basis) Is there any ongoing purging or deletion?	Is this system-application backed up? How frequently and what type of backup? Where are backup tapes stored?	Who are the users of the system-application?
OutlookSoft **Business Intelligence** "OutlookSoft Corporation is a Stanford, Connecticut based software company with products for business performance management including planning, consolidation, forecasting, budgeting, dashboards, and predictive analytics and reporting. Along with OutlookSoft, other vendors in the performance management space include SAS, Cognos and Business Objects." From Wikipedia This company has been acquired by SAP. Tim Strowe	2002	SAN	SQL		Yes. Backups are performed once per day. No tapes are used as this is backed up via TSM.	Primarily financial employees as this is a financial reporting tool.

Figure 6-2:
A data map.

Courtesy of John Collins and The Ingersoll Firm (www.theingersollfirm.com)

The information that you need to collect is spread out. Some of it's written, and some of it has to be learned though interviews. Have meetings to discuss what questions to ask and how to get truthful answers to your questions.

You can record the information in a spreadsheet or other document, but for extensive infrastructure and data mapping, you'll want to use a software solution or an automated solution specifically for e-discovery. By keeping your data map updated as changes occur, you keep it in ready-to-use condition. This reduces the risk of not having enough time to adequately prepare for the meet-and-confer session.

Most e-discovery vendors offer data mapping services. There are also ESI data map software vendors/consultants, such as

- **The Ingersoll Form:** www.theingersollfirm.com
- **Fios:** www.fiosinc.com/
- **Exterro:** www.exterro.com

Lawyers can request ESI from the laptops of specific employees, retired applications that you cannot access, home computers used for work-related purposes, and the content of flash drives and backup tapes. You always want the ESI map to identify data that's no longer accessible due to technical limitations, expired licenses, discontinued proprietary applications, and ESI retention policies.

Including an estimate of the cost to recover certain not reasonably accessible data gives the judge a way to weigh the impact of e-discovery against the potential usefulness of the ESI requested.

Overlooking ESI

You'll most likely overlook sources of ESI. Mobile workers' laptops, out-of-use applications or zip drives, or undisclosed backups created by project managers with a deep mistrust of hard drive reliability are all possibilities. Your opponent can request any or all of these data stores. To make yourself look good in front of the judge, as soon as you realize that ESI was overlooked, get in front of this train by disclosing the overlooked ESI. Depending upon when you think to look for ESI in these different places, you may be facing penalties. If overlooking ESI leads to late production, hopefully your lawyer can get your company out of serious trouble or monetary sanctions.

In *Phoenix Four, Inc. v. Strategic Resources Corporation* (2006), the court found that late production of ESI amounted to *gross negligence.* The defendant did not search its servers completely and was unaware of 25GB of data, which is roughly equivalent to 2,500 boxes of paper. The ESI was located on an unmapped hard drive partition such that

> ". . . someone using a computer connected to that server could not 'view' or gain access to that section of the hard drive and would have no way of knowing of its existence."

By locating the ESI late in the discovery process and producing it after the deadline, the court awarded monetary sanctions against certain defendants and their counsel for destruction and late production of evidence.

Describing data retention policies and procedures

You want legally defensible data retention and disposal procedures. Determining whether ESI has been disposed of in good faith or whether it was disposed in order to obstruct justice is a serious matter. You don't want the court to think you've disposed of the ESI for the latter reason.

With business records, you don't have much discretion. Local, state, federal, and international laws and an increasing number of industry regulations dictate the types of data you must retain, how long you must maintain specific types of data, and even the manner in which you store the data.

Retention is less tight with ESI like e-mail, documents, spreadsheets, and so on that is created or received by employees. Retention policies that rely on individual employees to correctly save and store — or get rid of promptly — are also less secure.

Here's an example of what might happen in a workplace harassment lawsuit in which the harassing conduct is objectionable e-mail sent over the past 12 months. As soon as the defendants find out that they've been named in the lawsuit, they start deleting everything — a massive information wipeout. In fact, their efforts are not only useless because the messages have already been backed up, but also because logs show the attempted cover up. This example shows that you may not have data retention policies and strong enough enforcement procedures in place.

During the identification stage of e-discovery, you need to describe the following to the court:

- ✔ Your written data retention policies
- ✔ Your methods for communicating policies to all users of company computers, networks, and digital devices — and reminders of the policies sent to users
- ✔ User training and documentation of that training

✔ Consent forms signed by users wherein they acknowledge understanding of the policy rules, agree to abide by them, and know the consequences for noncompliance

✔ Your methods for monitoring and enforcing compliance

Proving the reasonable accessibility of ESI sources

Rule 26(b)(2)(B) created and introduced the awkwardly worded concept of *not reasonably accessible* ESI. The terms *reasonably accessible* or *not reasonably accessible* in negotiations or court filings do not flow smoothly. Some people use *accessible* and *inaccessible* ESI. Not so fast. There's a reason why defendants on trial are found to be *guilty* or *not guilty*. *Not guilty* is not the same as *innocent*. And *not guilty* is a more correct and precise term.

Law is precise in this area. Using *accessible* and *inaccessible* misstates the Rule 26 standard, which is not to your advantage. Only ESI that exists on known storage media — all of which have been physically destroyed — can be defined with confidence as *inaccessible*.

While you're identifying ESI, make sure to describe the following:

✔ What ESI is reasonably accessible, what is not reasonably accessible, and why or why not

✔ The cost to produce various types or scopes of ESI regardless of accessibility

✔ Whether accessing and presenting legacy data will require legacy applications or consultants

The ability to argue that ESI is not reasonably inaccessible is related to costs and burden, so do your calculations.

Taking Lessons from the Mythical Member

In 1975, Fred Brooks Jr. published *The Mythical Man-Month* (Pearson) in which he describes differences between large and small projects. While Fred focused on software development projects, his principles are dead on for most schedule-driven team efforts, like identification. The book's cover depicts beasts struggling to pull their stuck limbs out of a tar pit, a metaphor for the Catch-22 of completing software projects on schedule and to specifications. Sound familiar?

One of his ideas, known as Brooks's Law, is that "adding manpower to a late software project makes it later." He explains that software development isn't like harvesting crops, which can be done faster with more workers. When new members are added to a software development team, those on the team need to drop what they're doing and bring new members up to speed. As the team size grows, so does the amount of time needed to coordinate work.

Electronic discovery has the same characteristics and symptoms described by Brooks. Every time you go through the process is like the first time because of the unique features of the legal case and people involved. The following are two other tar traps to be aware of during your identification processes:

- ✔ **Slipping behind slowly:** Identification needs to be completed in time for your lawyers to prepare for the meet-and-confer session. Falling behind may be barely noticeable because it happens one day at a time. Most slippage is caused by termites, not tornadoes.

- ✔ **Bending timelines:** You can't reduce the amount of time for some processes if one task needs to be finished before the next task can begin. As Brooks writes, "The bearing of a child takes nine months, no matter how many women are assigned." You may need creative ways to bend timelines and unblock bottlenecks.

Doing identification correctly saves you from having to do a lot explaining when disputes arise — and they will.

Chapter 7

Complying with ESI Preservation and a Litigation Hold

In This Chapter

▶ Drawing a bright line between duty to preserve and preservation

▶ Being guided by The Sedona Conference WG1

▶ Knowing what and when to hold

▶ Stopping ESI deep-sixing

▶ Stopping in the name of litigation

*W*hen you zero in on the locations that store responsive ESI, you preserve them and prepare to demonstrate good faith in your ESI preservation efforts. During litigation, you face heated disputes over your efforts to find responsive ESI and to destroy incriminating documents. If you can't prove that you're not guilty of willful mismanagement (legalese for *disappearance*) or negligent management (*oops, we lost it*) of digital devices or discoverable ESI, you're also facing punishment from the court. Failing to preserve a litigation hold brings sanctions, such as *adverse inference* jury instructions (juries can infer the evidence would've been incriminating), fines reaching into millions of dollars, and expenses for an expert to investigate suspected destruction of incriminating e-evidence. In the worst case, you lose.

In this chapter, you read about the preservation of reasonably accessible ESI, how to deal with not reasonably accessible ESI, and how to physically host and manage a litigation hold on your ESI. *Litigation holds* are affirmative acts to prevent the destruction of paper or digital documents. You read that courts may issue sanctions even when the destruction appears to be inadvertent. You get into the crevices of preservation duties; for example, a human resources department that processes terminations or exit interviews becomes the custodian of data received from departing employees, which may be subject to litigation hold. It's a safe bet that employees recently pink-slipped don't care about preserving ESI litigation hold. You need to be.

Distinguishing Duty to Preserve from Preservation

The e-discovery rules regarding the preservation process, as with other e-discovery processes, are grounded in two ideals:

- **Good faith:** Acting in good faith in this instance means making informed decisions about preserving ESI untainted by self-interest. Of course, using mistakes made by your opponent against them (and in your self-interest) is alright.

- **Reasonableness:** This vague standard requires taking affirmative action to preserve potentially relevant ESI. Preservation obligations supersede your company's electronic record retention and management policies that could destroy ESI.

No bright lines draw clear boundaries between good and bad faith, what is and is not reasonable, and what you need to preserve and what you don't have to preserve. To sort out the murkiness, you first need to recognize the difference between the duty to preserve and preservation:

- **Duty to preserve:** The duty to preserve potential sources of discoverable ESI is a pre-discovery obligation.

   The Federal Rules of Civil Procedure (FRCP) does not apply to pre-discovery or prelitigation. Case law is the governing law. Meeting your duty to preserve, in effect, requires that you have a well-thought-out information management (or electronic records management) program in effect. (Electronic records management is discussed in Chapter 14.) How well you meet this duty influences your ability to preserve when litigation — and therefore, the FRCP — triggers the need to do so.

   Periodically revising your preservation plan could mean the difference between winning your case and being sanctioned by the court.

- **Preservation:** The preservation phase loosely begins after the identification phase (see Chapter 6).

   Preservation means protecting ESI that you might need to produce from being cleaned up accidentally or on purpose. Figuring out what you'll be expected to produce so that you know what to preserve is tricky.

Following The Sedona Conference

When you know that litigation has begun or will begin, you take reasonable steps to hold on to relevant ESI for e-discovery, even if you're a third-party to the suit. Did we mention that preservation is tricky? Some comfort became available in mid-2008 when the first Working Group (WG1) of The Sedona Conference published guidelines and a decision tree. WG1 is the *Working Group on Electronic Document Retention and Production*.

WG1's 2008 guidelines provide important advice.

- ✔ For satisfying your duty to make decisions in good faith about the accessibility of ESI.
- ✔ To know what guidelines the court will use to judge whether your decisions.

The word reasonable is critical to distinguishing good from bad, and now the courts and litigants have a respected set of guidelines to evaluate what's reasonable.

The Sedona Conference WG1 guidelines

The Sedona Conference WG1 published six guidelines in July 2008.

- ✔ **Guideline 1:** When you anticipate litigation but no plaintiff has emerged or it's not yet possible to discuss litigation, you should make preservation decisions that follow the processes in the decision tree.

    Figure 7-1 shows the decision tree as a flowchart showing the processes (in rounded squares) and decision points (in diamond shape) that lead to two alternatives based on the conditions tested:

    - *Preservation is required.* You must preserve the ESI, which could be a hard drive or flash drive for example.

    - *Preservation is not required.* You don't have to preserve the ESI.

- ✔ **Guideline 2:** As soon as feasible, discuss all preservation issues in sufficient detail with other parties, so you can reach a mutually satisfactory accommodation and evaluate whether you need to seek court intervention or assistance. (You should undertake the latter only if you can't come to an agreement about how to preserve ESI with your opposing party.)

- ✔ **Guideline 3:** You should clearly identify the inaccessible sources reasonably related to the discovery or claims you don't plan on searching or preserving.

- ✔ **Guideline 4:** You need to be very careful when for business reasons you move potentially discoverable information that's subject to a preservation duty from accessible to less-accessible data stores.

- ✔ **Guideline 5:** In the absence of an applicable preservation duty, you can manage your information in a way that minimizes accumulations of inaccessible data, provided that you make adequate provisions to comply with preservation duties.

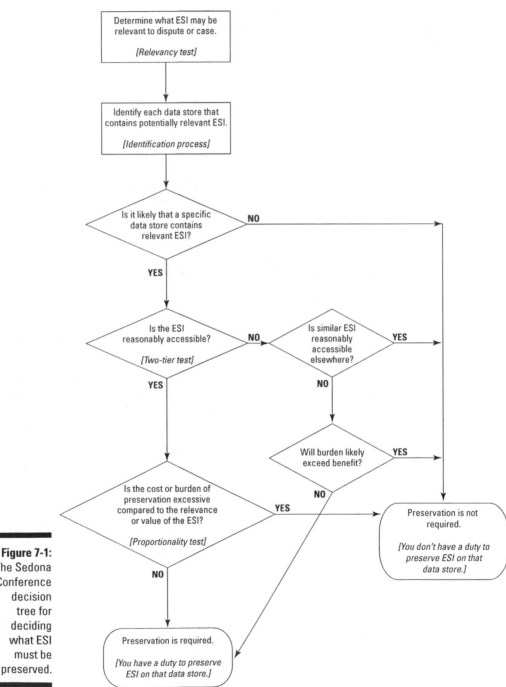

Figure 7-1:
The Sedona
Conference
decision
tree for
deciding
what ESI
must be
preserved.

> ✔ **Guideline 6:** You should encourage cooperation among legal and other functions and business units within your company to help ensure that preservation duties are met and that resources are effectively utilized.

Seeing the rules in the WG1 decision tree

The WG1's decision tree concisely represents these two subsections of Rule 26(b)(2):

> ✔ **The two-tier test of Rule 26(b)(2)(B):** You can object to producing ESI from sources that you identify as not reasonably accessible because of undue burden or cost.

> ✔ **The proportionality test of Rule 26(b)(2)(C):** The court may still order discovery of your not reasonably accessible ESI if the requesting party shows that the benefits outweigh the burden and cost.

You cannot ignore data storage media that fall into the *preservation is not required* tier. Under Rule 26(b)(2)(B), you must disclose the existence of ESI located on sources that are not reasonably accessible even if you have not searched them. Put another way, you must identify those sources that you don't intend to search or from which discovery won't be made.

You can download a copy of the free publication *The Sedona Conference Commentary on Preservation, Management and Identification of Sources of Information that are Not Reasonably Accessible* developed by WG1 from www. thesedonaconference.org/dltForm?did=NRA.pdf.

Recognizing a Litigation Hold Order and Obligation

A *litigation hold* is a preservation hold. It's an affirmative action by your company to prevent the destruction of physical or digital documents relevant to a lawsuit or government investigation. The purpose of the litigation hold is to stop routine or any other destruction of potentially responsive ESI and to make sure that ESI stays safe until the hold is released. Failed litigation holds have gotten some of the biggest headlines in e-discovery because a failed litigation hold is the most likely path to *spoliation* (destruction or extreme alteration of evidence).

When your action or inaction causes harm to your opponent's case, the court may impose a termination sanction. In other words, you lose on the spot.

You're free to preserve documents any way you see fit, as long as the methods and media are reasonable. If you preserve ESI by saving them to hard-to-access backup tapes, or without an index to facilitate search, you cannot later tell the court the ESI is not reasonably accessible — you should have kept it accessible.

Of the many questions surrounding the issue of a litigation hold, here are four of them:

✔ What triggers a litigation hold?

✔ When must a litigation hold start or be applied?

✔ Does starting a litigation hold late mean an automatic sanction?

✔ Does a litigation hold apply to ESI that's lost because employees left their positions or the company?

Figure 7-2 shows a master plan of the litigation hold process beginning with a triggering event and ending with the release of the litigation hold. You read about the process in the following sections.

Knowing what triggers a litigation hold

The first thing you have to do is recognize an event that can trigger the need for you to implement a litigation hold. Here are several events that rise to the level of a triggering event, of which the first two are easily identifiable triggering events:

✔ A preservation letter from opposing counsel or a government agency stating in effect, "We're going to sue you."

✔ A complaint is filed with, "We're suing you" language.

✔ A threat of litigation or an investigation, such as when companies in your industry are being sued or investigated.

✔ Knowing that there's a problem that could turn into a lawsuit.

If you suspect that there's a triggering event, ask your in-house counsel for an opinion. Get the opinion in writing, and keep it in case you have to defend your inaction or delayed action.

Knowing when to issue a litigation hold

Knowing when to issue a litigation hold is not simple. The latest date that you can justify issuing a hold is the date you receive the preservation letter or the date the complaint is filed. If there's no letter or complaint, start the hold when you anticipate litigation. *Zubulake* established that the duty to preserve attaches at the time litigation is reasonably anticipated.

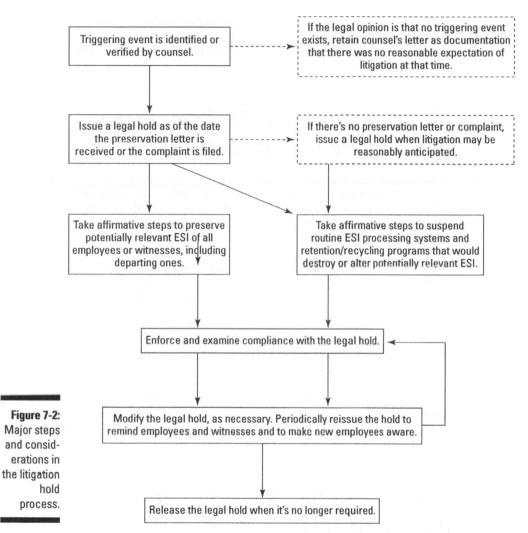

Figure 7-2:
Major steps
and consid-
erations in
the litigation
hold
process.

Because questions about a litigation hold are based on the facts of the situation, you need to be able to document what you did and why you did it, and to argue convincingly and intelligently that what you did was reasonable. If you document that, at the time, you did not recognize the trigger event as a red flag of foreseeable litigation, you have a chance at avoiding sanctions.

Any relevant evidence that's destroyed before the trigger date would be harmless because you were unaware of a need to preserve evidence. Destroying potential evidence after the trigger date is never allowed.

Your litigation hold decisions are analyzed in hindsight, which distorts what was reasonable. In hindsight, answers to *How could you not have known that*

the product design flaw would lead to multimillion-dollar lawsuits and the need for a litigation hold? can look very different. You want to preserve the thoughts and facts at the time of the decisions to demonstrate that you acted in good faith or reasonably.

Knowing when a hold delay makes you eligible for sanctions

Good news if you start late and didn't lose ESI relevant to the case: The legal issue is whether the opposing party was harmed by the delay or lateness of the hold, not the timing of the hold. If there's no evidence that relevant documents are destroyed, you dodged that bullet, but there's often a price to pay in terms of time and sleeplessness.

Trying to use a delay to your self-interest is a sure ticket to a sanction. In 2008, a paralegal filed a sexual harassment and constructive discharge action against her former employer and one of its partners. The law firm allowed the partner to continue working on his computer for over a year without taking any action to preserve discoverable ESI on the computer. The partner testified that because he had deleted the e-mail with explicit images and continued using the computer, the deleted e-mails had probably been overwritten and unrecoverable. Not surprisingly, the courts did not agree. Whether relevant documents ever existed on the partner's computer did not negate the fact, according to the court, that defendants failed to meet their obligations to preserve the partner's computer files. The jury was told that neither the law firm nor the partner took steps to preserve the partner's computer electronic records or e-mail (an *adverse instruction*).

Accounting for downsizing and departing employees

Downsizing companies redistribute computers, cellphones, PDAs, and computer files from departing employees. Additionally, digital devices might depart with the employee, be dropped accidentally in front of a moving vehicle, or become auction items on eBay. Employees who are retiring, being fired or promoted, or quitting create similar hard-to-hold situations. Unmanaged redistribution of equipment contributes to losing ESI pertinent to an existing litigation hold.

When ESI is gone, any explaining you do has little chance of avoiding sanctions. Arguing that key pieces of evidence are lost because an employee was promoted or fired won't get you sympathy from the court. Your obligation to manage litigation hold procedures effectively doesn't have escape clauses for employee departures.

Protection from losses because of employee departures or transitions includes the following actions:

- ✔ **Retain ESI of departing employees.** Keep all data from departing employees until you receive verification in writing that the data is not subject to litigation hold.

- ✔ **Suspend wiping of hard drives.** Don't wipe hard drives or redistribute computers.

- ✔ **Track who's leaving.** Check the names of departing employees against the names of employees whose ESI is subject to litigation hold. Record contact information of departing staff.

- ✔ **Keep new custodians up-to-date.** Issue litigation hold notices to new custodians.

- ✔ **Keep your e-discovery plan up-to-date.** Examine litigation hold procedures regularly to ensure that they're working.

Throwing a Wrench into Digital Recycling

The litigation hold requires that you suspend any routines that could delete or alter ESI. Doing so can be challenging. Here are some of the operations that need to stop:

- ✔ **Suspend automatic deletion systems, system upgrades, and recycling of back-up tapes.** You read more in the upcoming "Suspending destructive processes" section.

- ✔ **Tell employees not to install or uninstall software programs or defrag their hard drives.** These activities could cause the loss of potential ESI if employees mess up the install or defrag and destroy their computers.

Suspending destructive processes

Many company-wide information and e-mail systems are automated to perform (delete, overwrite, or archive ESI) tasks based on timing, volume limits, or other criteria. Any automatic system to purge ESI is fine, as long as there's a way to turn it off so you aren't destroying documents you need to preserve.

A common destructive process is the reformatting and redistribution of computers or hard drives. In *Padgett v. City of Monte Sereno* (2007), the defendant was sanctioned when an employee, who did not know of the pending litigation, reformatted the hard drive of a custodian of relevant ESI. The court held that the defendant failed to take adequate precautions to preserve the co-worker's computer equipment.

If you have an electronic records management (ERM) policy defining how to retain and dispose of ESI, you can be shielded from sanctions. You read about prelitigation ERM in Chapter 14.

ESI retention policies have shielded defendants from sanctions. In *Gippetti v. United Parcel Service Inc.* (2008), the plaintiff sought spoliation sanctions after alleging that the defendant had destroyed relevant ESI. The ESI at issue were UPS employees' driving records. The defendant responded that some of the requested documents were destroyed as part of their routine ESI retention policy. According to policy, driving records are deleted to cope with sheer volume. The court did not sanction the defendant because of their routine and reasonable policy. However, the court in *Doe v. Norwalk* (2007) recognized that not following a retention policy or not consistently following a policy is the same as not having one.

Verifying that you have an ERM program doesn't matter with the court if you don't follow it.

The court in *Keithley v. Homestore.com, Inc.* (2008) ordered severe financial sanctions and an adverse inference when defendants failed to issue a written document retention policy after its duty to preserve had arisen. The court fined them $250,000 and gave the jury an adverse inference instruction.

Don't overlook the risk of criminal sanctions, such as obstruction of justice. Read about sanctions in Chapter 5.

Where do you put a terabyte?

E-discovery can easily reach tens of thousands of documents and several terabytes. This may involve stopping routine document destruction, recycling of backup tapes, disk defragmentation or compression, and instructing employees to refrain from deleting documents. The point is that you may need to hold onto and put huge amounts of ESI somewhere during the litigation hold to preserve it. Here are two preservation protocols:

✔ **Preserve in place:** The litigation hold is put on ESI that may be material to your case at their source, typically the file or e-mail server. In-place litigation holds can be implemented, sometimes quickly, in one or both of the following ways:

• *Suspend routine destruction or recycling.* The IT department stops its standard procedures. For large automated tape libraries, it's not realistic to expect to suspend these operations immediately.

- *Restrict access or use.* Lock any potential material ESI where it resides on the network by modifying file permissions to restrict what can be done with or to the files or data. For example, permission to files could be restricted to read-only so users would still be able to read but not alter them.

✔ **Collect to preserve:** As the case advances, moving the ESI to central repositories may be necessary so that people (legal team, IT staff, vendors, remote users) can access the ESI from any location. Native ESI comes in various formats, so you need more than one repository. You want to use one repository for e-mail, another for documents, and so on. Rounding up the ESI helps minimize the risk of data or metadata spoliation if you do the following:

- Notify data users and custodians by sending a collection notice.

- Use a collection process that preserves the ESI, its metadata and embedded data; and that documents the chain of custody and authenticity.

- Tag the responsive ESI, move it to a new server, and verify that the transfer was successful.

Implementing the Litigation Hold

When the litigation hold is triggered, you and your counsel should meet to ensure that you have an appropriate policy in place to protect the relevant ESI and to avoid loss or destruction of the relevant ESI.

You take the following steps to begin the litigation hold:

1. **Review the scope of the ESI to be preserved.**

   Be aware that the scope may be larger than what is alluded to in a preservation letter. Include any IT people and both in-house and litigation counsel in this review.

   Be careful anytime you receive an overbroad preservation letter. Use your best collective judgment as to what will be relevant ESI. Ask your lawyer whether opposing counsel can limit the preservation request. Consider writing a letter to the opposing counsel (and keeping a copy) outlining what you will do, and the cost of what you won't do along with the offer to do it if the requesting party pays. If that fails, seek help from the court. Judges are not kind to parties who try to use a hatchet rather than a scalpel.

2. **Identify the relevant ESI, the key players in the litigation hold, and the various locations of the ESI.**

   You need to know what ESI is needed, who has it, and where it is. The data map is your guide.

3. **Determine what steps are necessary to both protect and collect the relevant ESI.**

   Verify that those steps are feasible and that they'd achieve what you expect.

4. **Implement a document retention plan if you don't already have one.**

   To implement the plan:

   - Notify all persons who might possess relevant ESI for the litigation hold and the steps they are required to take under the plan.

   - Monitor the implementation of the plan on an ongoing basis.

5. **Where necessary, limit access to systems or machines that may have relevant ESI.**

   In some cases, a person may want to rewrite history by getting rid of the device that stores it. You'll want to prevent them from doing so.

6. **Establish the format for production of the relevant ESI.**

When your company hires a litigation lawyer (separate from any in-house lawyers your company might have), that lawyer determines what's happened and collects any written documents that logs the steps you've taken. These logs will be used to demonstrate good faith compliance efforts.

Producing such documentation, including the actual hold notice, may not be ordered by the court. Hold notices are protected under attorney-client privilege and attorney work-product doctrine. You don't want to waive either protection. At some point, the judge may order you to produce your notices and memos. As with the logs, those documents are critical when an e-discovery dispute arises.

Courts give varying degrees of protection to the hold notice. At an early stage in one case, the court ordered the responding party to disclose information contained in the litigation notice, including the names and titles of 600 employees who received the hold notice. In *re eBay Seller Antitrust Litigation* (2007), the court said that details of the responding party's employees' ESI collection and preservation efforts would be fair game not only in the meet-and-confer session, but also in a deposition notice of a person familiar with those efforts. However, the defendant in the eBay litigation was not required to disclose the actual notice or any of its privileged contents.

Your lawyer has an obligation to oversee the litigation process and to ensure compliance. This is an ongoing obligation not just at the start of the hold.

Documenting that custodians are in compliance

Zubulake says you must notify the key players personally about the litigation hold, but notification isn't enough. Employees should understand the consequences of failing to comply, and know where to get help when they have questions. In addition, you need to get acknowledgments from employees and data custodians that they've received, understand, and are able to comply with a litigation hold. If they fail to comply, the blame falls on you because blame-shifting is not in the rules. Your lawyer needs to take affirmative steps to ensure that you're monitoring compliance correctly.

As you're documenting where ESI is and who has it, start a preservation log (see Figure 7-3). These come in handy during the e-discovery process.

Figure 7-3: Document all your ESI in a production log.

Custodian	Date	Method of Notification	Delivery Acknowledged	Date of Follow-Up	Questions	Updated Notice
Sally Doe	01/02/x1	Interoffice mail and e-mail	01/03/x1	01/04/x1	Sally had no questions on her obligation	02/01/x1 03/01/x2

Rounding up what needs to be collected

Rule 34 states that electronic records and communications are subject to subpoena and discovery for use in legal proceedings. Under Rule 34, the phrase *under control* doesn't require that you have legal ownership or actual physical possession of the documents at issue. Documents are considered to be under your control when you have the right, authority, or practical ability to obtain the documents from a non-party to the action.

A preservation letter that makes unreasonable or overbroad demands on a litigant or their operations won't be complied with and the courts won't enforcement it. Letters need to be specific and detailed. Don't send a "save it all" letter.

The contents of the letter help you achieve one or more goals:

- Makes sure the relevant ESI you think a person has is going to be there when you need it.

- Educates your opponent of their duty to prevent data destruction and data loss.

✔ Establishes a basis for your claim of spoliation against your opponent because your opponent can't claim ignorance.

✔ Establishes a basis for your claim of bad faith against your opponent for disregarding the duty to preserve relevant evidence.

You can issue a letter to a party or a non-party that you believe has ESI needed for your case.

Be sure to address the following points in the preservation letter:

✔ Spell out the nature of the dispute, litigation, or investigation.

✔ Name key individuals, dates, events, locations, departments, and any other facts that are known.

✔ Identify the types of ESI to be preserved. In this identification, you can either list general categories, such as e-mails relevant to an issue in dispute, or precisely identify specific e-mail on an issue between two or more named individuals.

✔ Warn the opponent not to delete, destroy, or modify any relevant material, even in the routine operation of its computer systems.

✔ Tell the opponent to suspend its normal retention policy and not destroy any relevant material until further notice.

✔ Ask them to distribute the preservation notice to all persons who may have relevant material in their possession and control, and document who's received the notice.

✔ Ask them to find out whether there's anyone else who should also receive the notice.

✔ Ask that the preservation notice be kept updated and send reminders of the preservation obligations to recipients.

✔ Provide the name of a contact person in case there are any questions about the litigation hold.

✔ Ask for acknowledgment that the preservation letter was received. This might be a certified mail receipt although, ideally, you want confirmation of receipt and that they intend to comply.

We present three sample preservation letters depending on the recipient. The preservation letters might be to a party, as shown in Figure 7-4; to a non-party, as shown in Figure 7-5; or to the client, as shown in Figure 7-6.

In Re: Preservation of electronically stored information

To whom it may concern:

This letter is to advise you that we are considering bring an action against your company for violating our anti-gravity machine patent. You have in your possession electronically stored information that is relevant to our claims and we are notifying you of your duty to preserve such information from spoliation.

You should preserve all electronically stored information relating to the development and marketing of your anti-gravity machine. This includes all hidden system files or metadata, presently located on or contained in any free standing computer or laptop, or on any part of a server, CPU or digital device containing data storage capabilities. Data storage devices include, among other things, hard drives, optical drives, floppy disk drives, CD-ROM and DVD drives, Zip drives, flash drives, data processing cards, computer magnetic tapes, backup tapes, drum and disk storage devices or any other similar method of electronic storage or system regardless of its name. Steps should be taken to preserve all electronically stored information relevant to this matter that may not be presently used by your company or has been deleted from your active system. Also preserve all digital images relating to the development and marketing of your anti-gravity machine that may be stored on any type of hardware used to store or manipulate electronic images. These include microfilm, microfiche and their repositories and readers. This is regardless of the image's format, such as jpg, .bmp, or some other advanced or proprietary form of digital image format.

It is important that you not destroy, modify or delete any of the electronically stored information that is the subject of this letter. You should take immediate steps to notify all persons who may have such information in their possession and control of their obligation to preserve. You should suspend any routine document retention and destruction policy that may result in the loss of relevant electronically stored information.

This preservation letter extends to anyone in your organization who may have possession or control of any electronically stored information relating to the development and marketing of your anti-gravity machine. This letter extends to all your subsidiaries and other ventures of any type and includes your successors and assigns. You should notify all such persons within your organization of the duty to preserve and document the name and location of each person receiving the preservation notice, as well as the date and time of such notice. You should regularly remind those persons of the continuing obligation to preserve.

This preservation notice includes any electronically stored information concerning the development and marketing of your anti-gravity machine that you now have, or may hereafter acquire. If anyone within your organization has any questions about this preservation notice, please contact the undersigned. I will be happy to discuss it.

Figure 7-4:
Preservation
letter to a
party.

Very truly yours,

Signed

In Re: Preservation of electronically stored information

To whom it may concern:

    This letter is to advise you that we are considering bring an action against XYZ company for violating our anti-gravity machine patent. You may have in your possession electronically stored information that is relevant to our claims and we are notifying you of your duty to preserve such information from spoliation.

    You are requested to preserve all electronically stored information relating to the development and marketing of XYZ's anti-gravity machine. This includes but is not limited to e-mails, spreadsheets, word processing documents, databases, Internet usage files and any other electronically stored information that may be relevant.

    It is important that you not destroy, modify or delete any of the electronically stored information that is the subject of this letter. You should take immediate steps to notify all persons who may have such information in their possession and control of their obligation to preserve. You should suspend any routine document retention and destruction policy that may result in the loss of relevant electronically stored information. You must take reasonable steps to preserve this information until further notice.

    This preservation letter extends to anyone in your organization who may have possession or control of any electronically stored information relating to the development and marketing of XYZ's anti-gravity machine. This letter extends to all your subsidiaries and other ventures of any type and includes your successors and assigns. You should notify all such persons within your organization of the duty to preserve and document the name and location of each person receiving the preservation notice, as well as the date and time of such notice. You should regularly remind those persons of the continuing obligation to preserve.

    This preservation notice includes any electronically stored information concerning the development and marketing of XYZ's anti-gravity machine that you now have, or may hereafter acquire. If anyone within your organization has any questions about this preservation notice, please contact the undersigned. I will be happy to discuss it.

Very truly yours,

Signed

Figure 7-5:
Preservation
letter to a
non-party.

In Re: Preservation of electronically stored information

Dear _____ ,

This letter is to advise you that we can reasonably anticipate that we will be in litigation over XYZ's anti-gravity machine and our patent on such. As such, you may be required to produce evidence to prove our case. Some of this evidence may be in the form of electronically stored information relating to the development of your patent for the anti-gravity product. Also any relevant information you may have concerning the development and marketing of XYZ's machine.

In order to properly protect the relevant evidence, it is important that you identify the location and person(s) in possession and control of any relevant information. We need to protect and preserve all relevant evidence, even if not in our favor. We should not destroy, modify or delete any of the electronically stored information that is the subject of this letter. You should take immediate steps to notify all persons who may have such information in their possession and control of their obligation to preserve. You should suspend any routine document retention and destruction policy that may result in the loss of relevant electronically stored information. You must take reasonable steps to preserve this information until further notice.

The information and documents may be in many different forms and they must be identified and preserved. This includes but is not limited to, e-mails, text messages, word processing documents, spreadsheets, memorandums, handwritten notes, voice messages, notes and engineering plans, regardless of the form or method of storage.

You should search for, protect and retain any documents relating to either your patent or XYZ's machine. This includes but is not limited to the following documents:

[list all potentially relevant documents]

You should instruct all personnel who may have such information in their possession and control to not alter, destroy, remove, or modify any related documents or information. You should notify them in writing of this obligation and document the person(s) and have them acknowledge receipt of the notice. You should ask if they have any reason to believe that someone else may have any information or documents relevant to this matter. If identified then a notice should be sent to that person. You are reminded to continually review and revise the preservation notice as needed and to assure continuing compliance.

If anyone has a question please have them call me at (555) 555-5555.

Very truly yours,

Signed

Figure 7-6:
Preservation letter to a client.

Judging whether a forensics-level preservation is needed

Preservation depends on people and actions that are out of your control. One method to ensure preservation is to make a forensics copy of the ESI on hard drives of computers or flash drives of handhelds. Computer forensics involves the use of specialized techniques for finding and recovering electronic evidence, preserving it, and authenticating and analyzing it.

Questions to ask at this time are the following: Does this case require a forensics level of data preservation? Would you benefit from the use of a forensics approach? These are important decisions to be made at this time. You might not implement forensics until later in the case or you may have no choice but to do so at this time.

Computer forensics methods and tools can be used to

- ✔ Discover, recover, and collect ESI
- ✔ Preserve documents, e-mail, and metadata
- ✔ Search and analyze the documents, e-mail, and metadata
- ✔ Authenticate the ESI
- ✔ Create and preserve the chain of custody

You often need computer forensics tools and techniques in cases that involve current or former employees. Asking the person who's suspected of committing a crime or who's suing you to preserve their ESI has obvious flaws.

Forensics is needed in s of fraud, employee misconduct, or misuse of corporate IT resources, theft of intellectual property, or crimes in which the perpetrator tried to hide their actions by deleting e-mail messages, files, or logs. However, it's an extra expense and disruption (while the forensics image is being made of the computer or handheld) so computer forensics may not be needed in the case if the effort is not proportional to the amount in controversy or other risks.

A computer forensics expert can help you understand the fundamentals of recovering, analyzing, and authenticating ESI. The use of computer forensic preservation is increasing even in matters that seem straightforward (one with no disputes). Cases starting with forensic analysis requests typically start or are expected to evolve into high-volume e-discovery matters. And some cases need the unbiased analysis provided by computer forensics. If you find yourself in need of a computer forensics specialist, check out Chapter 13, where we talk about how computer forensics and e-discovery work together.

Chapter 8

Managing e-Discovery Conferences and Protocols

In This Chapter

▶ Meeting the obligations of the meet-and-confer session

▶ Agreeing on the scope of e-discovery

▶ Selecting a timetable

▶ Designating the Rule 30(b)(6) witness

▶ Evaluating both party's interests

*W*hen you're served with a lawsuit, you must get your e-discovery plan rolling from day one. The first 120 days of litigation are perhaps the most critical days if you want to be successful. Your lawyer is required to meet with the opposing party in order to move the case forward and develop a plan to proceed. Among the most important aspects of this meeting — called the *meet-and-confer* meeting — are the discussions of issues related to ESI preservation, production, and protection.

In this chapter, you find out what goes on in the meet-and-confer session and how to help your lawyer prepare and successfully negotiate the process. Though it is early, it can be a make or break moment for your case. If your lawyer is properly prepared, he can provide both leverage and protection for your case.

Complying with the Meet-and-Confer Session

Early in the litigation stage, your lawyer meets with the opposition and discusses what ESI you have and how you intend to collect, preserve, and hand it over. The opposing side gives your lawyer the same information for their side so your lawyer can start building your case. This is the *meet-and-confer meeting*. This meeting is important to have because, as you can imagine, the two sides don't always agree on what ESI should be handed over and in what format. Hashing out an agreement on what is expected and setting time frames for discovery help you move forward with your case and build a strategy.

Rule 26(f) of the Federal Rules of Criminal Procedure (FRCP) says that the meet-and-confer meeting must be held by day 99. (See Chapter 1 for a discussion of the timing.) You may find that the meet-and-confer meeting happens earlier because a local rule takes precedent over the federal rule. The local rule may also allow for your attorney to report orally on the conference rather than in writing.

Check with your lawyer to determine whether you're governed by a local rule. You must comply with an applicable local rule even if it is at odds with the FRCP.

The meet-and-confer session is required unless there's an exemption (Rule 26(a)(1)(B) provides one) or the court says otherwise. Your lawyer needs to go into the meet-and-confer session armed with information you give him about your ESI, its condition, and an overview of your retention policies. This requires that you get the e-discovery team up and running in a short period of time (see Chapter 6 if you need to put your e-discovery team together).

Rule 26 requires that you and your lawyer confer in good faith. Failure to do so could result in sanctions. Rule 26(f)(2) instructs you to consider:

 ✔ The nature and basis of your claims and defenses

 ✔ The possibilities of promptly settling the case

 ✔ The required disclosures of discoverable information that may support your claims or defenses

 ✔ Any preservation issues

 ✔ A proposed discovery plan, which covers the following points:

   • Any changes in the timing or form of disclosures

   • The subjects that may require discovery and when you expect them to be completed, including any limitations that are requested

   • The issues relative to the disclosure of ESI including the form of production

   • Any issues dealing with privilege or protection and any agreements

   • Any changes or limitations or other suggested orders

It is not required that you agree, only that you confer in good faith.

Figure 8-1 is Form 35 that your lawyer submits to the court, detailing what was discussed in the meet-and-confer session.

Report of Parties Planning Meeting

[Caption and Names of Parties]
1. Pursuant to Fed.R.Civ.P. 26(f), a meeting was held on (date) at (place) and was attended by:

(name) for plaintiff(s)
(name) for defendant(s) (party name)
(name) for defendant(s) (party name)

2. Pre-Discovery Disclosures. The parties [have exchanged] [will exchange by (date)] the information required by [Fed.R.Civ.P. 26(a)(1)] [local rule ___].

3. Discovery Plan. The parties jointly propose to the court the following discovery plan: [Use separate paragraphs or subparagraphs as necessary if parties disagree.]

Discovery will be needed on the following subjects: (brief description of subjects on which discovery will be needed)

All discovery commenced in time to be completed by (date). [Discovery on (issue for early discovery) to be completed by (date).]

Maximum of ___ interrogatories by each party to any other party. [Responses due ___ days after service.]

Maximum of ___ requests for admission by each party to any other party. [Responses due ___ days after service.]

Maximum of ___ depositions by plaintiff(s) and ___ by defendant(s).
Each deposition [other than of _____] limited to maximum of ___ hours unless extended by agreement of parties.

Reports from retained experts under Rule 26(a)(2) due:
from plaintiff(s) by (date)
from defendant(s) by (date)

Supplementations under Rule 26(e) due (time(s) or interval(s)) .

4. Other Items. [Use separate paragraphs or subparagraphs as necessary if parties disagree.]

The parties [request] [do not request] a conference with the court before entry of the scheduling order.

The parties request a pretrial conference in (month and year).

Plaintiff(s) should be allowed until (date) to join additional parties and until (date) to amend the pleadings.

Defendant(s) should be allowed until (date) to join additional parties and until (date) to amend the pleadings.

All potentially dispositive motions should be filed by (date)

Settlement [is likely] [is unlikely] [cannot be evaluated prior to (date)] [may be enhanced by use of the following alternative dispute resolution procedure: [_____].

Final lists of witnesses and exhibits under Rule 26(a)(3) should be due:
from plaintiff(s) by (date)
from defendant(s) by (date)

Parties should have ___ days after service of final lists of witnesses and exhibits to list objections under Rule 26(a)(3).

The case should be ready for trial by (date) [and at this time is expected to take approximately (length of time)]. [Other matters]

Date: _____

/signed by all counsel

Figure 8-1:
Form 35
Report of
Parties
Rule 26(f)
Meeting.

The FRCP envisions a cooperative environment to reach a just result. If you don't do your best to cooperate with the opposing side, judges can sanction you for e-discovery misconduct. Here are a couple of examples:

- In the case of *In Re Seroquel Products Liability Litigation* (2007), the court found that the defendants failed to understand their own records and documents and to prepare them for production. The court was unimpressed by the defendant's preparation and participation, and agreed that they should be subject to sanctions, but reserved the type of sanction until a future date when the full impact of the defendant's misconduct could be determined.

- In *Mikron Industries, Inc. v. Hurd Windows & Doors, Inc.* (2008), the court refused to grant the defendant's request for a protective order that would have allowed them not to produce certain ESI because the defendant had not met and conferred in good faith. The court said that there should have been a substantive discussion regarding the defendants' difficulty in producing responsive ESI, the extent to which defendants have searched ESI, and the foundation for defendants' belief that a more thorough search of ESI, including backup tapes, would yield only information that has already been produced. The plaintiff's counsel stated that no meaningful discussion of the issues had taken place, and defendants submitted no evidence to dispute them.

Preparing for the Meet-and-Confer Session

Rule 26(f) requires you to address four important areas of ESI for the meet-and-confer session:

- Preservation of evidence
- Form of production
- Privilege or protection issue
- Any other issues

We discuss each of these in the following sections.

Preservation of evidence

You're expected to attempt to reach an agreement on what ESI to preserve. When you discuss the meet-and-confer session with your lawyer, be sure to give him this information:

✔ **Who has the ESI:** Simple enough, who are the custodians of the data?

✔ **How the ESI has been preserved:** Is it easily accessible or is it stored on a backup archive somewhere?

✔ **How much it costs to retrieve the ESI:** What will it cost in terms of time and money for you to get the ESI in shape to hand it over?

The court is generally unwilling to approve broad preservation orders that may be overly burdensome or impossible to comply with. However, if you agree to it, then the court is not sympathetic to your later complaints. Be prepared to deal with this issue and understand the costs and burdens associated with preservation.

If you created a data map (see Chapter 6), get it out now because it most likely contains all the information you need.

Your attorney has an ongoing obligation to make sure that your company is properly disseminating, understanding, and complying with the litigation hold.

Form of production

Production can be an extremely important issue. Rule 34 allows you to specify the form of production. If you can't agree to a form for handing over the ESI, you must hand over the ESI in the manner in which you usually maintain it or in another reasonably usable form. Refer to the Sedona Principles (www.thesedonaconference.org) for assistance in form production. In *D'Onofrio v. SFX Sports Group, Inc.* (2008), the court noted that the requesting party must be clear in what it is seeking.

The court in *Autotech Techs Ltd. P'ship v. Automationdirect.com* (2008) refused a request for metadata because the party had not requested it earlier. The court recognized that the requester was in the driver's seat and "must be satisfied with what it asked for." If you want the metadata — data about the data — you must ask for it. Metadata is data generated by the computer and can show when and who created something (for example, a Word document). It can also show if and when revisions were made. This could be crucial in trying to show the authenticity of a document being offered into evidence.

Your attorney should go to the meet-and-confer session with a good understanding of the format in which you'll produce ESI. Lack of specificity or an incomplete understanding of the technology could result in not getting you what you need. Be careful what you ask for because it may be all you get.

Privileged or protected ESI

The third area you should address with your lawyer is any possible privilege or protection issues for ESI. Be prepared to compromise with the other party to deal with any possible inadvertent disclosure. These agreements may become part of the scheduling order of the court under Rule 16.

One method to deal with inadvertent disclosure is the quick peek agreement, as shown in Figure 8-2. This agreement allows you to get a snapshot view of your opponent's ESI before they constitute a waiver of privilege or protection. Once the quick peek has occurred, you can establish what you want and the format you want it in. Your opponent can still claim a waiver.

We talk more about privileged and protected ESI in Chapter 10.

Discovery Quick Peek Agreement

The undersigned parties in an effort to aid in the discovery process pursuant to the Federal Rules of Civil Procedure Rule 26, do hereby agree as follows:

1. *[Responding party]* shall make relevant information requested by the *[requesting party]* available for inspection.

2. Provision of such requested information shall not constitute a waiver of any privilege or protection claims on the information so provided.

3. *[Requesting party]* shall review the information and designate the information it believes is responsive to the request.

4. *[Responding party]* shall review such designated information for information it believes is privileged or protected.

5. Following the review *[name of responding party]* shall produce the information it believes is relevant and not privileged or protected.

6. *[The parties shall request that this agreement be a part of the Scheduling or other pre-trial Discovery Order.] Optional*

Dated: _____

{Requesting Party}

Dated: _____

{Requesting Party}

Figure 8-2:
A quick peek agreement.

Any other issues regarding ESI

You must also address any other issues that may arise regarding the ESI. These issues might include sources of ESI, relevant time periods, and the custodians of the ESI — in other words, where is it and who has it!

A few crucial aspects of this last category of inquiry are trying to agree on

✔ Search protocols

✔ Issues related to accessibility of the ESI

✔ The cost or burden of restoring inaccessible ESI

For example, if your company converted its word processor from WordStar to Microsoft Word in 1987, you may want to argue that you can only produce ESI created after 1987. If you can't produce the earlier ESI, then you need to be prepared to discuss the costs and burden associated with the production of those documents. You should be familiar with what is necessary for conversion and whether the same information is available through other sources.

In *Williams v. Taser* (2007), the parties could not reach agreement on search terms and would not budge from their original positions. The court ordered Taser to run 21 specific searches and produce all presumptively responsive documents. The only documents excluded were those with a claim of privilege or protection.

Agreeing on a Timetable

One of the purposes of the meet-and-confer session is to establish a timetable for discovery. If the agreed-upon timetable is reasonable, the court uses it as the basis of the scheduling order.

The judge puts together a scheduling order to provide a roadmap for the completion of the case, and it includes dates and issues on discovery. A scheduling order may include any agreements you've entered into regarding e-discovery. The court issues a scheduling order after receiving the meet-and-confer report.

You should not overreach by setting an overly aggressive schedule. Likewise, after the schedule is set, you risk sanctions if you fail to comply. You can ask the court for additional time, but it's best if you can agree to an amended timetable with your opposing party.

Selecting a Rule 30(b)(6) Witness

During the course of discovery, you can take a deposition of any person that may have relevant information about the case. A deposition is not done before the court but the witness is sworn in by a court reporter and questioned by the attorneys. The testimony is recorded and reduced to writing.

In the interest of saving the time and cost of taking multiple depositions, FRCP Rule 30(b)(6) allows you to name the people you want to be deposed on behalf of your corporation, partnership, association, or government agency. The requesting party provides a description of the matters that they wants to examine. Depending on what they want, you can choose the best person to testify. This usually includes information on information pertaining to your system, data retention policy, implementation of the litigation hold, and location of ESI. But it can be much broader. Your attorney may object if she believes the requested information is not subject to discovery. The person selected as your Rule 30(b)(6) witness also testifies at the trial.

While you're preparing for the meet-and-confer session, think about who should serve as the Rule 30(b)(6) witness. This is the best time to do it and your selection will be discussed at the conference.

Making this decision before the meet-and-confer session is much more efficient. It is not necessary to engage in discovery to figure out whom to depose.

The person you select does not need to have any direct knowledge of the case or be the most knowledgeable on the issues in the case. For example, a person may know nothing about your specific case but is knowledgeable about the systems, platforms, locations of ESI, and policies of your company. If that is what is requested, that person is your best Rule 30(b)(6) witness. In fact, in some cases, it may be advantageous to have someone that is not directly involved with the case to avoid any emotions tainting the witness.

In determining who should be the Rule 30(b)(6) witness, you and your attorney need to review the subpoena and matters that are subject to the deposition. This review helps you narrow the field of potential witnesses. Then your attorney should meet with all the proposed witnesses to determine who she believes is most knowledgeable but also who she believes would be a better witness. You want to present your most convincing witness, and some people aren't convincing witnesses.

If you fail to designate a Rule 30(b)(6) witness, you can be sanctioned under Rule 37. While seldom done, you may risk the sanctions rather than expose the testimony because information might be revealed that is detrimental to your case.

You can designate more than one person and it need not be a current employee. Designate the person with care if that person has duties in the organization; the deposition could elicit testimony that may lead to additional discovery that you might not want revealed.

Take care in deciding who will be designated and properly educate them on the matters for examination and the process itself. Make sure they're comfortable being questioned by opposing counsel. Both your company and your Rule 30(b)(6) witness may be sanctioned for not being prepared. In *Ideal Aerosmith, Inc. v. Acutronic USA, Inc.* (2007), the court stated that there was no reason why the witness "could not have prepared himself, whether through documentation prepared by the consultant or conversations with him." The judge found that the Rule 30(b)(6) witness was unable to answer even the basic foundation questions.

Finding Out You and the Opposing Party May Have Mutual Interests

One of the great advantages of an effective meet-and-confer session is your ability to narrow the issues. One area that you'll probably agree on is the reduction in costs. This may, however, not be the case if you and your opponent have disparate financial resources. Expenses related to ESI can be both astronomical and disproportional. You have a duty in the process of discovery to consider whether the costs in relation to the amount in controversy — are the costs disproportional to the amount in controversy? Setting that aside, the costs of e-discovery nationwide are estimated to be in the billions of dollars.

The meet-and-confer session provides the opportunity to narrow the scope not only of discovery, but also of your entire case. After you determine the issues that are really in dispute, you can focus on discovery without judicial intervention.

If you're prepared and you participate in good faith, a lot can be accomplished to move the case effectively and efficiently to a conclusion.

Part IV
Processing, Protecting, and Producing ESI

The 5th Wave   By Rich Tennant

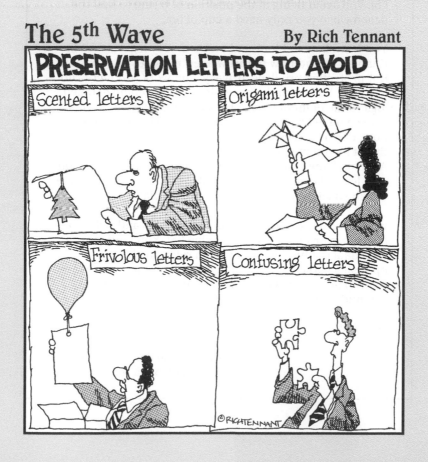

In this part . . .

Part IV takes you from the point of reviewing and processing ESI in Chapter 9, through protecting privilege and work product in Chapter 10, to the point where you package and produce on schedule all responsive, non-privileged ESI to opposing counsel in Chapter 11.

In many cases, ESI review takes the lion's share of the budget, and if done incorrectly, privileged documents can be leaked to the opponent, as you start to understand in Chapter 9. You learn why the key driver of costs, and waiver errors, is the number of documents that outside counsel must review for privilege and relevance. By filtering and staging multiple reviews to reduce the ocean of ESI, you avoid being in the position of trying to boil the ocean when you only need a cup of tea.

You learn how to block and tackle thorny legal issues in Chapter 10, and how to throw a few punches of your own. But protecting privilege, privacy, and work product is not all sport. You learn the necessity of maintaining detailed logs to the point of being obsessive/compulsive. At this stage, you're trying to argue that you don't need to produce ESI, regardless of its relevance, because you know that it's protected by privilege, work product, or privacy. Amidst all the challenges at this stage of e-discovery, you also learn the value of agreements with the opposing side, which you'll want the court to make official.

In Chapter 11, you find out about the costs and risks you face when producing and releasing ESI. You read that metadata is a hidden threat when releasing ESI to an opposing party because it might reveal things you wanted to keep under wraps. Mistakes here, as in prior stages, can undermine your trial strategies or worse.

"Oh, no!"

—Words you don't want to say,
or hear from a team member

Chapter 9

Processing, Filtering, and Reviewing ESI

In This Chapter

▶ Putting your finger on responsive ESI

▶ Trying until you get it right

▶ Doing a first take on the ESI

▶ Laying out the evidence

▶ Distinguishing hits and misses

▶ Getting statistical

▶ All eyeballs (and review software) on deck

*E*lectronic discovery becomes even more intense when the processing phase arrives. To get ESI ready for review and analysis, you might have any amount — a 1GB pile to multi-terabyte mountains — of discovery documents to process and index to get them into searchable shape for filtering. Using proprietary or commercially available software to index the documents and filter out duplicate and meaningless ones takes a big bite out of the volume of ESI to be reviewed. Review is the highest cost line item on most e-discovery bills, so less really costs much less.

During these procedures, ESI undergoes a bag-and-tag-and-bag sequence. Indexed ESI is stored on a secured accessible platform (bag) for filtering; files are tagged as relevant, privileged, confidential, discard, damaged, and so on; then files tagged as relevant, nonprivileged, and non-work product ESI are bagged in order to meet production deadlines. *Remember:* You must organize and index any ESI that you're planning to hand over so it's ready for your opponent to review. Not organizing and indexing ESI can carry a sanction and re-work.

In this chapter, you learn the art and science of processing, filtering, and review. You read why documenting every decision creates a shield to counter attacks from opponents. You read about systematic sampling and trial-and-error search methods to pare data. Search methods that amount to little more than wild grasps and shots in the dark won't survive challenge. Planning your process-filter-review work around the amounts at issue in the case, and then carrying out that plan, minimizes your cost and risk.

Planning, Tagging, and Bagging

After identifying the key custodians and relevant sources of ESI (see Chapter 7) and preserving and collecting ESI (see Chapter 8), you arrive at the costly tasks of processing, filtering, and reviewing the data and documents.

At the process, filter, and review stages, follow these steps:

1. **Define the outcome you want and what you need to achieve it.**

   Start by planning. Determine what needs to be done, the alternative ways in which it can be done, and then decide how you'll proceed. As you can read in Chapter 3, your emphasis in the plan might shift from the budget, to the scope, to the schedule as deadlines near and nerves fray.

2. **Perform an early case assessment.**

   Take a realistic look at the elements of the case, what types of e-evidence there are and their strengths, and the intent and staying power of both yourself and your opponent. You need to figure out your position. Then, like in poker, hold, fold, or bluff.

3. **Process and index the preserved ESI.**

   Preserved ESI is not in searchable condition until you've processed and indexed it using specialized software offered by many e-discovery vendors and consulting firms, such as Kazeon, FIOS, EMC SourceOne, Xerox Litigation Services, Clearwell, MindTalent, and Quest. Most software packages index the ESI prior to processing to expedite the searches. Several vendors provide litigation support platforms where ESI is filtered, searched, and reviewed for responsiveness, privilege, trade secrets, and other matters.

4. **Filter the processed ESI.**

   The ESI is put through multiple searches, including keyword, data, custodian, time frame, and conceptual filtering deduping; and near-duplicate processing, to separate the relevant responsive ESI from that which is not. The software may filter the ESI through the Reference Data Set (RDS) of the National Software Reference Library (NSRL) (www.nsrl.nist.gov). The RDS is a collection of digital signatures of known system files and software applications. Filtering out these non-responsive files reduces your load.

5. Review and analyze the filtered ESI.

Review is a fine-tuned filtering of the ESI to identify irrelevant, privileged, work product, and other ESI that is protected from disclosure. Redacting documents might be done at this stage. Review does not necessarily require someone sitting and reading each page. Review decisions depend on what's at stake, the time frame, ethical obligations, and the FRCP, as you read about in Chapter 10.

To bend (shorten) timelines when interim milestones or final production dates are closing in, these phases can overlap. For example, as the e-mail repository is processed, filtering can begin on that batch, and then the document repository can go into processing. As ESI moves along, you can be processing, filtering, and reviewing different batches or chunks of ESI concurrently. If documents are being processed in small chunks, these documents can be made available as they become available. This approach is called *rolling production* and can occur over a short time or over a year or more.

Taking a finely tuned approach

Searching data and files might seem like second nature to you. Who goes a day without searching the Internet, an address book, a retail Web site, a flight's status, or some type of database?

Computer search software, most notably Google Desktop (`http://desktop.google.com`), the Microsoft Windows search utility (part of the Start menu), and Internet search engines are handy tools for finding information, but they operate like excavators. They grab a lot and aren't too particular about what they grab. They're also not particular about what they don't grab. Also, search tools can demand too much precision. For example, if you search your laptop for a document containing the phrase "inadvertent disclosure," and you misspell the term in the document or as the search term, the search utility won't find the document. Of course, if you misspell the phrase both times the exact same way, you're in luck. Overall, basic search engines are strong, but sloppy. In contrast, e-discovery duties and the courts demand a more discriminating and intelligent search methodology that's capable of finer precision.

Finding exactly what you need

To visualize the complexity of the search task, look at the symbols representing files stored on a single hard drive in Figure 9-1.

Assume each wingding represents a file category, such as an e-mail message, a word processing document, a personal instant message sent or received, a music file, a photo, a computer virus or spyware, a trade secret or other proprietary document, a work product or privileged document, an encrypted file, a deleted file, and so on. General groupings are easy because of easily identifiable distinctions. The easiest method of identifying a group of files is to use the three-letter or four-letter file extension. But file extensions can be changed accidentally or easily to disguise the file and, therefore, can't be trusted. Computer forensics experts use software tools to discover all data that might exist on computers and other storage media, and then to retrieve the ESI in a way that a chain of custody and authenticity can support.

Consider the challenges. Unless a privileged document or e-mail is labeled as such, how can search software distinguish it from nonprivileged documents or e-mails? Computers don't really search; instead, they match. A résumé that states, "I don't have a Harvard MBA," would be selected by a search protocol looking for those words or credentials just as it would a résumé legitimately listing "Harvard MBA." Review would hopefully catch the discrepancy.

Similar problems exist with e-mail messages containing disclaimers that may or may not disqualify them from disclosure. Non-relevant personal e-mail messages and relevant case-related e-mail messages can look alike. (This is roughly the time when the litigation team complains about the lax e-mail usage policy that co-mingles business and personal messages.)

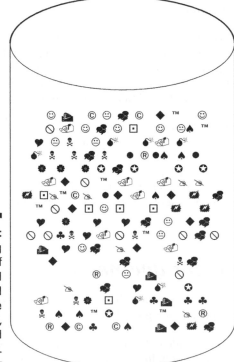

Figure 9-1:
A wingding view of files stored on a hard drive to be processed, filtered, and reviewed.

You now recognize the inherent problems with filtering methods and why your opponents and the court will scrutinize your methodology, not just your results. The good news is that your processing, filtering, and review procedures are judged in terms of whether they are reasonable relative to the issues and value of the case.

Enlisting an experienced technical expert to help define and defend your ESI search methodology is not only a smart investment, but also a necessary one. The expert may persuade the court that your efforts were reasonable and proportional to the case.

Litigators may need to explain and demonstrate with appropriate documentation that the filtering and review methods were reasonable, given the amounts at issue in the case. Your lawyer depends on you to a large extent for the documentation. In *U.S. v. O'Keefe* (2008), Judge John Facciola colorfully concluded that the selection of keyword search terms is "best left to experts" and not to lawyers.

Stop and identify yourself

Processing, filtering, and reviewing of ESI depend on the ability to identify and make distinctions, a job that cannot be done using an excavation approach. Here are a few of the many tricky identifications and distinctions that, if done correctly, reduce the volume of ESI to only what you're obligated to produce:

- ✔ **Identify duplicates.** Check your work e-mail account and you'll find messages that were sent to a distribution list or sent via a *reply all*. You can discard all but one of each of these messages as duplicates.

- ✔ **Distinguish final versions from drafts.** Being able to distinguish drafts of documents from the final official version not only reduces volume, but also reduces the risk of releasing plans that were never adopted or quality control problems that were remedied.

  Unedited drafts might be key evidence depending on the nature of your case.

- ✔ **Distinguish near-duplicates from one-of-a-kinds.** Documents may be converted to portable digital format (PDF) or compressed into a Zip file. Having the same document in different formats is unnecessary.

- ✔ **Identify documents according to creation or modification dates.** Documents whose created, generated, accessed, or printed dates are before or after the relevant date range are not material to the case unless the dates are misleading. For example, when a file is re-used or used as a template, the dates may be false, as shown in Figure 9-2. The file properties in Figure 9-2 show that the file was printed on February 20, 2008 and that the file was created on June 6, 2009 — more than 15 months later.

Figure 9-2:
A document's date properties may not be accurate.

| General | Summary | Statistics | Contents | Custom |

Created:	Saturday, June 06, 2009 4:57:00 PM
Modified:	Friday, June 12, 2009 2:00:26 AM
Accessed:	Friday, June 12, 2009 2:00:25 AM
Printed:	Wednesday, February 20, 2008 9:46:00 AM

Two wrongs and a right

If your memory of statistics is a bit rusty, here are terms you come across when sampling:

- ✔ **False positives:** A document or file is marked as *relevant* when it's not. False positives result in overinclusiveness. These errors increase the amount of ESI to review, which increases the time and cost of review, as shown in Figure 9-3.

- ✔ **False negatives:** A document or file is marked as non-relevant when it is relevant. The result is underinclusiveness. These kinds of errors result in files that should be reviewed and possibly produced being tossed into the discard pile (as shown in Figure 9-3). These errors increase the risk of accusation or sanction for not producing all responsive ESI.

  Keep the discards and sample them as well.

- ✔ **Just right:** A document or file is marked correctly as relevant when it is relevant, or marked non-relevant when it's not. Achieving perfection costs more and might require more time than you have.

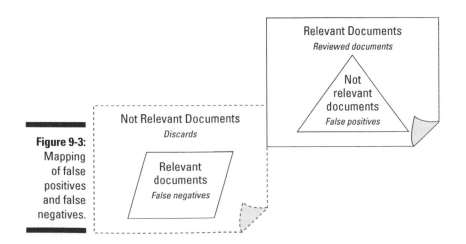

Figure 9-3:
Mapping of false positives and false negatives.

You process and search only the reasonably accessible ESI. If you process and review not reasonably accessible ESI, you can change its status to reasonably accessible because you deflated the basis of your argument against producing it.

Learning through Trial and Error

In uncharted or uncertain conditions, people often figure out what works and what doesn't through trial and error. Inventors Thomas Edison and Benjamin Franklin used this method. More importantly, the court expects that you use the trial-and-error approach and document your results with each trial.

The general trial-and-error process consists of the following steps:

1. **Select a sample upon which to run the trials.**

2. **Perform a trial run on the sample using a selected approach.**

   For example, on a sample set of e-mail messages, perform a search for relevant ones using a set of keywords.

3. **Examine and document the results of your approach, both good and bad.**

   Testing the results of a particular search method can flag problems like the overinclusiveness or underinclusiveness of the filtering technique.

4. **Identify limitations of your approach.**

5. **Make adjustments to the approach criteria.**

   If your search doesn't get you what you want or if it returns too much, you refine and redo the search. Searches involve two types of criteria:

   • *Objective:* Searches based on dates and custodians are objective criteria.

   • *Subjective:* Searches based on keywords and context based on judgments are examples of subjective criteria.

6. **Repeat Steps 2 through 5 until you obtain the results you need.**

You do a search to reduce the burden of review and the risk of sanctions for using a wild-guess approach. After, your legal team makes a final review of the relevant ESI before it's released.

Documenting the results of your trial-and-error method is critical for the following reasons:

- ✔ **Case law:** Judges look to your documentation for evidence of a systematic approach and not a self-serving approach.

- ✔ **Federal Rules of Civil Procedure:** The FRCP 26(g) requires good faith efforts, but also gives you some protection by mandating that efforts should be proportional to the costs and benefits.

- ✔ **Federal Rules of Evidence:** The FRE 502(c) waiver protection only applies if you took reasonable measures in your search. If not, your protection is gone.

Doing Early Case Assessment

Early case assessment tools can give you an initial perspective of the sources, scope, and types of potential relevant ESI. An early case assessment allows you to determine the position ESI puts your company in relative to litigation. Your attorney also needs the information you gather to prepare for the meet-and-confer session. An accurate early case assessment made by you can directly affect the case strategy and decision to fight or to settle.

Many e-discovery vendors provide a range of support services and automation tools for early case assessment. You should provide a short list of e-discovery vendors for your legal counsel to work with.

There's been considerable consolidation of e-discovery vendors, and that's expected to continue. An e-discovery vendor has the ability to work with a your company's IT staff to determine where documents are stored, in what format they are stored, and how the data can be retrieved in a way that doesn't alter it. Electronic discovery vendors typically have equipment and personnel to access active and legacy data from e-mail, word processing, and other systems to be read and retrieved. Vendors help you convert collected ESI into a format that allows your lawyer to review and produce it. Here are several e-discovery vendors:

- ✔ **Fios:** www.fiosinc.com
- ✔ **vdiscovery:** www.vdiscovery.com
- ✔ **AccessData:** www.accessdata.com
- ✔ **Kazeon:** www.accessdata.com
- ✔ **LexisNexis Applied Discovery Inc.:** www.applieddiscovery.com

For an extensive list of vendors, visit Socha Consulting at sochaconsulting.com/vendors.php.

E-discovery technology arms race

Rapid advances in the scale, security, and usability of e-discovery software have reduced the time lawyers, paralegals, and litigation teams need to search, dedupe, filter, review, disclose, and prepare documents for a hearing or trial. Electronic discovery services providers may offer individual services, project management, or comprehensive one-stop litigation support. Competition and improvements in technology have driven prices down. According to an estimate by *Legal Week* in the United Kingdom, a large e-discovery project undertaken in 2004 that took six months and cost more than £500,000 could be completed in 2009 within days and cost less than £10,000.

Vetting vendors

As you're selecting your e-discovery vendor, keep these tips in mind:

- ✔ **Get a good understanding of e-discovery issues, processes, and obligations.** You're mastering e-discovery by reading this book. Bravo. Preferably, you should become knowledgeable before you have to face e-discovery issues and the clock starts ticking down to the meet-and-confer session.

- ✔ **Meet vendors before you need them.** If you take the time to educate yourself about the vendors prior to actually needing them, you give yourself time to learn about vendors when you're not under the stress of litigation. Review vendors' Web sites to learn about their services and view their demos or Webinars. After this intelligence gathering, develop a short list of vendors and contact them. You need to know whether the vendor can support the volume and types of ESI your company has and get price estimates.

- ✔ **Get a live test using your ESI.** You need to get past the marketing team and meet with those who actually do the work. Have the vendor create load files to import a test set of your ESI into litigation support databases for a live demo.

- ✔ **Take the position that you're partnering with a vendor for the long run.** Every case is unique, and what's subject to discovery will differ. But you're not going to want to start from ground-zero with a new vendor each time you need one. Having a vendor on speed-dial hopefully won't be necessary.

- ✔ **Check references.** Ask vendors you're considering for references. Call and ask clients about competence, responsiveness, turnaround time, accuracy of cost estimates, and project management skills.

In June 2007, WGI of *The Sedona Conference* published an 84-page report *Navigating the Vendor Proposal Process: Best Practices for the Selection of Electronic Discovery Vendors* available from its Web site at www.thesedona conference.org/.

Breaking Out the ESI

ESI that's been put on hold is in no condition to be searched efficiently or effectively. It needs to be *processed*; that is, transformed into a searchable format. Processing is done using specialized software by an in-house technology staff or a third-party vendor or consulting firm. ESI must be processed following legally defensible procedures, which e-discovery support firms know.

Not all media you've identified and preserved may need to be processed. The type of case, the data sources, and the number of custodians influence how best to determine what needs to be processed. Risks stemming from reducing the amount of ESI include

- ✔ Excluding potential key evidence that's beneficial to your case
- ✔ Violating e-discovery obligations resulting in sanctions, an adverse inference instruction, or worse, even if there was no bad faith or gross negligence

The transformations done during processing depend on the software and the level of service provided by the vendor or consulting firm. Processing plug-ins or add-ins may be available to expand the range of processing. Relevant ESI might already be filtered during identification and collection stages if date restrictors and key search terms were used to extract relevant ESI from data repositories. Or the ESI may consist of entire laptops, network directories, workstations, or other media.

In any case, processing ESI, done either by third-party vendors or in-house IT staff, includes these tasks:

- ✔ **Standardizes file formats.** Files need to be converted.
- ✔ **Performs document-type specific data extraction.** Files may need to be extracted. For example, zipped files need to be unzipped, and e-mail attachments must be separated out.
- ✔ **Removes repetitive copies.** A first pass file deduplication is made to reduce the volume.
- ✔ **Removes system files.** Software files, such as Microsoft Office applications and non–user-created files, are typically not relevant and are removed.
- ✔ **Creates an inventory of ESI.** A list of the ESI is created to serve as documentation.

✔ **Extracts metadata.** Metadata might be extracted so it can be searched. Metadata describes a file or its properties, such as who created the file and when it was created or last accessed.

✔ **Detects e-mail threads.** We're all familiar with e-mails that contain replies, or *threads*. Because e-mail is the leading form of e-evidence, detecting the progression of messages is important.

✔ **Exports the ESI.** The resulting pool of ESI is exported in an appropriate review database. Subsequent filtering and review of the ESI is done on this pool, together with its index. The ESI may be exported in its native form for review or converted to image, text, or HTML. Native review is most common and beneficial because it preserves the metadata.

Review format might depend on the type of review tools the review team uses or it might be determined by agreements made about the form of production.

✔ **Creates an index and word-frequency list.** The processing software examines the files; finds words and names; and adds them to a master index of the words, terms, and filenames. This is similar to the index of a book. If you look up *meet and confer* in this book's index, you see a listing of the pages that contain the phrase.

The index created by processing is actually a database of every word, term, and name contained in the volume of ESI. It lists the frequency or number of times the word appears in the ESI repository.

Processing software can index several different types of data, most commonly e-mail, word processing documents, spreadsheets, PDFs, database files, and Web browsing history logs. When selecting processing software, be alert to its limitations and do the following:

✔ **Verify that the software is capable of processing your file types.** Not all processing software can process all types of files, such as object linking and embedded (OLE) files, an example of which is an Excel graph embedded within a Word document. Other tough files to crack are encrypted and password-protected files.

✔ **Check the capability of the software to create an index that meets your needs.** An index is a database that is limited in size. For example, Google Desktop only indexes 100,000 files per drive during the initial indexing period, which might be insufficient for users with large hard drives.

Provide your legal team with a list of your keyword search results because they'll need it at the meet-and-confer session. The index created during processing is a detailed view of potential keywords and their frequency.

New and improved techniques for processing and reviewing data are evolving to mitigate risks, lower costs, and improve efficiency. Even if you partner with a vendor or consulting firm, check on their capabilities.

Crafting the Hunt

You identify ESI that's likely to be relevant by performing searches using key-words and other methods that have the power to discriminate between hits (relevant ESI) and discards (non-relevant ESI) with reasonably high reliability.

Given the volume of ESI, you need the help of experts to devise a list of key-words and then test the results and refine the list via trial and error. Search terms and other restrictors need to be discussed internally with your entire e-discovery team and externally with the opposing party.

Most search results, or data sets, have false positives. Refining search que-ries can minimize those false hits. See the earlier section, "Using Trial-and-Error," for information on refining your search queries.

A single fire-and-forget search method is not scientific. An iterative process of examining, thinking, evaluating the process to determine if you can do better, and refining the process is a defensible method.

Deciding on filters

On all decisions about search methods, you should come to an agreement with the opposing counsel or by court consent regarding the search protocol so you can avoid discovery disputes.

Here are the filters that require decisions. These filters are fact-based objec-tives and produce rather clean results:

- ✔ **File size and type filtering:** You may notice files on your computer that start with a tilde [~] and a dollar sign [$], as shown in Figure 9-4, or that end in .tmp. These are all temporary files that you know you didn't create. One .tmp file can generate many of these types of files because they may serve as a backup in Windows.

  Filter out files that are 1K in size or that end in .tmp because they're not generated by the user and most likely are duplicates.

  In contrast, you can filter to select what file types to include in the ESI pool. When an agreement is reached with opposing party or the court on file types, for example spreadsheets and e-mail, then you use the filter to select those files. (You may need to use computer forensics software to confirm actual file types because the software doesn't rely on the file extension to find files.)

- ✔ **Custodian filtering:** Reducing the number of custodians whose files are in the ESI pool reduces the need to process and review data from their laptops, handheld devices, workstations, network directories, and e-mail accounts. But when users share equipment or have access to each other's accounts, to name just two scenarios, the ability to distinguish whose ESI to filter in or filter out weakens.

✔ **Date range filtering:** Distinguishing files based on date may or may not be straightforward. A file has several dates and not all of them are accurate. An e-mail thread can also have many different dates.

Figure 9-4:
File types to be filtered from the pool of responsive ESI.

~$80470510124 Ch09.doc	1 KB	Microsoft Word Docu...
~WRL2347.tmp	126 KB	TMP File
~WRL0146.tmp	126 KB	TMP File
~WRL3258.tmp	126 KB	TMP File
~WRL3663.tmp	126 KB	TMP File
~WRL3444.tmp	127 KB	TMP File
~WRL1370.tmp	127 KB	TMP File
~WRL4008.tmp	126 KB	TMP File
~WRL1572.tmp	126 KB	TMP File
~WRL0063.tmp	126 KB	TMP File
~WRL0523.tmp	127 KB	TMP File
~WRL3649.tmp	128 KB	TMP File
~WRL2171.tmp	128 KB	TMP File

Keyword or phrase searching

Keyword or *phrase searching* is the process of identifying ESI based on specific keywords or terms in order to find documents for attorney review. Keyword searches scrape only the surface of what might be relevant, and cannot guarantee that you found everything. That is, the ESI the search identifies are relevant, but the results are not complete.

Words that are misspelled, abbreviated words, slang, typos, and the like don't make the cut because searches are so exact. Even the auto-correct feature can change a word to something unintended. To relax the precision constraint, use software that supports a fuzzy search that looks for common misspellings or guesses at whether the word is what you want.

If you miss relevant ESI and the opposing counsel challenges you, the judge may have doubts regarding what else you might have missed.

Deduping

Deduping decisions might seem easy. If a file is a duplicate, put it into the discards. Some decisions about the deduping process are not clear and can become overwhelming. Deduplication can be done within each custodian's ESI or within a single ESI repository. Or the process can be applied across all custodians of each department or all ESI sources of a department.

Tag duplicates and near-duplicates to inspect closely later on.

Concept searching

Concept searching software uses the meaning of words or terms to find responsive documents. They don't just match letters or words; they use something similar to a thesaurus. A thesaurus finds synonyms, or words with similar meaning; hence, it's a concept finder. Concept searching also looks for categories or examples. For example, the word _automobile_ is one category in the broader category of _vehicles;_ it's also a broader category to _sedans, convertibles,_ and so on.

Concept searching may also be capable of finding things that are related, but not necessarily in categories.

Heeding the Grimm roadmap

In his 43-page opinion in _Victor Stanley, Inc. v. Creative Pipe, Inc._ (2008), Judge Paul Grimm put fear into the hearts of attorneys who might have attempted to structure their own keyword searches for e-discovery.

Judge Grimm made it clear that in order to have a keyword search acceptable for the court, one of the following two approaches need to be taken:

- **Collaborative search:** You need to confer with your opposing party in an effort to identify a mutually agreeable search-and-retrieval method. If the method is approved and you follow it, you can avoid disputes over the sufficiency of the method. Obviously, doing the search right the first time is always faster and cheaper than doing it again on an order from the court.

- **Best practices and data-driven search:** In order to have a defensible methodology in the absence of collaboration, you need to:

  - _Stay current:_ Know the current strengths and weaknesses of various methodologies, including The Sedona Conference Best Practices. Arm yourself with the knowledge to select the method that's most appropriate for its intended task.

  - _Prepare your defense:_ If your selection method is challenged, then expect to support your position with affidavits or the equivalent from qualified experts that reliable principles or methodology was used.

  - _Be capable of rapid course correction:_ Use appropriate data sampling, trial and error, and quality assurance to test your methods and core search assumptions.

Sampling to Validate

Sampling is a systematic approach to learn about a population. Sampling is a test or an audit. You take small samples of the population to study and learn from.

Given the huge population of preserved ESI, sampling is typically necessary in e-discovery. For large cases, consider it mandatory. People would rather have nothing to do with sampling because of its association with probability and statistics. Let's face it: Las Vegas is proof that people don't understand or have a healthy respect for probability.

Testing the validity of the search

How do you know that you did a reasonable job? The short answer is that you don't unless you used a systematic process.

The courts have made it crystal clear that a *black box approach* — a method that no one can verify — won't work. Figure 9-5 illustrates such an approach.

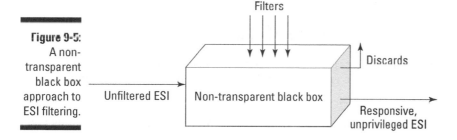

Figure 9-5: A non-transparent black box approach to ESI filtering.

You might have to validate your search methodology or show that your methods retrieved all the ESI they were supposed to retrieve. You must show how your methods work and that they actually did work. The best way to do the latter is through sampling.

Follow these steps when taking a sampling of your results:

1. **Take a statistically significant number of files.**

   The size of the sample depends on the population, or the total number of files, as well as several other mind-numbing factors beyond the scope of this chapter.

2. **Review the files manually for the ESI that you want it to identify or target to learn what the results should be.**

3. **Use your automated search methodology to perform the same search that you did manually.**

4. **Compare the manual results to the automated results.**

5. **Draw a conclusion.**

   If an acceptable percent of the target ESI detected in the manual search appears in the automated search results, the sample validates your search methodology. If the automated search did a terrible job of detecting target ESI, use trial and error to improve it.

Validating a methodology is tough because you have to be certain that your sample size is sufficient for the test. Luckily, e-discovery production doesn't require statistical certainty and confidence levels. By using trial and error with sample sizes and results, you have sufficiently defensible production. As Judges Facciola and Grimm pointed out, perfection has never been the standard of discovery production; Rule 702 sets standards for testimony by experts are in place to make the process rational, not perfect.

A legal hedge against imperfection in sampling is the clawback provision, which you read about in Chapter 10.

Documenting sampling efforts

No one is going to accept "trust us" as a response if your sampling and search methodologies are challenged. Keep the following in a running journal:

- ✔ Minutes of meetings discussing or determining sampling techniques and search terms
- ✔ Logs of trial-and-error testing
- ✔ List of key words and terms, dates, file extensions, and custodians that you used
- ✔ Reports on the results of trial-and-error testing
- ✔ Invoices or logs of the time and costs involved in sampling efforts

You want to be transparent and be able to explain exactly what you find and why.

Doing the Review

Your team of lawyers and paralegals review all the processed and filtered ESI.

As you're processing the ESI, use the following tags for a first-pass review:

- **Responsive:** ESI that matches the desired set of criteria for the case or that's selected by one or more of the filters.

- **Irrelevant:** ESI that's not important or pertinent to the dispute.

- **Privilege:** Documents that you're not required to provide because they're protected against disclosure by attorney-client privilege.

- **Private:** Personal content, but may be discoverable.

- **Work product:** Written notes, reports on conversations with you or witnesses, research, and confidential materials that your attorney develops while representing you. Work product is not discoverable.

- **Redact:** Text to be removed or obscured from a document so that the redacted parts remain confidential and protected. Files whose content include content that must be produced as well as privileged or confidential content need to be redacted to remove what's privileged.

- **Corrupt:** Files that have been damaged and cannot be opened.

- **Encrypted:** Files whose contents are disguised and that can't be read until they're decrypted using the cipher key.

- **Password protected:** Files that require a password to open.

- **Hot:** Slang for documents, e-mail, text messages, or the like that contain relevant content that may impact the outcome of the case. Also referred to as *smoking gun* documents or e-mails.

- **For further review:** Files that need further attention.

If the case proceeds, you can continue to refine the ESI pool for second and third-pass reviews.

Choosing a review platform

You input all the ESI and their information, including their tags, into a review database. The review database might be an in-house application, your e-discovery vendor's software, or a third-party-hosted solution. That database might be hosted on an Internet-accessible platform. If the hard drives were imaged (preserved) using computer forensics software, that software's database review capabilities are typically used (see Chapter 13). The trend is toward using a Web-based review platform.

An Internet-accessible platform is essential if your reviewers are geographically dispersed or even in different time zones. To accommodate and increase convenience, vendors and consulting firms may offer Internet-based review platforms, a service known as *cloud computing*. Many of the Internet features that support business operations are customized to support litigation and the review process.

Here are some of the litigation support software products and models:

- **Cloud computing:** This model is based on the utility model. You don't own electricity-generating equipment (or water or gas). You pay for usage. With cloud computing, users access services via the Internet without owning the IT infrastructure that supports the services.

- **Software-as-a-Service (SaaS):** Basically, SaaS is a rent-a-service. It's also referred to as *hosted applications*. Many ESI review software packages require huge up-front capital investments for licensing fees, user fees, and training. With SaaS, you rent capabilities when you need them; that is, you get delivery of the services you need on demand. These services are like movies-on-demand and video-on-demand.

    Pricing is per page or per gigabyte for data processing, plus a hosting fee and subscriptions are another option. The SaaS model has several benefits, including scalability to the size of your case, 24 hours a day and seven days a week support from the vendor (pass the headache of IT maintenance to the vendor), and around-the-clock availability to reviewers via the Internet. One complaint leveled against this model is security, but, then, lawyers used to avoid using e-mail to communicate with clients for that same reason.

- **Dashboards:** In e-discovery, dashboards are information portals that provide the litigation team with real-time actionable information to help. These can be used to track status, timelines, percent completion, and estimate the cost of e-discovery activities, for just a few examples.

- **Drilldown:** When you want to drill down to get the details, being able to simply click for the details saves a lot of time. Drilldown capabilities are part of every business executive's arsenal and now are available for e-discovery. For example, summary metrics are linked to their detailed components. When a summary metric is clicked, it displays details about the review or reviewer.

Be sure to train everyone who is tagging ESI. Despite what anyone says, the software is not intuitive.

How to perform a review

Human review is not necessary for all documents, e-mails, and other ESI because it's fallible and it's impossible. You are not going to get perfection and, if you want perfection, you're not going to get done with the review. *Hot documents* (those most likely to contain relevant ESI or privileged content) warrant the effort of human review.

Consensus is that review is the most expensive e-discovery process. By this time, you've reduced the volume of ESI using sampling, filters, deduping processes, and any other appropriate tool. The actual content of the now-current pool of responsive ESI needs to be understood somehow. What does the e-evidence reveal, expose, or support? You need this information about the strengths and weaknesses of your position when your lawyer walks into the meet-and-confer session.

Issues to consider when performing a review are

- **Preserve the link or relationship between documents or e-mail messages and their attachments.** Most databases provide a utility to protect against separation.

- **Link duplicate files.** All files need to be tagged consistently.

- **Preserve metadata by maintaining native file formats.** Even if you don't plan to hand the ESI to your opponent in its native format.

- **Verify that tagging and redaction are consistent before preparing the ESI for disclosure.** You want to redact trade secrets if the rest was relevant. It could also be ordered as part of a motion to produce or protective order. You read more about redacting in Chapter 11.

Chapter 10

Protecting Privilege, Privacy, and Work Product

In This Chapter

▶ Recognizing the vast amount of ESI available

▶ Knowing the rules of evidence and procedure

▶ Finding out what's privileged, protected, or not

▶ Asking for protection (or forgiveness)

▶ Steering clear of waivers

▶ Making agreements that protect ESI

*A*ny game you play comes with established rules you need to follow and penalties you incur for breaking them. When litigation triggers, you're in a high-stakes game involving charges, pleas, evidence, and so on. This game has rules that govern evidence discovery, and breaking these rules (intentionally or not) can have serious consequences for the outcome of your case. Consider e-discovery the Super Bowl of discovery where the plays you run are controlled by Federal Rules of Civil Procedures (FRCP) and Federal Rules of Evidence (FRE), and are refereed by the courts.

In state cases, state rules apply and may vary from the federal rules. Because the general concepts involved apply to both state and federal rules, we focus the chapter discussion on federal rules.

The amount of information that's stored electronically (ESI) is staggering, but not all this ESI is eligible for discovery. The rules governing discovery of ESI are devised to protect certain types of communication from disclosure. In this chapter, you find out what ESI is protected from e-discovery because of privilege (communication considered confidential, such as doctor/patient), privacy (trade secrets and the like), or work product (materials prepared in the preparation of the case). You also discover how to assert that certain ESI deserves protection and how to protect ESI if inadvertent disclosure occurs.

Facing the Rising Tide of Electronic Information

Just envision the explosion in the number of servers and hard drives of handhelds that retain a copy of e-mail messages that have been copied and forwarded. There's no indication that the exponential growth of business and personal text messaging (via iPhones, BlackBerrys, and social networks) is abating. These venues exchange more e-mail messages in one day than the U.S. Postal Service handles mail in a year.

Because of this digital deluge, you may often have hundreds of thousands of documents that you must review for potential confidential information or privileged communication. Therefore, the cost of e-discovery and, with it, the cost and other burdens associated with filtering protected or privileged ESI, has escalated.

In *Rowe Entertainment v. Williams Morris et al.,* the estimated costs of filtering through ESI for two of the multiple defendants would conservatively be over $370,000 and take upward of two years to complete. The ESI included hundreds of thousands of documents.

Imagine having 200,000 documents stacked in front of you and trying to find two documents that may be confidential or privileged. This *needle-in-the-haystack* scenario is a common occurrence, and the haystack is getting bigger. On television, cases get finished up within an hour — unless the show is a miniseries; then it may take as long as four hours. The reality is that the e-discovery process can take years.

Respecting the Rules of the e-Discovery Game

Certain sections of the FRE and FRCP serve as the rulebook for the e-discovery game. Therefore, knowing how the rules are evaluated and applied is essential for managing the e-discovery process. Additionally, these sections help you identify whether ESI deserves protection because of privilege, privacy, or work product.

Targeting relevant information

FRE 401 defines *relevant evidence* as evidence that goes to prove the existence of any fact that helps prove or disprove a fact of importance to the outcome of the case. Only relevant evidence is admitted into court. You might think that this rule helps limit ESI targeted for discovery, but e-discovery may encompass a body of ESI that's much broader than what is considered relevant evidence.

You can discover ESI that might not be admissible at trial if the ESI could reasonably lead to the discovery of admissible evidence. Therefore, when planning for e-discovery, allow for the possibility that the amount of information discovered will be much larger than the amount that's admissible evidence in court.

Conversely, relevant evidence may not be discoverable. For example, ESI that is not reasonably accessible because of undue burden or cost may be protected from e-discovery. However, for a good cause (such as the ESI requested is important to the case and cannot be obtained through any other means), a court may order its discovery.

Generally, e-discovery may be limited when any of three conditions are met:

- ✔ **You can obtain the ESI from other lower-cost sources.** For example, a request for voluminous financial records that might otherwise be available in summary form in documents filed with the SEC or other government agencies and available to the public.

- ✔ **The ESI is unreasonably cumulative or duplicative.** For example, when a fact has already been disclosed, obtaining thousands of e-mails that indicate the same fact is unnecessary and duplicative.

- ✔ **Your burden or cost of the e-discovery outweighs the usefulness of the information discovered to sufficiently prove something important to the trial (in legal terms, this is the information's *probative value*).** This situation might occur when a party requests all the e-mails of all the employees of a large company, even those e-mails unrelated to the litigation issues. The cost of production far outweighs what may be discovered by looking at every employee's e-mail. The same may be said if the cost of production, even if it's probative, far outweighs the amount in controversy. It makes no sense to force production costs that exceed the amount in controversy.

When determining which ESI is discoverable, courts assess the amount of information in controversy in the case, the importance of the discovery to the issues of the case, and the resources of the parties involved to avoid undue burden.

Seeing where relevance and privilege intersect

Confidential communication and information differs from what is legally considered privileged communication. Privileged communications have significantly more protection under the federal rules (FRE 501 and FRCP 26 and 45) than do confidential communications or information. In either case, certain information and communications may be subject to some protection from e-discovery *but only when the information is not relevant to the case* (see the preceding section).

Trusting that your communications are confidential can only go so far when litigation starts. Only communications legally recognized as privileged communications are not subject to e-discovery.

You don't have to disclose privileged communication even if it's relevant to the issue in the case.

Determining which communications are privileged

A communications *privilege* is meant to protect certain relationships as developed under common law. FRE 501 allows the courts to apply common law and reason in establishing privileges. This means that courts may differ in what they consider privileged information. Although state rules may differ from federal rules, generally privileges apply to communications in these types of relationships:

- ✔ **Attorney-Client:** If you talk to your attorney about a legal matter, you should be able to expect that the conversation is confidential and not be used against you. If these discussions were allowed to be used in court, it would hinder the ability of attorneys to prepare cases with clients who were afraid or reluctant to be candid. The wheels of justice would get jammed.

  To be covered by attorney-client privilege, the communication must have been made in confidence and not further a crime or fraud.

- ✔ **Physician/Psychotherapist-Client:** Communications with a doctor that relate to diagnosis or treatment of a physical, mental, or emotional condition are covered by the privilege.

- ✔ **Husband-Wife:** Communications that were intended to be confidential and made during the marriage are considered part of the sanctity of marriage and have a privilege.

- ✔ **Religious Leader–Follower:** If you communicate in confidence to a clergyman, that communication is protected by privilege. *Confidence,* for this purpose, means that the communication was made privately and was not intended to be told to anyone else.

- ✔ **Accountant-Client:** Some states recognize this privilege as similar to the attorney-client privilege. However, the federal government recognizes it only in a very narrow privilege — in IRS matters, a situation almost never available in third-party actions.

- ✔ **Self-Incrimination:** The Fifth Amendment provides a privilege against self-incrimination if you have a reasonable apprehension that an answer might tend to incriminate you. It must be of a criminal act. It applies only to testimonial evidence. Generally, the privilege doesn't apply to business entities to the same degree as individuals.

Covering work product with protection

The United States Supreme Court in *Hickman v. Taylor* recognized that certain trial preparation materials should be protected under the work product (trial preparation materials) doctrine. These are materials that reveal your attorney's strategy and may include evaluations of your case's strength or weakness, reflections from interviews of witnesses, tactics, or similar information. Imagine getting a copy of the opposition's game plan while preparing for the Super Bowl.

Work product is not privileged within the meaning of the FRE, but it is safeguarded by FRCP 26(b)(3) and FRCP 45(d)(2), which grants protection to documents and tangible things that meet two criteria:

- ✔ They're prepared in anticipation of litigation or for trial.

- ✔ They're created by or for a party or its representative.

Even work product protection is limited. Work product may still be subject to e-discovery if two conditions are met:

- ✔ The material is otherwise discoverable under the FRCP or FRE.

- ✔ Your opponent shows a substantial need for the materials to prepare his case, and you can't obtain the material by alternate means without undue hardship. This means that the information sought is essential to your opponent and crucial to the case.

Even if required by the court to disclose work product, be sure to disclose only those materials that contain facts related to the case. Courts generally don't require you to disclose the attorney thought process. This ESI generally remains protected. ESI containing thought process, legal theories, or opinions of your attorney or other representative should not be disclosed unless by specific order of the court.

Similar to the work product protection is the protection afforded government agencies in the *deliberative process* (the process of forming governmental decisions and policies). Documents reflecting advisory opinions, recommendations, and deliberations in this process are protected.

Here is how you invoke the court's protection against e-discovery successfully:

1. **Verify that the ESI is a trade secret or proprietary research.**

   You do this by

   - Determining the value of the ESI both to the company and in the market (that is, internally and externally).

   - Evaluating how easy it would be for someone to duplicate your trade secret or proprietary research.

   - Estimating the amount of time and effort that you spent in development.

   - Identifying the level of disclosure within your business and the measures taken to protect the information.

2. **Assert that the ESI is a trade secret or proprietary research.**

   You do this by proving that

   - The information has separate economic value.

   - You have made an effort to maintain its secrecy.

Managing e-discovery of confidential information

While you're involved in litigation, you may get a hold of some nonprivileged ESI that's relevant to the other party's claim or defense. The court can order you — or even a third party — to disclose relevant evidence. In the words of Anna (to the King) in *The King and I:* Getting to know you, getting to know all about you.

When you're managing the disclosure (or not) of information through e-discovery, you can do the following:

- ✔ **Request ESI for information from the other party (under FRCP 26), or from third parties through a subpoena (under FRCP 45).** For example, if a third-party vendor (such as Yahoo! or AOL) maintains e-mails or other records on its server, you can subpoena those e-mails or other ESI for use in the litigation.

  Third parties can't object to discovery of ESI based on confidentiality, privilege, or work product protection of another party, but could object on their own behalf. The party whose protection or privilege may be violated must make the claim of privilege to the court. Although the third party could seek to avoid disclosure on other grounds, such as not reasonably accessible or undue cost or burden.

- ✔ **Don't disclose ESI that's protected under federal rules (which means it isn't subject to e-discovery).** Parties in a lawsuit can ask for any information, but it doesn't mean they'll get it!

You can protect confidential information through an order of protection, issued by the court under FRCP 26, which relieves you of the duty to disclose. (We discuss this further in the section, "Getting or Avoiding a Waiver," later in this chapter.) Commonly protected types of confidential ESI include

- *Trade secrets,* for example, the secret formula for Coca-Cola.

- *Proprietary research,* which includes research on a new product or improvement.

- *Other valuable proprietary information* that is meant to remain private, such as corporate strategic plans for an expansion. It might also include ESI such as personally identifiable information (PII) that not only identifies a person but can be used to trace a person, such as name. address, birth date, and Social Security Number.

Privilege, protection, and e-discovery complications

A plaintiff brings an action for divorce alleging infidelity on behalf of the defendant spouse. Further, the plaintiff seeks custody of the two children born of the marriage alleging the defendant is an unfit parent. To attempt to prove infidelity, the plaintiff's attorney makes a demand for all e-mails, cellphone and texting records, and a mirror of the hard drive on both the company computer and laptop of the defendant. This action is in state court.

In addition to the divorce, the defendant's company (owned by the defendant) is involved in a patent infringement suit. This matter is in federal court.

E-mails and text messages involve communications between the defendant and the defendant's attorney in both matters. They discuss strategies in the divorce and potential settlement offers in the patent infringement case. Privileged communications.

The hard drives contain copies of correspondence with the attorney as well as spreadsheets prepared for the attorney in the patent infringement suit. In addition, the hard drive at the office contains information on pending merger negotiations with another company.

There is also confidential research data on new product development unrelated to the patent case. Both confidential and work product ESI. Probably not relevant to the divorce.

Further, there is correspondence between the defendant and the defendant's psychiatrist concerning emotional problems the defendant has been experiencing. It includes a diary that the defendant writes in each day and then takes to the psychiatrist as part of this therapy. Most of the entries relate to his relationship with the plaintiff spouse and the children. Physician-patient privilege.

A first pass review indicates at least 20,000 e-mails and 140,000 other documents that may show initial relevance. A review of the facts indicates that there is probably privileged, work product, and confidential ESI in the e-discovery request. The complexity of issues and two separate trials — one in state court and one in federal court — multiplies the difficulty and expense of e-discovery. See Chapter 9 for a look at the role of the IT professional in helping to determine the protocol to use to filter for privileged communications, confidential material, and work product.

Listening to the Masters

Judges can use Special Masters under FRCP 53 to handle ESI-related disputes, and you can request that the court appoint one. A Special Master can help cut costs by:

- ✔ **Facilitating the e-discovery process:** Special Masters work with both you and your opponent to resolve such issues as relevance and privilege protection.

- ✔ **Monitoring compliance:** The Special Master can watch over the process to assure everyone complies with discover and maintain appropriate timetables.

- ✔ **Assisting in technical disputes:** For example, a technical dispute might involve the form in which the ESI is to be produced. A Special Master would work with you to determine the most cost-effective form of production.

- ✔ **Adjudicating legal disputes related to ESI:** In the case of a legal dispute regarding work product protection, the Special Master can determine the scope of the information to be protected.

- ✔ **Assist in developing preservation protocols:** Special Masters work with you to develop appropriate protocols as discussed in Chapter 9.

- ✔ **Work with the parties to establish e-discovery agreements:** Special Masters can assist you in developing the terms of an agreement to protect from privilege waivers. See the upcoming section, "Leveling the Playing Field through Agreement."

Getting or Avoiding a Waiver

An intentional disclosure of ESI serves as a waiver of any confidentiality, privilege, or work product protection. And if the privilege or protection is waived, the waiver generally applies to all other ESI concerning the same subject matter. So, it's (logically) a *subject matter waiver*.

You do have some say on a subject matter waiver. If the sheer volume of ESI involved under a subject matter waiver would impose costs for review and filtering that are disproportionate to what is at stake in the litigation, the courts could limit the scope of the waiver. Rule 502(a) of the FRE limits a waiver to the communication or materials disclosed and not to the entire subject matter of the communication. The court may expand the waiver beyond Rule 502 if it deems the expansion appropriate.

But with the expediential growth of e-discovery and technology, filtering all the ESI before making the appropriate protection claims becomes increasingly more difficult. Not only are the costs and delays apparent, but the possibility of inadvertent disclosure can seem virtually inevitable — like death and taxes.

Asserting a claim

You have various options related to avoiding or limiting a waiver. You can

✔ **Assert confidentiality:** Your attorney may claim that certain ESI is not relevant or may request (with a motion) a protective order under FRCP 26(c)(1). She must accompany the motion with a certification that you've conferred in good faith or made a good faith attempted to confer with the other parties to resolve an issue. (Conferring includes the meet-and-confer session that we discuss in Chapter 6.)

The court can issue the protective order for good cause to protect against annoyance, embarrassment, oppression, or undue burden or expense. Undue burden — in the case of a trade secret — could include serious injury to your business or putting your business at a competitive disadvantage.

✔ **Assert privilege or work product protection:** You don't use a protective order to assert privilege or work product (trial preparation materials) protection as a reason for withholding information. Instead, follow these steps:

1. *Expressly set forth the claim of privilege being asserted.*

   Translating from legalese, you have to tell the requesting party that you're claiming privilege.

2. *Provide information about the nature of the ESI withheld to the requesting party to enable them to analyze your assertion.*

   That means you tell the other side what it is that you're not giving them.

Preparing a privilege log

Privilege logs list the ESI that you're withholding as privileged or protected. Figure 10-1 shows one of the many privilege logs that Dow Chemical submitted to the Environmental Protection Agency (EPA). CREW (Citizens for Responsibility and Ethics in Washington) made the request for those documents under the Freedom of Information Act (FOIA).

	#	Exemption/Privileg	From	To/cc/bcc	Subject	Date	Time	Size
Dow 2-Ex	315	Ex. 5 -- Deliberative Process Privilege Ex. 7(A) -- Law Enforcement Proceedings	Milt Clark	▫ James Augustyn	Re: Fw: Reach L Tech Memo	▣ 09/28/2007	03:35 PM	3,293
Dow 2-Ex	316	Ex. 5 -- Deliberative Process Privilege Ex. 7(A) -- Law Enforcement Proceedings	Catherine Garypie	▫ Cynthia Faur;Gerald Phillips;Gregory Rudloff;James Augustyn;Jason El-Zein;Jeff Cahn;John Steketee;Leverett Nelson;Marc Greenberg;karl.richard;Wendy Carney;Mary Logan;RALPH DOLLHOPF	⬗ Final Confidentiality Agreement/Ltr	▣ 10/15/2007	10:49 AM	80,465
Dow 2-Ex	317	Ex. 5 -- Deliberative Process Privilege Ex. 5 -- Attorney Client Privilege Ex. 5 -- Attorney Work-Product Privilege Ex. 7(A) -- Law	Jeff Cahn	▫ "Wright, Peter (PC)";Catherine Garypie;Leverett Nelson;Frederick Mueller;Robert Kaplan;"Steven M. Jawetx";James Augustyn	⬗ RE: The Dow Chemical Company- Saginaw River/Wickes Park sediment cleanup AOC	▣ 11/13/2007	7:34 AM	450,048
Dow 2-Ex	318	Ex. 5 -- Deliberative Process Privilege	Gregory Rudloff	▫ Gerald Phillips;Sypniewski.Bruce;Margaret Guerriero;Hak Cho;Jose Cisneros;John Steketee;Jeff Cahn;James Augustyn	⬗ Dow Hot Issues Paper	▣ 11/14/2007	03:00 PM	44,166
Dow 2-Ex	319	Ex. 5 -- Deliberative Process Privilege Ex. 7(A) -- Law Enforcement Proceedings	Mark Durno	▫ RALPH DOLLHOPF;Jason El-Zein;Brian Schlieger;James Augustyn	⬗ Region 10 Site - 39 ppt Dioxin ARAR	▣ 11/27/2007	07:30 PM	73,731

Figure 10-1:
Privilege log submitted by Dow Chemical to the Citizens for Responsibility and Ethics in Washington.

When developing a privilege log, record the following items:

- ✔ **Document number:** Remember to number the documents sequentially.

- ✔ **Type of document or information withheld:** For example, identify the document as an e-mail, memo, and so on.

- ✔ **Names of parties:** Who's involved in the communication.

- ✔ **Date and time:** When the document was prepared.

- ✔ **Privilege or protection claimed:** Such as whether it's attorney-client privilege, or work product protection.

- ✔ **Description or summary of contents:** Allows your opponent to determine whether a privilege or protection exists.

The court could allow you to prepare the log on a category basis if the amount of material is too voluminous.

Responding to ESI disclosure

Disclosure of ESI doesn't automatically eliminate the claim of privilege or protection. Notify the recipient of the ESI about your claim. When you do, the recipient must

- **Promptly return, sequester, or destroy the ESI.** They may not disclose it until your claim is resolved.

- **Retrieve the ESI.** If the recipient disseminated the ESI to others before you notified them of your claim, they must take reasonable steps to recover the ESI.

- **Turn over ESI to the court.** The recipient may also send the ESI to the court to be held under seal until the claim is determined. While you are asserting the claim, you must keep the ESI secure until resolution of the matter, which may be many years later.

Some courts have held that if your attorney knows or has reason to know that protected or privileged ESI was inadvertently disclosed, he has a legal and ethical duty to notify the responding party and take action.

If your opponent objects to your assertion of privilege or protection, the court may review the ESI or a portion of it (called *in camera review*) to determine whether the ESI should be protected from discovery.

Applying FRE 502 to disclosure

In federal courts, inadvertent disclosure of ESI protected under the attorney-client privilege or work product protection can't be deemed a waiver. FRE 502 is one of the federal rules of evidence that the courts use to determine what evidence will be admitted into court. Rule 502 covers the attorney-client privilege and work product protection. Also, intentional disclosure in a federal case or to a federal office or agency (for example, the IRS or SEC) waives the privilege or protection only for the ESI disclosed. It is not a subject matter waiver.

If the intentional disclosure is meant to mislead or is put forth in an unfair manner, it will be considered a subject matter waiver and applies to all related ESI.

Many states use the federal rules as a guide, but they vary on the waiver rules. State rules generally conform to the approaches presented in Table 10-1.

Table 10-1	State Approaches to Waivers
Approach	*What It Means*
Lenient	An inadvertent disclosure is never considered a waiver.
Middle of the road	If you used reasonable care to identify attorney-client privileged or work product protected ESI, then an inadvertent disclosure doesn't constitute a waiver. Most states follow this rule, which is also the basis of FRE 502.
Strict	Disclosure is a waiver. No further discussion is necessary.

You must take great care not to waive other privileges or protections that you can secure by party agreements, such as quick-peek, attorney-eyes-only, or clawback agreements. (See the section "Leveling the Playing Field through Agreement," later in this chapter.) After the ESI is out there — whether disclosure is inadvertent or intentional — it is already disclosed. Suppose that the ESI is a memo from in-house counsel to outside (or out-house?) counsel discussing a possible settlement figure. Clawback, quick-peek, attorney-eyes-only, waiver, no waiver — the form of protection doesn't matter. You really can't take back what the other side has learned about your case.

Check out Table 10-2 for a rundown of disclosures and related waivers under various circumstances.

Table 10-2	Waivers (or Not) in State and Federal Scenarios	
Type of Disclosure	*Incurs*	*With These Specifics or Results*
Inadvertent in federal court action	No waiver	If you took reasonable steps to prevent disclosure and prompt action to rectify the disclosure.
Inadvertent to federal agency	No waiver	If you took reasonable steps to prevent disclosure and prompt action to rectify the disclosure.
Under agreement	No waiver for only the parties involved in the agreement.	The agreement must be incorporated into a court order to apply to other parties.
In state court	Waiver or no waiver according to the rule that most protects the disclosed ESI (in federal court)	A waiver under a strict test in a state court is subject to FRE 502 in federal court.
In federal court	No waiver under FRE 502	No waiver in any subsequent state court action.

Type of Disclosure	Incurs	With These Specifics or Results
Metadata	Possible waiver	In some states, an attorney who allows disclosure of metadata containing information for which a privilege or protection is claimed has probably committed malpractice.

FRE 502 treats an inadvertent disclosure as a clawback agreement (see the next section).

Establishing and implementing a protocol to identify and filter privileged, confidential, and protected work product before the litigation is the best defense. See Chapter 9 for how-to information.

Leveling the Playing Field through Agreement

You can take additional steps to protect against unintentional disclosure. FRE 502 provides relief for inadvertent disclosure of items privileged under the attorney-client privilege or protected as work product. But you must manage other claimed privilege or waiver by party agreements.

All parties involved in litigation benefit from reduced costs and timely e-discovery. Therefore, facilitating the e-discovery process with agreements can help promote savings of both time and money. In the meet-and-confer session, you should try to determine the extent of e-discovery, any privileges or other protection that the other party claims, and methods of reducing the possible extraordinary costs that come from producing and protecting ESI.

Checking out the types of agreements

You can produce agreements on a number of common e-discovery solutions that help protect against waiver.

Here are some common types:

 ✓ **Quick-peek** agreements allow you to take a quick peek at your opponent's ESI based on an agreed filtering protocol. A quick peek is not a waiver of privileged or protection.

After this quick initial review, you specify the ESI you want. Filtering only the specified documents for privilege, confidentiality, or protected work product saves your opponent time and effort.

✔ **Attorney-eyes-only** agreements save time and expense by stating that the material requested is reviewed by your attorney only. Any review of confidential, privileged, or protected information is not deemed a waiver, and your opponent can still assert privilege or protection later.

✔ **Clawback agreements** provide that you may take back any ESI that you've disclosed and later believe is protected or privileged. The clawback allows for more liberal and timely e-discovery while still protecting the ability to claim privilege, confidentially, or work product protection. Clawback agreements should contain express language on the following:

- Inadvertent disclosure or production of ESI that is protected by privileged or work product protection (could also be expanded to include confidential information) doesn't constitute a waiver and can't be admitted into evidence in court.

- Upon request, you return the privileged or protected ESI and any copies expeditiously.

- If you receive privileged or protected ESI, you must notify your opponent and return it in a timely manner.

- You must provide the names of all persons who have had access to the privileged or protected ESI and take reasonable steps to secure the return of any privileged or protected ESI it may have disseminated to third parties.

- If this agreement becomes a subject of litigation, the successful party will be entitled to costs and attorney fees incurred to enforce it.

When you assert the claim, your opponent should return the ESI. If your opponent challenges the assertion, she may sequester or deposit the ESI with the court until a resolution of the dispute.

Shoring up your agreements by court order

You should try to incorporate every agreement into a court order. An agreement alone may not extend the waiver protection to other actions or subsequent litigation, especially for state court litigation. Generally, any ESI disclosed by court order is not deemed a waiver in other matters because the disclosure isn't voluntary.

Agreements may also be incorporated into various court orders, including:

- ✔ **Scheduling orders under FRCP 16,** in which, after receiving a report from your meet-and-confer session or consultation with the attorneys, the court enters an order managing the time frames of the case, discovery, and an agreement relating to asserting privilege or protection.

- ✔ **Protective orders under FRCP 26(c),** where the court may protect you from annoyance, embarrassment, oppression, or undue burden by forbidding or limiting discovery.

- ✔ **Discovery management orders under FRCP 26(b)(2),** in this case, the court may alter the extent of discovery.

If the agreement is made part of a discovery management order under FRCP 26(b)(2), you can later assert that the disclosure was not voluntary and was pursuant to an order of the court. To make this assertion avoids the future privilege or protection arguments. If you don't incorporate your agreements in a court order, they're merely contractual in nature.

Chapter 11

Producing and Releasing Responsive ESI

. . . .

In This Chapter

▶ Dealing from the top of the data deck

▶ Redacting information properly

▶ Deciding how to handle metadata

▶ Keeping the links of the custody chain tight

. . . .

*E*lectronic discovery may seem like it's just about producing documents to the other side. But its purpose is to allow your lawyer to obtain the factual information that he needs to prepare a case for trial, or maybe even negotiate a settlement.

In this chapter, you find out about the final e-discovery stage to achieve a production or release that's relatively smooth and efficient. Disputes will arise if agreements aren't met or if the other party believes your production is insufficient — especially if you don't produce metadata or privilege logs that identify ESI that you excluded because it was privileged. We also tell you about the final work to be done, such as redacting work-product information, and work to be produced, including the chain of custody.

The actual production is done by one of three parties: a third-party litigation services provider, outside counsel's litigation support department, or your in-house litigation support team. But this chapter is useful to you because you need to hand over all the ESI in the manner your lawyer needs it.

Producing Data Sets

The production stage, or disclosure, begins with ESI that you've preserved and processed and that has survived numerous filters and the scrutiny of privilege review. Files that include content that must be produced, as well as privileged or confidential content, need to be redacted to remove the privileged information, as you can read about in the section "Redacting prior to disclosure," later in this chapter.

All ESI that's non-relevant or protected by a rule or court order is filtered out, leaving the responsive ESI data sets that will be produced or released to the requesting party. You see the steady reduction in volume in Figure 11-1 from unwashed to refined and responsive ESI. Figure 11-1 also shows that production that's improperly done forces you to cycle back to prior stages for do-overs.

After you produce ESI, the dispute doesn't end. Judges' rulings on post-production motions might also change what you have to produce or the format in which you produce the files. You see a lot of activity during this stage involving technical, legal, or judicial issues.

Do-overs increase costs and anger judges. Follow the e-discovery plan to the letter, and you minimize having to do work over.

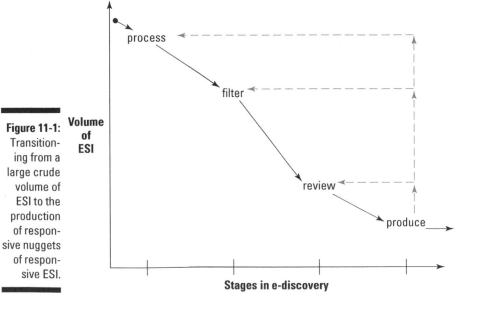

Figure 11-1: Transitioning from a large crude volume of ESI to the production of responsive nuggets of responsive ESI.

Botched redaction compromises security

The United States military composed a 42-page PDF file to publish its report about the 2005 death of Nicola Capilari, an Italian agent, and the wounding of Italian journalist Guiliana Sgrena. Because the U.S. report included sensitive military information that could be used by an enemy, it was heavily redacted before it was released. Unfortunately, those performing the redaction didn't understand the properties of Adobe Acrobat. They used the black highlighter tool, which on paper would have left a black mark. However, in Adobe Acrobat, black highlights can be removed or changed to a pale color, which would reveal the contents underneath. The report's redacted classified information was revealed. This error could have been avoided if commercially available software, such as Redax, had been used to redact text from documents created by Adobe Acrobat.

Packing bytes

In the pre-digital age, production consisted of packing paper documents into boxes and delivering them to the requesting party. With e-discovery, you have two basic methods of production:

- ✔ **Deliver:** You deliver the ESI on physical magnetic media, such as CDs, DVDs, or portable hard drives. Like with paper, the ESI is packaged and sent to the requesting party.

- ✔ **Release:** You make the ESI available to the responding party. ESI may be *hosted* (stored) on a *litigation services platform* (a server). Authorized users can access the server via a secure Internet connection or a *virtual private network* (VPN, which is an encrypted tunnel for accessing a server via the Internet). You give log-in permissions to requesting parties to access your data.

Several of the steps you use to secure and provide access to ESI if you use the release method are:

- • *Implement strict information security protocols.* You may expect that your litigation service provider or host has multiple layers of security, but verify that to be sure. Find out if they've had any incidents, infections, or intrusions. Companies that have been victimized by security breaches aren't eager to report them. Consider the nightmare of having your ESI infected by malware, spyware, or a hacker. Malicious malware can destroy or corrupt files. Even if a virus or hacker doesn't compromise the integrity of the ESI, verifying and proving it would be time-consuming and carry a big price tag.

- *Share secure access. costs for hosting the ESI between you and your opponent.* You each have secure and separate log-in access to the data sets being produced, and the receiving parties can review and designate the documents they want and the format in which they will receive the documents.

  The military's model of *trust, but verify* is a good one for you to adopt.

- *Track access and activity in an access log that doesn't get overwritten.* All networks have logging capabilities that log access and activity at the level of detail that you set. The logs are like network metadata that you may need if access or release is challenged. For example, if your opponent claims that you failed to release content that you'd released and that someone on their team had accessed, you can prove your opponent's claims are false. If for some reason, access was denied, you'll know where the problem is.

- *Track the production history for each file to ensure defensibility.* As data sets are released, production is logged. You have deadlines and schedules to meet. These logs are your verification if timing for the release is disputed.

Whether physical delivery or digital release, production timing is done in one of two ways.

- ✔ **All at once:** You pack and produce in one swoop. For cases that involve a small volume of ESI, this method makes sense. There may be other reasons related to case strategy to hold off production until the drop-dead deadline.

- ✔ **Rolling production:** You produce batches of ESI according to set schedules. Or if documents are processed in small chunks, these documents can be made available as they're ready. Rolling production can occur over a short time or over a year or more.

Staging production

Rolling productions are done on an agreed-to or negotiated schedule. Consider a rolling production when your team has a lot of information that they have to review and produce within a short time frame.

Some other considerations to think about with a rolling production are

- ✔ **Use a pilot method to test and debug.** A rolling production allows the receiver to receive a sample of the production and test it. A pilot test, like marketers use to test a new product, gives the opportunity to identify problems early in the production so they can be fixed so that deadlines are met.

✔ **Prioritize the release of your ESI.** Not all ESI is of equal value. E-mail messages or Excel spreadsheets with financials might be higher priority (value) than the minutes of meetings. Requests for critical custodians' data or those whose depositions are scheduled can be processed and released first rather than last. Prioritize the order in which ESI will be processed and produced on a rolling basis.

With rolling production, you must come up with a process to manage the review of documents and ensure that everything is rolled out as scheduled. With rolling production or production involving many final reviewers, you want processes in place for final reviews to ensure the following:

✔ **Non-repetitive review:** It's possible that reviewers will accidentally review the same documents multiple times. Repetitive review can cause delays or inconsistent coding, which opens an entirely new can of worms. At this stage, the focus is usually meeting schedules or deadlines, whatever the cost.

✔ **Complete review:** If you aren't sure about what's already been reviewed, you also can't be sure about what hasn't been reviewed. Make sure you don't miss documents.

✔ **Non-duplicate review:** The first deduping filtering may not have detected duplicates, for example, leaving duplicate e-mails from multiple custodians. Now is the time to remove the duplicates.

If a custodian's e-mail box and messages must stay intact for an investigation, don't attempt to do anything to it. For example, do not dedupe the mailbox because that would violate the order to keep it intact.

Regardless of the method you use, when production is complete, you certify your production as complete. In a letter sent by counsel to the opponent, you certify that you have produced all information within your possession, custody, or control related to the claims and defenses in the litigation.

Being alert to native production motions

Situations may arise in which the opposing counsel, after receiving your production, determines that the ESI is not searchable, or reasonably searchable. For example, a complaint might be that the spreadsheets produced in image format don't provide the information (for example, formulas, metadata, or macros) needed to analyze the documents fully. The opposition could make a motion to the court that you must produce the spreadsheets in native format. You return to the review stage, or more specifically, you roll back to the files before processing occurred. (Refer to Figure 11-1.) Then you can proceed to review and produce the spreadsheets in native format.

Make sure your lawyer specifies what production file formats and priorities are needed at the meet-and-confer session so you don't waste your time and effort producing evidence that the other party may challenge. If your lawyer doesn't tell you what she and the opposing party agreed to, ask her.

If there's no agreement and no court order specifying the forms of production, you can produce the information in the manner you ordinarily maintain it or in a reasonably usable form.

Producing reasonably accessible metadata that enables the receiving party to access, search, and display the information is mandatory unless your lawyer negotiated some sort of *Get Out of Jail Free* card with the opposing counsel or the court. However, don't agree to something that you think or hope you'll never have to keep.

While agreements between litigants cannot violate the rules, case law, or court orders, it's possible to wipe out protections they provide you at your own hand. GeoStar learned this lesson in the *In re: Classicstar Mare Lease Litigation* (2009).

Defendant GeoStar took the position that GeoStar's original production had met and satisfied the legal requirements. (In fact, it did.) GeoStar had produced its financial documents in PDF and Excel format and also converted its documents to TIFF documents with DII load files so that the documents could be loaded into the parties' Summation or Concordance databases, two widely used litigation platforms. Concordance and Summation are proprietary legal software that allow a firm's staff to organize case files in an electronic format. It's not uncommon for firms to request either of these formats so that they can automatically load them into the database.

Although the plaintiffs did not initially specify the form of production, one sought an additional production of the documents in their native format. The plaintiff didn't contest that the documents already had been produced in reasonably usable forms, but claimed that review of the documents in their native formats would save hundreds of hours in search time. GeoStar argued that it had the option to produce documents in their native format or in an alternative format that was "reasonably usable" and that did not "significantly degrade" the searchability function of the documents. They cited a decision in *United States v. O'Keefe* (2008) which held that

> ". . . production of the electronically stored information in PDF or TIFF format would suffice, unless defendants can show that those formats are not 'reasonably usable' and that the native format, with the accompanying metadata, meet the criteria of 'reasonably usable' whereas the PDF or TIFF formats do not."

The exchange that took place between counsel for the West Hills plaintiffs and counsel for GeoStar Corporation reads as follows.

"This letter responds to your prior letter and emails regarding documents produced by GeoStar Corporation. You asked that we produce the financial and accounting records in their native format. I do not know, however, whether you have the software to be used in connection with that information. GeoStar runs two software packages for its financial records: (1) Creative Solutions; and (2) Oil & Gas Information Systems. It is my understanding that the latter program may cost in excess of $15,000. Although we could provide you with the data housed in these programs, it would be useless without the software in which to import that data. We will provide you with the financial records in a format that will allow you to upload them into your Summation or Concordance database, and we can provide you with the data in its native format if you choose to buy the software."

GeoStar has a bulletproof defense until that final part of the last sentence. The court caught that last sentence, where counsel for defendant unwisely stated in a letter to plaintiff's counsel that the documents would be provided also in native format if plaintiff chose to buy the $15,000 software needed to make native format documents useful. In hindsight, this attempt at humor or sarcasm or spirit of cooperation was a mistake. To the court, even if the initial production in non-native format met Rule 34 requirements, defendant (under no pressure to do so) had agreed to the additional native format production. The court compelled the production in native format, but found it "only fair to shift the reasonable cost of copying and delivering" the native format production to plaintiff because defendant already had produced the documents and plaintiff had not specified a native format production.

Redacting prior to disclosure

One of the last tasks to perform or verify before you disclose ESI is *redaction* — taking out anything the opposing party doesn't deserve to get. Redaction sounds simple enough, but it's tough to specify with electronic content. A file may contain privileged information, as well as relevant, nonprivileged, and discoverable details. You're obliged to produce the latter while protecting the privilege.

Electronic redaction is different from standard redaction — the latter requires the use of a marker or redaction tape and a lot of hoping for the best. Electronic redaction involves completely removing content from an electronic document and making it irretrievable and unavailable for viewing, printing, searching, or copying.

If you redact info without using the proper software, you run the risk of not doing the job properly and giving confidential information to the other side. Always use a proper redaction software to redact your privileged information.

Redacting information the wrong way

You want privileged or private content to *not be there.* Notice the wording. Redacting should not be thought of as a cover up. Adobe Acrobat's PDF files and Microsoft Word's documents are notoriously vulnerable to botched redaction. Actually, it's the naïve individuals at the helm who are responsible for such mistakes because they do not know what they're doing.

In *Schaefer v. GE* (May 2008), legal counsel for the plaintiff improperly redacted documents by simply placing black bars over the text set for deletion. Although a court order mandated that the revealed information be sealed, the flawed documents were e-filed and available for download. When GE realized that people who read the material covered by the black lines could copy and paste the content into Microsoft Word, GE's attorneys filed an unsuccessful motion to dismiss. Plaintiff's counsel was able to withdraw the documents at issue and re-file properly redacted copies. While the error won't materially affect the outcome of the case, the negative press may undermine the company's potential and existing client confidence.

Facebook's confidential settlement of a lawsuit brought by ConnectU, a social site, was revealed when the Associated Press (AP) reported that redacted portions of a PDF transcript of a court hearing with details of the settlement could be easily revealed. Redaction was done by whiting out portions of the PDF. Specifically, white rectangles were placed over the white text in order to cover it and make it undiscoverable. When techno-literates copied the content of the PDF and pasted it into another document, they removed the whited-out overlays, making all contents fully readable. Figure 11-2 shows a document with some portions whited out.

Figure 11-2:
Whiting out text of a document is just that, white out, and not a redaction.

> With this Proclamation, The Sedona Conference® launches a national drive to promote
> to facilitate cooperative, collaborative, transparent discovery. This Proclamation challenges the bar to achieve these goals and refocus litigation toward the substantive resolution of legal disputes.

Another botched redaction was done to a Word document by selecting the text and highlighting it in black, as shown in Figure 11-3. Then the file was sent via e-mail. The receiver selected the same text, and changed the black highlighting to yellow. Not only was the document no longer redacted, but the receiving party knew exactly what their opponent didn't want them to know.

With this Proclamation, The Sedona Conference® launches a national drive to promote ███████████████████████████████████ to facilitate cooperative, collaborative, transparent discovery. This Proclamation challenges the bar to achieve these goals and refocus litigation toward the substantive resolution of legal disputes.

The text in Figures 11-2 and 11-3 are from The Sedona Conference Cooperation Proclamation that you can download and read in not-blocked format from `www.thesedonaconference.org/dltForm?did=proclamation.pdf`.

Redacting the right way

Redaction software rather than do-it-yourself highlighting is your safest approach. A number of redaction software products are available that ensure that you don't make common redaction mistakes. If you have large amounts of redaction, you can automate the process using intelligent redactionware. Automatic software searches for text strings, just as the search feature in a word-processing program does. Another option is intelligent software that works on the principle of matching patterns, such as finding all credit card or Social Security numbers. Redax is an example of software to redact text from documents created by Adobe Acrobat. To prevent redacted text hidden in a PDF from becoming discoverable, you can use Adobe Acrobat software's encryption feature to make it impossible for documents to be altered by unauthorized persons, while still enabling anyone to view them.

Most redaction software offers the ability to add a reason for redactions or comments, such as *Private* or *Highly Privileged*. Sometimes the reason is actually printed on top of the redaction entity. This level of documentation can provide a good defense if results are challenged.

Documents have a history

An example of botched document editing involved SCO Group. On March 3, 2004, SCO filed a breach of contract lawsuit in Michigan state court against DaimlerChrysler for violating the terms of its Unix software agreement with SCO. The complaint's electronic version contained its modification (change) history revealing the history of SCO's litigation plans. When the change history was examined, it revealed that up to February 18, 2004, SCO was planning to sue Bank of America in federal rather than state court, for copyright infringement rather than breach of contract!

The National Security Agency (NSA) published a document on proper redaction technique in December 2005. You can download the PDF from the agency's Web site at www.fas.org/sgp/othergov/dod/nsa-red. Redactionware allows you to process any document type and gives you a range of powerful tools to specify what information needs to be redacted. Once the redactions are confirmed, the information selected for redaction is completely and permanently removed from the document. The software produces a clean document that can't be reverse engineered back to its original content.

No-risk redaction of any kind does not exist. Human oversight is still needed for several reasons, including the following:

- **Automated redaction cannot identify and, therefore, cannot block a search term contained in a scanned image.** Text in an embedded image is not searchable.

- **Embedded tables or graphs, or handwriting on scanned documents should be manually redacted.** Software is not robust enough to trust it to detect and redact this information with reasonable reliability.

- **Legal teams may use optical character recognition (OCR).** Redaction tools are only as good as the OCR results. For instance, if the OCR software incorrectly identified "there" as "where," the redaction search won't find it unless the software has the capability of fuzzy search.

It is the responsibility of your legal counsel to properly redact all documents prior to production. Improper redaction creates the risk of inadvertent disclosure that might not be protected for using faulty redaction methods.

Over-redacting carries its own problems. If your results appear to be overly redacted or are, in fact, redacted more than needed and the other side challenges your claims of privilege, a court may second-guess you for the entire case, putting it at risk.

A lawyer who has produced insufficiently redacted information can be in violation of various ethical rules and subject to malpractice.

Providing Detailed Documentation

Documentation can be your get-out-of-sanction card when you're ordered to prove you did or didn't do something. ESI needs documentation, too. Every piece of media should be tracked as it moves through the stages of e-discovery by each person or company handling it. Here's what to do:

- Document the history of document productions, as you read in the section, "Packing bytes" in this chapter.

- Track every piece of media as it moves through e-discovery processes by each person, firm, or enterprise handling it.

If you redact without cause, you may be forced to reproduce

Magnatrax Litigation Trust, Plaintiff, v. Onex Corporation (2009) is a fraud case arising out of the 2003 bankruptcy of Magnatrax. The final deadline for fact discovery in this matter was February 29, 2008. But the parties continued to file motions to compel and request protective order into the third quarter of 2008. The prolonged discovery process spawned four discovery hearings. The process ranged from contentious to abusive. The court expressed its displeasure with the parties' behavior several times.

The plaintiff insisted that the defendants' redactions were evidence of an intent to hide evidence. In contrast, the defendants contended that all their redactions were consistent with the court's December 2007 and March 2008 orders. The plaintiff referenced one document, in redacted and unredacted form, to its motion for sanctions.

But the defendants provided the court with a credible excuse for the improper redaction of

this document. Without more, the court could not find that the defendants' redactions were evidence of a willful intent to hide information from plaintiff. The court was able to tell from the state of the record, however, that the defendants had unnecessarily prolonged the time and expense necessary to complete document production in this matter.

The parties had a confidentiality agreement in place from which the defendants could have sought additional protection from the court. They didn't. Instead, according to the court, the defendants improperly relied on the court's December and March orders. The court's March order merely sanctioned the redactions the defendants had put before it; it did not give them leave to redact other documents. The court found that the defendants had absolutely no cause to unilaterally redact thousands of documents only to be forced to reproduce them later.

The EDRM (Electronic Discovery Reference Model, www.edrm.net) recommends including the following information in a production history log:

✔ Date sent

✔ Sent to whom, with full contact information

✔ Means by which it was sent, with the shipper's tracking info

✔ Description of media sent, including a copy of the label

✔ Identification of the components being produced, including

- images

- searchable text

- native files

- load files (can be loaded into a review database)

- • extracted metadata or extracted fields (for example, an e-mail's author, recipients, date sent, subject, and so on) with a load file to define document breaks and relationships between e-mails and attachments
- ✔ Document IDs of production
- ✔ Location of the copy of media sent
- ✔ Document request to which the production is responsive
- ✔ Comments

The load file facilitates uploading the production into a litigation support database application. It links the native (original file, such as an Excel file), near-native (for example, a comma-delimited Excel file), and near-paper files (for example, an image or TIF of the Excel file) to the Document ID. Various load file formats depend on the software application. Some of the common load files include `.dii` (Summation), `.lfp` (IPRO), and `.opt` (Concordance/Opticon).

You can capture the production history log in fields in a database such as Access or an Excel spreadsheet. Often, the paralegal maintains and updates the production history log.

Figure 11-4 shows a production log.

Figure 11-4:
A production log.

Document	Date Produced	Manner of Production	Form Produced	Person Producing Document	Hash Value	System ID#

Showing an Unbroken Chain of Custody

The production history log also is an important link in the chain of custody. At the production stage, it's equally important to maintain that chain as during collection and other prior processes. *Chain of custody* is the process by which handlers of the ESI, computer forensics specialists, or other investigators preserve the ESI. The chain of custody is necessary documentation. It documents that the e-evidence was handled and preserved properly and was never at risk of being compromised. The documentation may need to include

- ✔ Where the ESI was stored
- ✔ Who had access to the ESI
- ✔ What was done to the ESI

You must carefully document each step so that if the case reaches court, lawyers can show that no one altered the ESI as the investigation progressed. Without a documented chain of custody, proving that ESI has not been altered after the fact is impossible. Computer forensics toolkits perform the necessary recordkeeping and documentation of proper handling.

A chain of custody doesn't only apply to the ESI at the file or document level. A chain can also be applied to or at different levels, including the following:

✔ The hardware, such as laptops, PDAs, cellphones, and any other digital device

✔ An entire data set

✔ Files

With respect to the preservation and collection of ESI, you should document all actions done to hardware as part of an electronic chain of custody. Chain of custody logs track how ESI is gathered, analyzed, and preserved for production. This means documenting which files were opened, every search and action performed, and the time and date of every step. These logs typically include a description of the forensic acquisition methodology used, minimize susceptibility to attack, and enhance credibility before a judge, particularly against an allegation of tampering.

Just as hardware or storage media containing ESI must be treated as evidence, the same rule applies to each individual file. *File-level chain of custody* is a technical process to determine or validate what had happened to a file prior to being admitted in a case. Chapter 13 discusses the computer forensics techniques used to perform this level of authentication, to ensure that each piece of evidence was handled properly, or to determine that it wasn't.

Keeping Metadata Intact

The form or forms of production would have been agreed to at the meet-and-confer session. The four forms of production are

✔ **Native:** Files are produced in their original (native) format with metadata intact. Examples are load files, extracted metadata, searchable text, and eXtensible markup language (XML). The EDRM developed a standard XML load file. Many e-discovery software and service providers are XML-compliant because of that format's benefits. Here are the big benefits of XML:

- Reduces the costs of moving data from one program to the another, as well as one company to another.

- Minimizes errors.

- Crashes (cuts) cycle times for production and delivery of ESI.

- Minimizes e-discovery disputes because of it is a very adaptable load file format.

✔ **Near-native:** As the term implies, this format is very similar to producing the file in its original format. Near-native files are extracted or converted from their original form into another searchable format.

✔ **Near-paper:** These are files that are converted to a non-searchable image file. They're called image files because they're basically pictures of the text or data.

✔ **Paper or hard copy:** The files are printed and produced on paper. Obviously, they're also non-searchable and most likely will get you into trouble with your opponent and the court. You need to produce in a format that is potentially easily reviewable by your opponent.

Some litigants want to produce only in native form because of the cost involved in converting the native files to images for an image production. Others prefer not to produce in native format unless specifically requested to do so to keep the opposing party from having the metadata. If you must produce metadata — and you can safely expect that you'll need to — there are two forms of production:

✔ Native file, which inherently has its metadata intact

✔ Image format with extracted data, including metadata and the full text of the file

When you use one these two forms of production, ESI has its own built-in evidence that, when handled properly, demonstrates, among other things, no one has changed the ESI since it was preserved.

The decision to request and produce extracted data and metadata will be influenced by the manner in which the documents were collected, processed, and reviewed. If the data wasn't preserved properly, the ESI that's produced may reflect the dates it was collected or reviewed as the creation or modification dates, which will be misleading. For example, when you download a file, the creation date and time is that of your download and not the original. These errors may raise questions about the collection, processing, and review processes. Get in front of this train by being aware of and upfront about the inconsistent date issues.

To be as safe as possible, you'll want to provide these basic extracted data or metadata fields as recommended by the EDRM.

✔ **Documents:**

- Creation date

- Date last modified

- Author
- Title
- History of changes

✔ **E-mail:**

- Author
- Recipients, including those who were cc:ed (copied) and bcc:ed (blind copied)
- Date and time sent
- Date and time received
- Subject
- Attachment relationship to original e-mail (and metadata fields listed for e-documents)
- Forwarded e-mails, attachment documents, and files

Court grants plaintiff's motion to compel re-production

White v. Graceland College Center for Professional Development & Lifelong Learning, Inc., (2009) was a wrongful termination case. The plaintiff filed a motion to compel a re-production because of insufficient production. While reviewing e-mails and attachments produced by the defendant, the plaintiff noticed discrepancies in the dates. *Sent dates* of the e-mails differed from the *created dates* of their attachments. The plaintiff contended that those dates were relevant to the issue of when the decision to terminate her employment was made.

The defendant claimed that the decision to terminate the plaintiff was made on July 2, 2004, but an attachment to a relevant e-mail showed a created date of June 9, 2004. In order to determine the actual dates, the plaintiff's computer forensics expert needed to review e-mail from both the sender's Sent items and the recipient's inbox. And he needed access to the computer that created the e-mails and their attachments.

In response, the defendants explained that the discrepancies were "due to the documents being templates," which were modified as needed. The defendants claimed that not all of the e-mails sought for re-production were available from the sources specified. Specifically, defendants indicated that e-mails of the Vice President of Human Resources were not available prior to 2005, and that e-mails previously produced were the only versions available and could not be located for re-production in the locations specified by the plaintiff.

Lacking any explanation from defendants regarding why the e-mails were unavailable, the court granted the plaintiff's request and ordered the defendants to re-produce, in their native format, the e-mails and attachments from both the e-mails' recipients and senders. If defendants were unable to do so, they were ordered to provide an explanation for why they could not.

No mistake left unmade

In *Drew Heriot & Drew Pictures Pty LTD v. Byrne*, (2008), a copyright-infringement case, the parties sought to settle the issue of copyright ownership over a made-for-television movie called *The Secret.*

The defendants made a motion concerning documents that the plaintiffs had produced in response to the defendants' request. On July 25, 2008, the defendants served the plaintiffs with their *First Request for Production of Documents*, which included a request for "... [a]ll documents relating to United States visa applications filed by or on behalf of Heriot."

To comply with the defendants' production request, the plaintiffs hired a document vendor, which provided OCR scanning and other discovery services for the case. The subsequent process by which the plaintiffs eventually produced the documents included the following steps:

1. The vendor created a master database of the documents provided to it by the plaintiffs, which the plaintiffs could then review.

2. During April and May 2008, plaintiffs hired paralegals and other non-lawyers to conduct a preliminary review of the documents in the master database. The reviewers coded the documents using general pretrial discovery codes. One general code was immigration, which the plaintiffs used to flag e-mails and other documents that pertained to Mr. Heriot's immigration to the United States.

3. The plaintiffs searched for responsive documents in their master database.

4. Once identified, these responsive documents were coded for subsequent copying and inclusion in the production database.

Several months into the litigation, the plaintiffs' document vendor made a processing mistake that resulted in the production of privileged materials. Nearly two months later, while preparing for depositions, the plaintiffs learned of the inadvertent production. The plaintiffs claimed the materials were protected by the attorney-client privilege. The defendants argued that their privilege was waived through disclosure.

The Court reviewed the documents over which the plaintiffs asserted attorney-client privilege. After an exhaustive page-by-page review of these documents and an entry-by-entry review of the privilege log, the Court *reserved* (delayed) its ruling on whether they are protected by the attorney-client privilege.

The ruling was delayed because many of the documents contained multiple e-mails and forwarded e-mails that intermingled privileged and unprivileged documents. Some of these e-mails were entirely unprotected and in no way could be claimed as covered by the attorney-client privilege. One document, for example, contained an e-mail that stated nothing more than an individual's Christmas wishes. Forcing the Court to read individuals' good tidings may have salutary effects, but efficiency and clarity are not among them.

This pile of jumbled documents created a huge intractable problem because the Court might have had to order the defendants to redact all or part of the documents. The following quote details the judge's strong opinion, anger with the defendants, and final decision. You don't want to be on the receiving end of this type of reaction from a judge.

"Describing how Defendants should redact multiple e-mails contained in multiple unpaginated documents is not only burdensome, it is a waste of this Court's time. The party asserting privilege, not the Court, should organize the documents in a manner that enables an efficient and effective determination of privilege.

"Because Defendants failed to accomplish this task, the Court will withhold its ruling on whether the documents are protected by the attorney-client privilege until after Defendants submit an amended privilege log and a revised compilation of documents for in camera review. The revised compilation of documents should be separated chronologically on a e-mail-by-e-mail basis such that each listed 'document' contains only one e-mail-and labeled so the Court can efficiently rule on each. If a series of e-mails belong together in a 'chain,' Defendants should group and label those e-mails accordingly. Defendants should also place Bates numbers or other means of identification on each page, something they failed to do on the documents they submitted to this Court. Additionally, the amended privilege log, which is to be submitted under seal (along with the revised compilation of documents), should describe, in sufficient detail, the circumstances surrounding each e-mail and Defendants' argument as to why it should be considered privileged. Finally, the amended privilege log must 'comport[] with this district's case law.'"

The judge's decision was that privilege was not waived because the disclosure was inadvertent and the plaintiffs acted promptly after discovering the disclosure mistake. The judge, however, delayed making a decision on attorney-client privilege until the plaintiff submitted an amended privilege log and a revised compilation of the documents.

Part V
Getting Litigation Ready

The 5th Wave
By Rich Tennant

"So far he's retrieved a cobra, 2 pythons, and a bunch of skinks, but not a single email or IM we can use as evidence in a court of law."

In this part . . .

In this fifth part, we look at ESI as evidence, specifically admissible e-evidence, and forensics methods to recover and preserve it. In Chapter 12, you learn that for evidence to be admissible, the first hurdle is proving that it's relevant to a disputed issue. Although the relevance rule requires only ESI that's closely related to facts that matter in the case, just *how close* is vague. You realize that rules of evidence are subject to judgment, as are the federal rules of civil procedure. Having learned about the federal rules and the challenges to privilege, you're prepped for the judgment calls and exceptions to rules that you read of in this chapter.

Chapter 12 also covers advanced e-discovery strategies and issues, some of which are the use of experts, sanctions, depositions, and cost-shifting when you're being financially crushed by big "undue" burdens.

Authenticating evidence in civil trials is relatively new, as you learn in Chapters 12 and 13. Traditionally, authentication was primarily argued in criminal cases; that is, until case law (*Lorraine v. Markel Am. Ins. Co.*) brought it into the civil sphere. You begin to understand persuasive methods for authenticating evidence, including those that fall under the scope of computer forensics. Also, you discover how to keep the chain of custody intact because you can't untaint tainted e-evidence.

"Life is tough, but it's tougher when you're stupid."

—John Wayne, actor and American icon

Chapter 12

Dealing with Evidentiary Issues and Challenges

. . . .

In This Chapter

▶ Having your witness accepted as an expert

▶ Proving your ESI is what you say it is

▶ Looking at the hearsay rule

▶ Supplying the best evidence

. . . .

During the e-discovery process, you focus on the applicability of the Federal Rules of Civil Procedure (FRCP). But when it comes to submitting evidence for consideration by the court, you have to turn your focus to the Federal Rules of Evidence (FRE). These are the rules used by federal judges to determine what evidence will be admissible in court. Each state has its own rules of evidence, but most are close to the federal rules. Just because something is subject to discovery does not mean that it is admissible in court.

If you want to admit your evidence in court, you must lay a proper foundation for its admissibility. You must prove — *authenticate* — that the ESI is what you say it is.

In this chapter, you travel the evidentiary highway and find out what is necessary to authenticate and admit ESI into court.

To be successful, you need to consider evidentiary issues from the onset of the case. First, give some thought to the records management for purposes of getting ESI authenticated for admission to the court (see Chapter 14 where we discuss setting up a record management system). After all, you don't want to go to the expense and time collecting evidence to have it thrown out of the case at some point.

Looking at the Roles of the Judge and Jury

In legal cases, the judge determines the law and the jury determines the facts. If there is no jury, then the judge serves both roles. When there is a jury, there is a complex interplay between the judge and jury on evidentiary questions.

FRE 104 provides that the court determines the preliminary questions of admissibility including:

- ✔ The qualification of a person to be a witness
- ✔ The admissibility of evidence
- ✔ The existence of a privilege
- ✔ Whether a condition has been met if relevancy is based on a condition of fact

The court is bound to the rules of evidence except when considering privilege. For example, a judge could allow hearsay evidence (an out-of-court statement offered as proof) if a witness is not available to testify.

After the judge has admitted the evidence, the jury decides what weight to give it. Evidence is often contradictory, with both sides taking a different view of what is offered. The jury has to decide what it believes, including the credibility of the witnesses.

If the judge makes a preliminary ruling not to admit your evidence, the jury never hears or sees it. If there is not a jury trial, the judge doesn't consider the excluded evidence while ruling.

Qualifying an Expert

Experts are not just those in scientific or technical areas but also the broad category of specialized knowledge. For example, a stockbroker giving testimony of a stock market analysis. Experts might become such from experience, skill, or knowledge as well as education. A person who has years of experience in working with a certain software program may be considered an expert without any formal training.

In *Galaxy Computer Services, Inc. v. Baker,* the court allowed a person to testify as an expert who had no degree in computer science, was not an expert in computer language, was not a computer programmer, but was a member of the High Crime Investigation Association and completed three postgraduate training courses in computer forensics. The weight given to the witness's opinion is a matter for the jury.

If a witness is determined to be an expert, they may testify in the form of an opinion or otherwise. For example, the testimony could be about various theories of a particular issue, and the jury decides which theory is correct.

FRE Rule 702 covers experts. The question of whether that person is an expert is determined by the judge. Under FRE Rule 702, a witness may testify whether:

- The testimony is based upon sufficient facts or data.

- The testimony is the product of reliable principles and methods.

- The expert has applied the principles and methods reliably to the facts.

The facts and data relied on do not have to be admissible in court if they are of the type normally relied upon by experts in the field. Experts are allowed to give their opinions on facts that are determinative of the case (for example, if you had data wrongfully deleted from the computers). Under FRE Rule 705, the expert may give their opinion without first setting forth the facts or data underlying that opinion. The court may order that it be disclosed prior to giving the opinion.

In *Daubert v. Merrel Dow Pharms., Inc.,* the court set forth a non-exclusive checklist to use in assessing the reliability of expert testimony. The factors are

- Can the expert's technique or theory be objectively tested for reliability?

- Has the expert's technique or theory been the subject of peer review and publication, for example, in an academic journal?

- What are the techniques or theories known or potential error rate?

- What standards and/or controls were used in applying the technique or theory?

- Does the technique or theory have general acceptance in the appropriate scientific community?

These factors might be applied to various degrees by different courts but provide a baseline for determination. They are also instructive in non-scientific cases. Additionally, courts may apply other factors as determined by the discretion of that judge.

Getting Through the Five Hurdles of Admissibility

Judge Grimm in *Lorraine v. Markel American Ins. Co.* went into great detail on the admissibility of ESI. This case has become the principle case in this area. It has formed the basis of *The Sedona Conference Commentary on ESI Evidence & Admissibility,* which can be found at www.thesedona conference.org.

This case established the following rules when getting ESI admitted:

- ✔ Is the ESI relevant as determined by Rule 401 (does it have any tendency to make some fact that is of consequence to the litigation more or less probable that it otherwise would be)?

- ✔ If relevant under Rule 401, is it authentic as required under Rule 901(a) (can you show that the ESI is what it purports to be)?

- ✔ If the ESI is offered for its substantive truth, is it hearsay as defined by Rule 801, and if so, is it covered by an applicable exception (Rules 803, 804 and 807)?

- ✔ If the ESI is in original or duplicate form under the original writing rule, or if not, is there admissible secondary evidence to prove the content of the ESI (Rules 1001-1008)?

- ✔ Is the probative value of the ESI substantially outweighed by the danger of unfair prejudice or one of the other factors identified by Rule 403, such that it should be excluded despite its relevance?

This creates a roadmap of the steps to get ESI admitted before the court. It's your guide to making sure the jury considers the evidence you want it to. We talk about each of these hurdles in the rest of the chapter.

Admitting Relevant ESI

The first major hurdle is *relevance.* To be admissible, the ESI must be relevant. ESI relevance means that the ESI has the tendency to make the existence of a fact more probable or less probable. In other words, that something did or did not happen. The fact in question must be of consequence to the case.

Authenticating ESI

Authentication comes down to three steps:

- ✔ You prove the ESI is what you're saying it is.

- ✔ The judge makes a preliminary determination of whether the ESI has sufficient probative value for a jury to rationally believe that the ESI is what it purports to be.

- ✔ The jury decides whether the ESI is what it purports to be.

You can authenticate evidence either directly or circumstantially:

- ✔ **Direct evidence** is testimony by the person who created the evidence (for example, an e-mail).

- ✔ **Circumstantial evidence** is outside evidence such as distinctive characteristics, content, and appearance. For example, an e-mail that contains details in response to a conversation between two persons might indicate that it was authored by that person.

FRE Rule 901 on authentication provides examples of authentication. Here are some ways you can have ESI authenticated:

- ✔ **Testimony by a witness with knowledge that it is what it is claimed to be:** The author or person who created it testifies to its authenticity. A person who has general knowledge of how that evidence is routinely made can also testify.

- ✔ **Comparison with specimens that have been authenticated:** Expert witnesses can compare something to ones that have already been authenticated.

- ✔ **Distinctive characteristics:** Appearance, contents, substance, internal patterns, or other distinctive characteristics, taken in conjunction with the circumstances.

    For example, e-mail that contains unique facts that are known to the persons alleged to have sent it. Some courts have developed a reply letter doctrine for authentication. If an e-mail is clearly in reply to another, and you can establish that the person received the first e-mail and the contents refer to that first e-mail, the judge can authenticate the reply e-mail. Also, an expert could offer testimony of the technical transmission and internal identification (metadata) to authenticate it.

- ✔ **Public records, reports, or data compilation:** You only need to show that the office where the records were obtained is the legal custodian of those records.

- ✔ **Evidence produced by an accurate process or system:** This can be used for ESI that is automatically generated by computers, such as metadata.

The ultimate decision is up to the jury. The jury might hear contradictory evidence and not believe it is authentic.

Self-authenticating ESI

Judges do consider some ESI as self-authenticating. Rule 902 contains a list of items that you don't need to authenticate. They include the following:

✔ Public documents under seal.

✔ Certified copies of public records.

✔ Newspapers and periodicals.

✔ Trade inscriptions and the like. Inscriptions, signs, tags, or labels purporting to have been affixed in the course of business and indicating ownership, control, or origin. An e-mail that identifies the company and contains information showing the origin of the e-mail might be authenticated by some court using this rule.

✔ Documents that are acknowledged with a notarized seal or its equivalent.

✔ Business records if accompanied by a declaration of the custodian or other qualified person certifying that:

- It was made at or near the time of the occurrence by the person with knowledge of the matters or from information received from a person with knowledge of those matters.

- It was kept in the course of regularly conducted activity and it was the regular practice of such activity to keep such records.

If the maker does not have personal knowledge of the details of the business record, then he must have received it from someone who does have knowledge and a duty to transmit that knowledge to the person recording it (for example, minutes sent to the secretary of a corporation). Some courts have allowed the authentication as a business record even without the business duty to transmit the information if the recipient had a business duty to verify the accuracy of the information received.

If you intend to offer self-authenticated ESI, you must notify your opponent in advance so they can prepare to challenge it.

Following the chain of custody

Documenting your chain of custody of all ESI includes recording each step of the gathering, reviewing, and preserving process. The chain of custody is important if the ESI might have been altered or changed at any time from its creation to the introduction as evidence. This may be especially important if the data was analyzed in any way. For ESI, it might mean the use of forensic analysis. To maintain a proper chain of evidence, a proper document maintenance plan is vital. You need to detail the process of storage, collection, and review. You should refrain from altering the originals in any way.

Hashing is very important in establishing that the offered ESI is what it was originally. *Hashing* is a method used to provide ESI with a unique number. This allows you to later identify the ESI and determine whether it is in its original form or has been altered. This numbering identification is called its *hash value*.

To ensure reliability of the ESI, follow these steps:

1. **Establish a document maintenance and collection procedure before any litigation.**

2. **Establish a system of document identification within that maintenance and collection procedure.**

3. **Identify the ESI in a manner that will provide reliability of the data after it's produced for discovery.**

   An example might be hash values.

4. **Maintain a log of all activity relevant to the ESI including obtaining, accessing, storing, and transferring the ESI.**

   This should be coordinated with the preservation log.

5. **Regularly review to make sure there is compliance with the procedures established.**

Keep in mind these two tips while you're going through the collection process:

- ✔ Allow only trained persons access to any ESI. Access should be limited to those with a legitimate need to have access.

- ✔ Designate a person who has ultimate responsibility and control of the ESI.

Authenticating specific types of ESI

The general rules of authentication apply to all forms of ESI. It does not matter whether it is an e-mail, a word processing document, or a text message.

Table 12-1 sets forth the typical rules applied in some specialized forms of ESI.

Table 12-1	Getting Specialized ESI Authenticated					
Method of Authentication	*ESI Types*					
	E-mail	Digital photos	Web site postings	Text messages	Chat rooms	Computer stored data
Witness with personal knowledge	✓	✓	✓	✓	✓	✓
Expert testimony	✓	✓	✓			✓
Comparison with other authenti- cated examples	✓					
Distinctive characteristics	✓		✓	✓	✓	✓
Trade inscriptions	✓					
Business records	✓		✓	✓		✓
Public records			✓			
Official publications		✓	✓			✓
System capable of reliable result		✓	✓			✓

Analyzing the Hearsay Rule

When you clear the authentication hurdle, your evidence might still not be admitted if it violates the hearsay rule.

Hearsay is an out-of-court statement offered by a person to prove the truth of the matter asserted. Hearsay is not just limited to verbal utterances as you might assume; it includes documents and ESI that are offered to prove the truth of what is said in the contents. If you offer an e-mail to prove the truth of the contents, and the person who wrote it is not available, your evidence is hearsay.

Exceptions to the hearsay rule can allow the evidence to be admitted. The jury gets to decide what weight to put on your evidence.

Two applicable provisions of the FRE provide exceptions to the hearsay rule. Rule 803 has 23 exceptions to the rule, while Rule 807 provides a residual exception. The key to the exceptions is that the ESI must have some circumstantial support for the court to believe that it is trustworthy. For example, authenticated business records would have that trustworthiness.

Some of the Rule 803 exceptions most applicable to authenticated ESI are

- **Present sense impression:** Describing or explaining an event or condition made while the person making it was experiencing it or right after. An example might be an e-mail made right after an event that describes what happened.

- **Excited utterance:** Made while under the stress of excitement caused by the event. An example might be a text message or a Twitter tweet made while at the scene of an accident.

- **Existing mental, emotional, or physical condition:** Relating to the emotional state of mind, a sensation, or the declarant's physical condition. This may go to show intent, planning, and motive. For example, an e-mail where the person writing it states how angry they are with their employer and would like to take revenge for a perceived wrong.

- **Recorded recollections:** This is often used to refresh the recollection of a witness who wrote it down at one point but now has forgotten some of the details.

- **Ancient records:** Statements in documents more than 20 years old.

- **Learned treatises:** Statements published in treatises, periodicals, or the like that have been established as reliable authorities.

- **Business records:** This rule is the same as for authentication. They go hand and hand. See the previous section, "Self-authenticating ESI," for a discussion on business records authentication.

The next major exception to the hearsay rule is provided in Rule 807. Your evidence must have an equivalent that guarantees the trustworthiness applicable to other hearsay exceptions and:

- Be offered as evidence of a material fact. If the fact it is offered to prove is not material, it cannot be admitted.

- The statement offered must be more probative on the point than any other evidence that you can get through other reasonable means.

- The general purpose of the rules and the interests of justice will be best served by admitting the evidence.

If you plan to use this rule, you must let the other party know in advance so they can properly prepare any challenge they might make.

If the ESI is offered to prove the truth of what is in it, then the hearsay rules apply. You might go through discovery and authentication and still not get it admitted into court.

Providing the Best Evidence

The best evidence rule provides that to prove the contents of a writing or ESI, you must provide the original. A copy is allowed as long as there is no question of its authenticity. If you can't reasonably obtain a copy, then the rules allow testimony to determine the contents (such as testimony of a person who read the contents or by an admission against the party who offered them).

In the area of ESI data stored in a computer or similar device, such as a server, an original is any printout or other output readable by sight, shown to reflect the data accurately. If the contents are voluminous, they may be presented in the form of charts or summaries with the originals made available to the other party for copying.

Generally, the best evidence rule does not create a problem for ESI. Electronic images, such as a TIFF or a PDF, are acceptable original printouts. One issue that you might be confronted with is whether a printout is actually an original if it does not contain the metadata. Typically, metadata is not produced on paper copies of the documents, such as word processing or spreadsheet documents. It can be argued that without the metadata, a printout is not a true copy of the original; it is not an identical but a fraternal twin. You should consult with your counsel to determine whether to disclose the metadata.

Probing the Value of the ESI

Even if evidence is admissible, the court may still use its discretion not to admit it. For example, Rule 403 allows a judge to exclude relevant evidence if the judge determines that the prejudice to the other party outweighs its probative value. The judge may also exclude it if there is a determination that the evidence will cause confusion or is a waste of time or needlessly cumulative. For example, you don't need 1,000 e-mails that all say the same thing to show the one fact contained in them.

Chapter 13

Bringing In Special Forces: Computer Forensics

In This Chapter

▶ Organizing a forensic defense

▶ Taking a scientific approach

▶ Crossing computer forensics with e-discovery

▶ Fortifying with forensics

▶ Showing strength

*Y*our case may require the recovery of deleted files or e-mails, the analysis and interpretation of metadata or Internet history to reconstruct the timeline of events, or the proof of illicit or unauthorized use of the company's computer networks. If there's a possibly that the admissibility of ESI will be challenged or there's been deliberate attempts to destroy evidence (for example, an employee stealing confidential data or sending harassing e-mail), then preserving and maintaining ESI using computer forensics methods in accordance with the National Institute of Standards and Technology (NIST) ensures its admissibility in court and prevents spoliation. The courts may require a forensic exam of one or more of your company's computers if your opponent shows a good cause for one. In these scenarios, your lawyer may recommend that a computer forensics expert join your e-discovery team to make a forensically sound copy of one or more hard drives. A forensically sound copy (also called an *image*) is an accurate and complete duplicate of the source evidence on a hard drive. The computer forensic tools and methods used to create the image also include ways to verify that its contents haven't been altered.

Either by choice at the outset of e-discovery or later by court order, you may want or need to go the extra mile in effort and expense by employing a computer forensic expert to preserve, recover, restore, or search ESI. Computer forensics, like special teams in football, may not be on the field very much, but those specialists can play pivotal roles in the game. Learning from the experience of others is always less expensive than finding out for yourself.

In this chapter, you can find out more about the functions that computer forensics experts can perform in your e-discovery efforts, including preservation, indexing keywords, authentication, recovery, and maintenance of the chain of custody. You'll want to select a vendor whose commercial and proprietary tools have the ability to recover, reconstruct, and analyze data all of your types of ESI, then to catalog and export to a document management tool, such as Concordance or Summation, for review.

Powering Up Computer Forensics

Some cases may require more than the standard e-discovery procedures (which we cover in Chapters 6–8). Cases with complications may necessitate taking your e-discovery up a notch. Computer forensics tools are used by experts to recover hidden or lost ESI, reconstruct the timeline of events, interpret the meaning of the evidence, and authenticate when the ESI was created and by whom. In brief, if there's ESI that you need to find or that needs to be admitted into evidence by the court, you need computer forensics. You want to take action on this procedure as soon as possible. After you've produced the ESI and it's rejected by the court because you can't authenticate it, you find out firsthand about the support that computer forensics can bring to a disputed issue in a case.

 In a class action lawsuit in which investors claimed they'd been defrauded, state prosecutors brought suit against financial advisors. The defense received an agreement from the prosecutors that they would not dispute their e-mails. One e-mail in particular was pivotal exculpatory evidence that investors hadn't been deceived. As such, defense decided at that time that they didn't need a computer forensic expert. During testimony by the defendant, his lawyer presented one key e-mail that the prosecutor refused to accept. The judge held that, to be admissible, the e-mail had to be authenticated. Of course, it was too late for the defense because there are no do-overs with electronic evidence.

Knowing when to hire an expert

You'll want to hire a computer forensics specialist when you suspect that ESI has been accidentally, intentionally, innocently, or maliciously compromised or you're concerned that illegal activity has been covered up in one or more of the following ways:

  ✔ **Withheld:** ESI exists and is known about, but has not been produced. When the collection basket was passed around, this ESI didn't make it in.

✔ **Deleted:** ESI is no longer available or accessible through the operating system.

Delete is a misnomer because when you delete a file, its physical presence doesn't change. The file stays put until the operating system snuffs it out.

✔ **Disguised:** The file extension is deleted or changed to hide the ESI's true identity. For example, an Excel spreadsheet could be changed from .xlsx to .jpg or .wav to throw off the search for spreadsheets.

✔ **Tampered with:** Contents of the file or its metadata (identifying information) are changed to try to get rid of the original and throw off anyone who examining it. Tampering with a file is one of the most common tricks to rewrite history, so to speak. For example, performance reports, messages, or contracts can be recast in a different light by doing a little digital editing.

✔ **Planted:** ESI is made to exist. Keep in mind that there's no perfect crime when e-evidence is involved. People who plant evidence leave a trail and usually make mistakes. Lazy people who try to plant ESI create the easiest-to-detect plants because they don't invest the effort required to plant hard-to-detect e-evidence.

✔ **Password protected:** The file cannot be opened without the password. Company policy or a user's personal habits or paranoia might be to safeguard their files by sealing them with a password. If the password is written on a sticky note attached to the monitor, getting into the files is not challenging.

✔ **Encrypted:** The file can be opened, but the contents are scrambled by an encryption algorithm or key. Encrypted files are practically impossible to decrypt without knowing the key and the method of encryption. Don't bother looking for sticky notes for the key because the keys are digital.

✔ **Headerless encrypted files:** The files have been encrypted and are impossible for the operating system to detect because they have no header. Files don't get tougher to open than these.

Typically, normal e-discovery processes don't detect complicated files or conditions. You need the power of computer forensics — digital archeology — to detect or uncover these files or conditions and interpret what they indicate. Computer forensics may be the only way to recover or restore deleted content or attempts to hide and disguise files.

Knowing what to expect from an expert

Here are the functions that you'd hire an expert to perform:

- **Recover ESI proving that someone has done something or an action or event has happened.** This situation is the most straightforward. You want convincing evidence of what's been done. Examples are e-mail showing illicit activity or correspondence capturing details of the theft of intellectual property.

- **Recover ESI proving that an alleged action or event didn't happen.** Proving a negative might be tougher than the situation in the preceding bullet. What the expert can do after examining the ESI is provide plausible alternative explanations for what's observed in the ESI.

- **Examine and interpret the opposing party's or third-party's ESI.** In some cases, you might need the expert to examine another party's ESI to assess whether it support the allegations.

- **Evaluate the evidentiary strength of the ESI.** Your lawyer might need an expert to interpret the strength of the ESI, particularly prior to the meet-and-confer session, so he can negotiate from a position of strength.

- **Rebut the findings of the opposing party's expert.** If your opponent retains a computer forensics expert, you'll want to counter with your own. Your expert can examine the expert's report for inconsistencies, omissions, or illogical conclusions.

Prior to retaining an expert, your lawyer will interview her to verify her credentials, to verify that there's no conflict of interest with any of the parties in the case, and to verify whether she can help prove or help build the case. However, there's the possibility that the computer forensics expert will draw conclusions from the ESI he or she has examined that might not be the conclusions you want. Your lawyer may decide not to use that expert.

Judging an expert like judges do

Since the 1990s, the Supreme Court has demanded strict standards for the admissibility of scientific expert testimony in federal courts. In its defining *Daubert v. Merrell Dow Pharmaceuticals* (1993) opinion, the Supreme Court created what's called the Daubert test or Daubert standard. The Daubert test looks at the relevance of the evidence. For testimony to be allowed in court, it must be closely tied to the facts of the case so that it helps the judge or jury (referred to as the *triers of fact)* understand the issues being disputed. Because the triers of fact rely on the expert to understand the evidence, a strict standard for experts is crucial.

In some courts, the Federal Rule of Evidence 702 may apply. Rule 702 governs the admissibility of expert testimony and states the following:

> "If scientific, technical, or other specialized knowledge will assist the trier of fact to understand the evidence or to determine a fact in issue, a witness qualified as an expert by knowledge, skill, experience, training, or education, may testify thereto in the form of an opinion or otherwise."

Your expert's credentials and conclusions need to be sufficient to withstand the opposing counsel's attempt to discredit them.

Your expert needs sufficient time to do the following:

✔ Acquire the ESI without altering it.

✔ Authenticate it.

✔ Analyze it.

✔ Prepare a report explaining the findings.

As such, involving an expert as early as possible is to your advantage.

Doing a Scientific Forensic Search

A *computer forensics investigation* is a process that uses science and technology to examine ESI. Computer forensics' distinctive characteristic is that it uses the scientific method, or forensic science. Here's the general sequence of steps in the scientific method:

1. **Raise a question, issue, or concern.**

2. **Observe systematically, or identify and collect or record data.**

   Your observations are not proof, but information on which to formulate a hypothesis.

3. **Develop one or multiple working hypotheses.**

   A *hypothesis* is an educated guess or idea to explain observations. A hypothesis should offer a rational explanation of an event based on what's observed or not observed.

4. **Test the working hypotheses based on analysis of a representative sample of the evidence, and do one of the following:**

   a. Accept the hypothesis.

   b. Reject the hypothesis.

   c. Modify the hypothesis.

5. **When you have evidentiary support for the hypothesis, you accept it and reject the others, and it becomes a theory (or a conclusion).**

 A *theory* is an explanation of a set of related observations that's been proven or verified by unbiased researchers or investigators. Theories tend to remain until new information or evidence causes them to be displaced by a new theory. For example, the early theory that the earth is flat was replaced with the theory that the earth is round. So far, the round-earth theory remains unchallenged.

6. **If or when new evidence appears that's not consistent with the theory, then conduct the scientific method again.**

 A hypothesis is tested and perhaps re-tested as new evidence is recovered or examined. Once evidence is found to refute the theory, the testing and sampling begins again.

Either formally or informally, cases start with working hypotheses, which may then lead to the development of a theory that tells a compelling or convincing story based on the evidence.

Electronic discovery requires you to run a lot of search queries and record which documents are associated with each of the queries.

Testing, Sampling, and Refining Searches for ESI

Data sampling is done to check for responsive material without taking the time — or incurring the expense — of doing a full review. Finding ESI can consist of a series of tests, samples, and refining searches to refute a hypothesis.

Doing a series of refining searches is considered a best practice; doing just one search is not a best practice! If you have to defend what you did or didn't do, you want to be on the side of best practices.

Here's how you scientifically examine an e-mail:

1. **Do intelligence.**

 The process begins with an analysis of the situation or intelligence scan to gain a basic understanding of the issues surrounding the incident.

2. **Formulate a hypothesis.**

 You can hypothesize that there are no responsive e-mail messages on any of the five e-mail server backups whose contents are within the relevant date range.

3. Create a forensic copy to be used for the analysis.

Acquire the ESI of one of the servers, which you read about in the upcoming section "Acquiring and preserving the image" in this chapter. You then use this forensic copy, and not the original, to perform the following steps. The forensic software creates an *index* (listing) of the words (including names) found in the files as it's creating the forensic copy. The original storage devices holding the ESI are stored in a secure location and never examined because examining a file changes its meta-data and could alter its contents. The generally accepted method is to examine the forensic copy to keep the original evidence untainted.

4. Test.

Run a search (also called a *query*) for e-mails using key words, key phrases, and the names of people related to the case. During e-discovery, every document in the search results must be reviewed for relevance, privilege, and protection, not just the most relevant ones. Because of the necessity to review everything, determining the scope of the search becomes more difficult.

- Over-inclusive searches drive up costs of downstream production and review, as we discuss in Chapter 9.

- Under-inclusive searches increase the risk of challenges to your search methodology's thoroughness, which put you on the defensive.

5. Draw conclusions.

Review the results of the query to determine the number of responsive e-mails. Reviewing for privilege and protected documents is also done during this stage.

- *If you find no responsive e-mails, accept the hypothesis.* You can conclude that a full review of the other servers isn't worth the time and cost.

- *If you find responsive e-mails, reject the hypothesis.* You can conclude that you need to search the other servers (if you're sure the e-mail messages are not available anywhere else).

The results of this type of scientific sampling also create a sample that you can use for further testing. For example, the discards — the e-mail messages that were not tagged as responsive — create a sample that you can use to test the adequacy of the search terms, phrases, and names used in the query. You get extra mileage because you can use the *output* (results) of one scientific method as input for another test.

Attempting to reverse engineer the scientific method by forcing the ESI to fit a self-serving hypothesis is a doomed method because it's unreasonable. Hearing from the judge that you did something unreasonable will most likely be followed by something that requires a lot of explaining, effort, or expense.

Applying C-Forensics to e-Discovery

A computer forensics expert can support the e-discovery process by identifying more possibilities for finding relevant ESI. Forensics experts can help identify places to look, signs to look for, and additional sources. These sources may be earlier versions of memos or spreadsheets that still exist on the computer's disk or on backup media.

A computer forensics professional ensures that

- ✔ ESI is protected against damage, destruction, or compromise by anyone else who investigates the computer.
- ✔ The system is protected against malware, such as viruses, worms, and Trojan horses during the analysis process.
- ✔ Extracted ESI is properly handled and protected from later mechanical or electromagnetic damage.
- ✔ A continuing chain of custody is established and maintained.
- ✔ Business operations are affected for a limited amount of time, if at all.
- ✔ Any client-attorney information that is inadvertently acquired during a forensic exploration is ethically and legally respected and not divulged.

The computer forensics specialist takes these steps to identify and retrieve ESI that may exist on a computer system:

- ✔ Protects the computer system during the forensic examination from any possible alteration, damage, data corruption, or virus introduction.
- ✔ Discovers all files on the storage media. This includes existing normal files, deleted yet remaining files, hidden files, password-protected files, and encrypted files.
- ✔ Recovers all or as much as possible of discovered deleted files.
- ✔ Reveals contents of hidden files to an extent, as well as the contents of temporary or swap files used by both the application programs and the operating system.
- ✔ Accesses the contents of protected or encrypted files if possible and if legally appropriate.

✔ Analyzes all possibly relevant data found in inaccessible areas of a disk. This includes but is not limited to *unallocated* space on a disk (which is currently unused, but may be the repository of previous data that is relevant evidence), as well as *slack* space in a file (the remnant area at the end of a file, in the last assigned disk cluster, that is unused by current file data, but may be a possible site for previously created and relevant evidence).

✔ Provides an opinion of the system layout; the file structures discovered; any discovered data and authorship information; any attempts to hide, delete, protect, encrypt information; and anything else that has been discovered and appears to be relevant to the overall computer system examination.

✔ Provides expert witness testimony.

Following procedure

The series of processes in a computer forensic investigation is shown in Figure 13-1. Investigations, like the Scouts, start with being prepared.

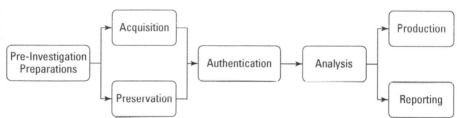

Figure 13-1: Processes in a defensible computer forensic investigation.

Procedures performed by computer forensic experts include acquiring and preserving the ESI, then authenticating and analyzing it, after which the ESI is produced along with a report. All ESI on a storage medium is acquired in a *forensically sound manner,* which preserves the ESI from any material alteration, so the ESI is in pristine condition.

Except for the forensically sound manner, the steps in computer forensics and e-discovery are quite similar. Computer forensics methodologies meet the tough standards for criminal investigations, wherein the prosecutor must provide evidence showing guilt beyond a reasonable doubt. In civil cases, the plaintiff needs to show only that the defendant is liable by a preponderance of evidence.

Computer forensics examinations may be part of e-discovery when exams are warranted by the facts of the case or by the law. Courts may allow forensic imaging of a hard drive or device if you show good cause. However, courts have been reluctant to order forensics exams largely because of the costs and burdens they inflict, but courts will order these exams if warranted. For example, in a 2007 trademark infringement action, *Koninklijke Philips Electronics N.V. v. KXD Technology*, the court ordered the defendant company to submit a report from a computer forensic expert explaining the circumstances surrounding the destruction of data, warning that the court might appoint a neutral computer forensic expert to verify the defendant's claim.

Preparing for an investigation

If you're not prepared and don't have a plan, basically, you're lost. A strong opponent will destroy you single-handedly.

A forensic exam may be done voluntarily as a defensive move at the outset of a case and under your control. For an example of how this effort can be used as part of a defense, see the nearby sidebar about *Williams v. Massachusetts Mutual Life Insurance Co.* (2007). Or a court may order a forensic exam at any point in the case and assign a neutral expert, such as a Special Master, who has the technical and legal expertise to help the court resolve the parties' disputes.

If the investigation is performed by a special master or someone hired by your opponent, you may need to sign a form prior to a forensic investigation of your company's computers or other electronic media. Figure 13-2 shows a general reference guideline prepared by the United States Secret Service for consent forms pertaining to the search of computers and electronic media. The Secret Service recommends that you consult your district attorney or assistant U.S. attorney regarding consent language applicable to your jurisdiction.

Here's how a forensic expert prepares for an investigation:

1. **Conduct interviews with IT staff members, archivists or records managers, and data custodians.**

   Your expert needs to find out and document as much as she can about responsive ESI and how it's managed.

2. **Determine relevant time periods.**

   Start rigorously filtering down the volume of responsive ESI in a defensive manner.

3. **Learn which file types are relevant.**

   In forensics, experts determine a file's type by looking into the file's header and ignoring the file extension. This process also aids in the filtering-down procedure.

4. **Identify key words, phrases, or concepts to be used as search terms for filtering.**

   Queries that are written to search the forensic copy of the ESI use these terms. Your expert makes several passes through the ESI using various search filters.

Consent to Search Electronic Media

I, _____ , hereby authorize _____ , who has identified himself / herself as a law enforcement officer, and any other person(s), including but not limited to a computer forensic examiner, he / she may designate to assist him / her, to remove, take possession of and / or conduct a complete search of the following: computer systems, electronic data storage devices, computer data storage diskettes, CD-ROMs, or any other electronic equipment capable of storing, retrieving, processing and / or accessing data.

The aforementioned equipment will be subject to data duplication / imaging and a forensic analysis for any data pertinent to the incident / criminal investigation.

I give this consent to search freely and voluntarily without fear, threat, coercion or promises of any kind and with full knowledge of my constitutional right to refuse to give my consent for the removal and / or search of the aforementioned equipment / data, which I hereby waive. I am also aware that if I wish to exercise this right of refusal at any time during the seizure and or search of the equipment / data, it will be respected.

This consent to search is given by me this _____ day of, _____ 20 _____ , at _____ am / pm.

Location items taken from: _____

Consenter Signature: _____

Witness Signature: _____

Witness Signature: _____

Figure 13-2: A general consent to search electronic media.

Building a defense

In an employment discrimination case against an insurance company, *Williams v. Massachusetts Mutual Life Insurance Co.* (2007), the employee (Williams) filed a motion asking the court to appoint a neutral computer forensic expert. Williams requested that the expert inspect the company's computer hard drives and e-mail system to recover an e-mail message from October 24, 2002, which he claimed existed. At his deposition, Williams testified that he had in his possession a hard copy of the e-mail message and that it described a discriminatory policy. (Later, when asked to produce the hard copy, Williams said that he couldn't locate it.)

The company opposed Williams' motion because it was based on a flimsy speculation.

The company also explained that the October 24, 2002, "e-mail" being referred to was probably an October 24, 2002, memo from the senior vice president, which the company had produced and which did not describe any discriminatory practices. The company went on to say that it had undertaken its own computer forensic analysis, which failed to identify any e-mail message like the one Williams described.

In the court's view, Williams presented no credible evidence that his employer was unwilling to produce or had withheld relevant ESI. The court would not appoint a neutral computer forensics expert to help Williams confirm his speculation about a document he could not produce or verify the existence of.

You may have performed one or more of these steps during e-discovery. You might need to do some of the processes over because your opponent or the court was not satisfied with how you did them initially. Another reason for voluntarily performing these processes is to have a forensics copy for your own use. Not all of these steps are necessary in all cases.

Computer forensic specialists sometimes investigate in extreme secrecy for a company, so other people don't know exactly what they're doing or what information they've unearthed.

Acquiring and preserving the image

In criminal cases, courts are fussy about evidence being in pristine condition. Not surprisingly, processing and searches are done on an exact physical duplicate of a hard drive, or a portion of one. The creation of a forensic copy is the *acquisition*. A *forensic copy* is the end product of a forensic acquisition of a computer's hard drive or other storage device. A forensic copy is also called a *bit-stream copy* or *image* because it's an exact bit-for-bit copy of the original document, file, partition, graphical image, or disk, for example. All metadata, file dates, slack areas, bad sectors — everything — are the same in the image as in their original forms.

Acquisition isn't the same as collecting or copying files from one storage medium to another. Examples of specialized forensics software tools are Kazeon (www.kazeon.com), Digital Intelligence (www.digital intelligence.com), X-Ways WinHex (www.x-ways.net/winhex), X-Ways Forensics (www.x-ways.net/forensics), Paraben (www.paraben.com), EnCase (www.guidancesoftware.com), FTK (www.accessdata.com), and Nuix (www.nuix.com). Forensics tools are used to acquire the drive and create the image of that drive. A drive can be imaged without anyone viewing its contents.

Acquiring a hard drive is like undergoing the carbonite freezing process that Han Solo went through. The ESI is preserved and can be safely transported.

You get only one shot to physically capture the first original image. If you even think you may need a forensic image in the future, nothing much is lost by spending a little more time to create it in the beginning.

Key benefits of creating forensic images include

- ✔ Preserving ESI in a generally accepted way.
- ✔ Having a working copy of the original to examine.
- ✔ Having multiple copies for examiners, decreasing the amount of time they need to complete examinations.

Authenticating with hash

As part of the acquisition process, the image is authenticated as an exact physical duplicate of the original. That authentication is necessary because the expert can't investigate the original so the copy must be authenticated as an exact duplicate. But authentication of the forensic copy doesn't authenticate the ESI itself, which you read in Chapter 12. Authentication of the ESI is done by the expert based on an analysis of various factors such as the content of ESI, when files and e-mails were created and by whom, other metadata such as when files were modified, attempts to hide or destroy data, and so forth.

As part of the imaging process, a forensic hash value (or *hash* for short) is calculated based on the contents of the image. The *hash* is a digital fingerprint that identifies the image, just as a human fingerprint identifies an individual. The hash is used for verification and authentication of file data, as well.

In its simplest form, a hash algorithm adds up the assorted bits in a data string and provides a value. MD5 (Message Digest 5), SHA-1 (Secure Hash Algorithm 1), and SHA-256 are complex algorithms used to produce a forensic hash. MD5 checksums are 32-digit hexadecimal numbers, SHA-1 checksums are 40, and SHA-256 checksums are 64. Theoretically, there are 2^{128} possible MD5 hash values. Hash values are the proof that the original and forensic copies are identical, allowing the processing to be done on the image instead of the original. An example of an MD5 hash values is e0d321e5f316bef79bfdf5a008876577. An example of a SHA-1 hash is 34821cfe609d3996f057252c45ec2156f5857806.

Recovering deleted ESI

Deleted ESI is typically considered to be not reasonably accessible. However, a computer system never actually deletes files, although they can be overwritten when the FAT uses the space for another file, so deleted ESI may be retrievable using computer forensics software and methodologies. Most documents, e-mail messages, log files of Internet activities, photos, and other file types can be analyzed without the application that produced them.

Deleting ESI in an attempt to get rid of it is never a smart move because sanctions for spoliation (deliberate destruction of evidence) are not mild. The temptation to use software to wipe, scrub, or remove incriminating ESI from hard drives has driven people to make bad decisions. You can safely assume that wiping ESI during an ongoing investigation will be fatal to your case. Even if the files can't be recovered and the scrubbing software's been removed after use, the computer forensics expert is able to detect that the software had been installed and removed.

In *Kucala Enterprises, Ltd. v. Auto Wax Co., Inc.* (2003), a patent dispute case, the defendant obtained a court order to inspect Kucala's computer files. Owner John Kucala learned that Auto Wax planned to use EnCase forensic software to image and examine his computer. Kucala stalled the inspection for two months. Against his lawyer's advice, the day before the inspection, Kucala installed Evidence Eliminator on his computer and eliminated an estimated 15,000 files. The forensic investigation could not recover the files, but it could prove that Evidence Eliminator had been used the prior day. Kucala's attempt to talk his way out of his self-created mess only further angered the judge who found that

> "Any reasonable person can deduce, if not from the name of the product itself, then by reading the website, that Evidence Eliminator is a product used to circumvent discovery. Especially telling is that the product claims to be able to defeat EnCase, the forensic imaging program used by Auto Wax to inspect Kucala's computer. Kucala knew that Auto Wax planned on using the EnCase software, and he proceeded to install Evidence Eliminator anyway, even after he was advised by counsel not to use it."

Kucala not only lost the case, but also had to pay Auto Wax's court and attorney's fees.

Computer forensics software makes this retrieval of deleted files possible by converting all contents of a hard drive into a single searchable file — called an *image* — that is entirely accessible. As such, even files that have been deleted can be recovered and made available for review. The image is made to another hard drive or other storage media. After a hard drive is imaged, all work is performed on the image and never on the original, or non-forensic, copies of the original. Non-forensic copies of the original cannot be verified as exact duplicates of the original, so any challenge to the integrity of the analysis would succeed.

Analyzing to broaden or limit

A forensic image is, in effect, a single huge database file in which each file becomes a record. The forensic toolkit has superpowers to search using keyword or other searches to find responsive ESI. If a generally accepted forensic toolset is used, the results are considered verified if the person who performed the work is skilled in the software.

For unstructured ESI, such as e-mail and instant messages, disregard for spelling or the use of slang, abbreviations, or code complicates the search. To compensate, the search engines have features to help structure a query and catalog the results. Broadening searches and limiting searches are two types of search options to use with keywords or search terms.

Broadening searches

The following are search-broadening options:

- **Stemming:** Variations of the root of the search word are found. For example, the search for *invest* also finds *investment*.

- **Synonyms:** Synonyms of the search term are returned, like when you're using a thesaurus. For example, *crisis* might also find *problem*.

- **Homonyms:** Words that sound the same (or similar) are found. For example, *personnel* also finds *personal*.

- **Fuzziness:** Different spellings of a word, misspellings, or variations involving digits are found. For example, a search for *offshore* also returns *offshoor*, and *Rule 502* might find *Rule 52*.

  You can specify the degree of fuzziness, with 1 being the least fuzzy. Fuzzy search makes sense for first and last names, names of cities, companies, and other proper nouns that are prone to typos or variations.

Limiting options

The following are search-limiting options:

- ✔ **File size:** You can limit the search to files of a certain size, or a range of file sizes.

- ✔ **Date range:** You can search within a range for when the file was created, accessed, or modified (CAM). Here's what these time stamps mean:

  - *Create:* Identifies the date and exact time, to the second, that the file was created on that particular storage media. The file's Create time stamp changes whenever it's copied to new media — even within the same storage device.

  - *Access:* Specifies the last time the file was opened or accessed, but not changed in any form.

  - *Modify:* Indicates the date and time that a file was modified or changed. On files that have been copied to new media, the Modified time stamps might be older than the Created time stamps. The reason is that the file in its original location had been modified before it was copied to the new location, thus created at a later date in the new location.

CAM time and date stamps are only as accurate as the time and date stored in the CMOS chip of the computer. The CMOS chip (which stands for Complementary Metal Oxide Semiconductor) is like an alarm clock that always knows the exact time, even when the power goes out. Like some alarm clocks, the CMOS chip is powered by an on-board battery — to retain all the information necessary to start the computer properly. If something goes wrong with the onboard battery, the CMOS loses all these settings, which causes the computer to effectively lose its mind. Therefore, not checking this information makes it almost impossible to validate the accuracy of the times and dates associated with relevant computer files. You can check current time at this Web site: `http://time.greenwich2000.com`.

Expressing in Boolean

You can combine search options to broaden or restrict results using Boolean searching.

Boolean searching uses connecting words to develop a *search expression.* Anyone familiar with online database searches is familiar with this type of query. Here are standard connectors to form a search expression:

- ✔ **and** narrows the search by requiring that the file contains more than one search word. For example, *new and client and commission* returns files containing all three of those words.

✔ **or** expands the search by broadening the resulting set of files. Files that contain any of the words are found. In effect, using the *or* connector in a single search (for example, *client or customer or buyer*) is like doing three separate searches (one search for *client*, one for *customer*, and another search for *buyer*) at once.

✔ **and not** subtracts files that have the specified word in it. For example, in a search with the terms *and not customer*, files containing *customer* are excluded from the search results.

When using the search expression *and not*, make sure it's the last connector in the search expression because whatever follows it is going to be excluded!

When combined, these operators may become much more powerful than a non-Boolean search. But a mistake in the formation of the expression can throw off the results.

The order in which the expression is processed is based on the connector. It isn't simply processed from left to right.

The software organizes the files according to categories or status such as the following:

✔ E-mail messages

✔ Documents

✔ Spreadsheets

✔ Databases

✔ Graphics

✔ Executables

✔ Folders

✔ Slack space

✔ Encrypted files

✔ Deleted files

✔ Files from the Recycle Bin or Trash

✔ Data carvings or data-carved files

You can view contents of files regardless of whether they were deleted, unless they were also overwritten. *Data carving tools* search through unallocated space on the storage medium looking for remnants of a file by searching for headers of known file types. The remnants are blocks of data, which are called *carved files*. Because the files no longer exist even as deleted files, what's left of them is carved out of that space.

A computer forensics examination can be limited to specific devices or hard drives of key custodians. It doesn't need to be performed on every device or hard drive.

Producing and documenting in detail

The forensic toolkit has reporting capabilities that generate reports in various levels of detail, with some becoming extremely detailed.

Forensic software's reporting engine allows you to create detailed reports and output them into the following formats (also called *protocols*), or others, with links back to the original evidence:

- **Native format:** Files as they existed on the media with metadata intact.
- **HTML:** HyperText Markup Language is the protocol of the Internet. HTML files can be opened and read in any Web browser.
- **PDF:** Portable Document Format is a convenient, popular, and well-supported format for publishing documents.
- **XML:** eXtensible Markup Language is a universal data format that's used to allow data export to virtually any IT system. Like HTML, this format uses tags to identify the data.
- **TIFF:** Tagged Image File Format is widely used to archive documents and photos when maximum quality is important.
- **RTF:** Rich Text Format is a file format standardized by Microsoft for creating formatted text files. It's a universal format, meaning it can be read by nearly all word processors.

You can save reports to a CD or DVD with hyperlinks to supporting information that's contained on the CD or DVD. This effective, self-contained method makes it easy to deliver necessary reports and supporting documentation.

Reporting procedures are important to the success of the case. The investigator performing or participating in the investigation may be required to testify in court, so all procedures need to be documented. The following recommendations help ensure proper documentation:

- **All reports of the investigation should be prepared with the understanding that they will be read by others.** Authorities, opposing counsel, the court, the press, and the general public might read the report.
- **The investigator should never comment on the guilt or innocence of a suspect or suspects or their affiliations.** Only the facts of the investigation should be presented, and opinions should be avoided.

Reinforcing E-Discovery

Computer forensics can support e-discovery in recovery and also in

- ✔ **Finding ESI.** Computer forensics can get into the computer's registry to find what software has been installed, or it can scan slack space to find out what's been done or written. A common reaction to seeing what computer forensics can find and recover is "wow." That's followed quickly by delight, relief, or panic.

- ✔ **Providing plausible interpretations of what the facts demonstrate.** Facts are easy to find, such as which Web sites someone visited or what was typed in a chat room. But analyzing the facts to interpret what they mean is much more difficult. Analysis of these facts or clues to figure out why someone visited those particular Web sites requires more critical thinking and hypothesis testing. Investigators' abilities to interpret what those facts mean, or could mean, depend on their technical expertise and competence.

- ✔ **Examining the opposing counsel's e-evidence for alternative interpretations.** ESI can support conflicting theories. An unbiased investigator may interpret and draw inferences supported by the messages, files, or other ESI that differ from those of the opposing side.

- ✔ **Assessing the strength of the ESI in support of or against a party.** This is a key benefit to gain from computer forensics. This information and advice allows you to decide whether to negotiate or to *litigate on* (as in *party on*). Having this knowledge at the meet-and-confer session can be a hefty bargaining chip.

Depending on the case, you may want to involve a computer forensics expert to avoid or at least decrease the risk of charges that you haven't produced ESI in good faith. You can see the logic of this approach. With e-discovery, data custodians may be the ones who self-identify and self-collect the potentially responsive ESI. In contrast, computer forensics investigators collect everything from a storage device and follow strict evidence handling protocols that document each step in preserving the chain of custody of the ESI.

Of course, if a laptop or other computer is withheld from the expert, the problem has gone full circle. Computer forensics experts also can assist in handling e-discovery issues, such as providing technical specifications for discovery or devising search strategies in a neutral capacity.

Fighting against forensic fishing attempts

You've seen TV detectives desperately wanting to enter and search a person's car or apartment, but they couldn't without probable cause. Without probable cause, they'd be on a fishing expedition — trying to find evidence to justify having broken into the car or apartment. The same principle applies to forensics. You can't use forensics to find out whether there's any incriminating e-mail or other ESI that simply "suspect" or believe must be in there.

Forensic fishing expeditions won't be allowed by the courts because showing both a good cause and a reasonable need are requirements. Good cause usually arises from suspicious circumstances that suggest spoliation, such as a story of a midnight hacker erasing all of your files or the loss of a laptop with all of your records just before a deposition. Generally, courts order full forensic copies of hard drives only if they have a good cause that's supported by specific, concrete evidence of the alteration or destruction of electronic information.

In a case involving the theft of trade secrets (*Ameriwood Ind., Inc. v. Liberman*, 2006), the court gave the employer (the requesting party) access to its employee's computer to recover ESI that was not reasonably accessible. The court allowed the company to make a forensic copy of the employee's computer and search for otherwise inaccessible ESI, the deleted files, and slack space because the company demonstrated the need for the forensics.

Fighting with forensics on your team

An investment in computer forensics can help your company prove that something did or did not happen. Computer forensics can reduce legal fees by bringing a case to resolution more quickly than it would have ended otherwise.

In another employment case, the employee brought an Employee Retirement Income Security Act (ERISA) action alleging that her employer fired her in unlawful retaliation for her complaints about the employer's failure to make timely contributions to her retirement account. The employee contended her firing took place in part because she met with an attorney and the employer had used a spyware program to review her e-mail to learn about the meeting. The employer acknowledged installing the spyware program on employee computers, but denied using the program. To aid in its defense, the employer hired a computer forensics expert to analyze forensic images of hard drives of the employee's business and personal computers. The results of this investigation proved that the spyware program had been deleted from the employee's business computer by antivirus software before the spyware copied any keystrokes or saved any screen shots. The court granted the employer's motion for summary judgment and dismissed the case.

Defending In-Depth

The forensic investigator, working as a neutral expert or special master for the court or hired by one of the parties, must be able to defend her methods, interpretations, inferences, and conclusions. Maintaining the integrity of the ESI as e-evidence requires a standardized, defensible approach to data handling, preservation, and analysis.

The opposition will try to find mistakes in the forensic investigation. Your defense should include evidence that one or more of the following documented procedures have been performed. Documentation needs to show that the investigator

- Acquired the e-evidence without altering or damaging the source.
- Authenticated the acquired e-evidence by verifying that it was the same as the original.
- Analyzed the data and files without altering them.
- Used systematic sampling techniques that included agreed upon keywords, phrases, concepts, date ranges, and file types.

Also, as part of the defensive strategy, the work must be

- Performed in accordance with forensic science principles.
- Based on current industry best practices.
- Conducted with verified tools to identify, collect, filter, "bag and tag," store, and preserve e-evidence.
- Documented thoroughly and in detail.

Part VI

Strategizing for e-Discovery Success

The 5th Wave   By Rich Tennant

"The short answer to your evidentiary challenge is, 'No.' The long answer is, 'No, and get out of my chambers.'"

In this part . . .

This sixth part helps make you a master of e-discovery from four perspectives. In Chapter 14, you find out about the latest in archiving business records and how it differs from data backups. You see the impact of the decision to do archiving within the framework of the *Zubulake* five categories of data, which you read about in Chapter 2. You learn a proactive approach to information management based on an enforced policy and how such an approach can put you in a position of strength when e-discovery hits.

In Chapter 15, we switch views from internal to external. You see e-discovery from the perspective of the judges and what they have in their toolkit to encourage parties to play fair and dissuade gamesmanship.

For large-scale, high-stakes, or unusual cases, you may find that the case cannot be resolved and you're headed for trial, as you read in Chapter 16. You discover the value of partnering with one or more e-discovery vendors whose expertise you need.

Chapter 17 covers e-discovery from the small end of the continuum. Even when there's a $15,000 contract in dispute or a $50,000 fraud charge, ESI may be the star witness. You discover how proportionality principles and computer forensics techniques influence these cases.

"The central problem with e-mail, as I see it, is not the smoking gun. It is the smoke."

—Kenneth J. Withers, Director of Judicial Education and Content for The Sedona Conference

Chapter 14

Managing and Archiving Business Records

• •

In This Chapter

▶ Meeting the legal requirements

▶ Rethinking documents and records

▶ Doing ERM defensively

▶ Constructing ERM programs

▶ Acing compliance

• •

*C*hanneling the flood of documents and messages rolling through your company into an archive or into a discard bin is a critical step toward being ready for litigation. Ad hoc e-mail management, for example, can lead to legal disputes or outright disasters. Early case assessments can be done with confidence only when active and archived electronic business records can be found, collected, and put on litigation hold on-demand (read that *quickly and easily*). What the e-discovery team needs from IT is well-managed ESI that makes it as simple as (economically) possible to identify and preserve responsive ESI. That level of simplicity is never going to happen unless you've indexed, classified, and categorized the ESI so that it's process-ready and legal-review–ready; and expired ESI is banished on cue. In practical terms, investing in tech solutions to achieve e-discovery zen may seem cost-prohibitive . . . that is, until you've faced the fire for being unprepared.

In this chapter, you read about IT's role in litigation-readiness. That role is following proper electronic records management (ERM) and implementing the policies, practices, and software to make it happen. You find out why layering ERM software on top of bad practices simply automates bad practices. Simplicity and certainty are the antidotes to chaos and complexity. Simplicity here means *automation* because the less human effort needed to manage ESI and ensure compliance, the better. For processes that you can't automate, you cover those gaps with data retention and disposal policies and procedures that provide users with the certainty to know what to do, what not do, and what will happen when policies are violated.

Ratcheting Up IT's Role in Prelitigation

Managing ESI is not only a technology matter. It's one of the most serious sources of legal exposure and risk your company may face. In the race for revenue, it's tempting for managers to overlook legal risks even though the price for not being prelitigation-ready has been paid by numerous companies.

Corporate records management policies and practices are now under great scrutiny thanks to the incidents of massive and hugely stupid attempts to get rid of evidence by document shredding and deleting. These incidents have created a new environment in which electronic records retention and destruction decisions are judged more harshly.

Laying the cornerstone of ERM

Records management, either paper or electronic, includes the creation, retention, continued access, and discarding and destruction of business records. The cornerstone of a defensible ESI management system and e-discovery protocol is a well-designed (or *reasonable* in legalese) ERM policy and program. ERM policies and programs do double duty in terms of managing the likelihood and the impact of litigation risk. They do the following:

- **Minimize or reduce risk associated with the case.** You've heard the cliché that information is power. Against your opponent in a lawsuit, you don't have much else. ESI is the negotiating tool or bargaining chip — a situation that moved ERM from a back-office task to a business-critical function for which IT has a major responsibility. ERM helps prevent the risk of not being able to prepare a powerful position for the meet-and-confer session. Or not being able to show your opponent that you're ready to respond to whatever they throw at you.

- **Transfer or offset risk associated with the court.** ERM helps minimize the risk associated with not being able to fulfill the duty to preserve when litigation strikes or is reasonably foreseeable. Taking early preventative measures by implementing an ERM designed with e-discovery in mind saves you legal grief down the road. Risk skyrockets for companies with sloppy prelitigation ERM practices. Having a rock-solid ERM program is like insurance to offset risk. When challenged, you have the ERM defense to save your hide.

Pitching your tent before the storm

The left side of the Electronic Digital Rights Management (EDRM) diagram (shown in Figure 14-1) is broadly called *information management*. For e-discovery purposes, this is the prelitigation or presubpoena stage when your company is operating its business as usual, continually producing ESI and using it to do business.

Figure 14-1:
The information management stage of the EDRM diagram is when you develop an ERM.

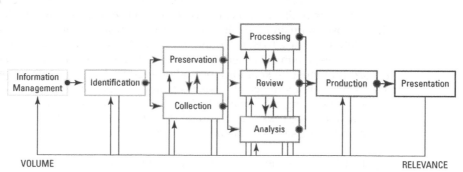

According to a 2009 e-discovery survey report published by HP, 51 percent of respondents chose to improve the information management stage through technology. However, many ERM programs don't adequately deal with the requirements of this stage. When IT doesn't take into account how their programs impact the volume and accessibility of ESI, it's possible that no one will know — until a lawsuit comes up. If there's validity to the quote "adventure is just bad planning," plenty of adventure is in store for the e-discovery team.

The amended Federal Rules of Civil Procedure (FRCP) exposed the weaknesses in many companies' ERM policies and programs. Most likely, ERM problems were known, but so what? The cost to fix the problems was too high until e-discovery rules changed the status quo. As every application developer and network administrator knows, it's not until software programs, policies, or networks are tested rigorously in a realistic situation that deficiencies and unexpected performance are detected.

If you don't have an ERM policy and program in place that are designed to meet litigation demands, you'll undoubtedly get in trouble sooner or later. We're talking very costly fines, sanctions, and lost judgments, and not gentle tap-on-the-wrist reprimands. And if your ERM schedule is hit or miss, the court may order a computer forensic expert to find, audit, and report on your ESI; and order your company to pay the bill. Face it, for IT, there's no escaping a key role in prelitigation. For IT departments, adding a litigation focus to their business focus is their destiny.

Telling Documents and Business Records Apart

ESI is a new term. *Documents* and *business records* are not. Although these terms are used rather generally, you need to use them more precisely when discussing their management.

Not every e-mail, instant message, memo, photo, PDF, word processing file, or other type of file is a business record. A *business record* is any document that records a business dealing, operation, or transaction. Much more complex definitions are tossed around, but this simple definition captures it all. For example, if e-mail is used in any way to transact business, it's a business record that must be kept for a period defined by law — usually seven years. The e-mails are evidence of business transactions or contracts, as well as evidence of changes to quarterly financial statements or a labor contract. Federal and state laws may mandate that the e-mails and their metadata and attachments be saved as business records.

Figure 14-2 shows the useful distinction between documents and records. Documents are under the control of the person (user) who created or received them. The user can save, send, delete, edit, or tag the document for retention or destruction according to a document management policy. Typically these actions take place without much hands-on control from IT. Control via policies. An e-mail policy may direct employees to empty their e-mail inboxes and voice-mail boxes at regular intervals; or direct them to clear out early versions of memos or documents and tag the final version for retention as a business record. You can read about policies and enforcement in the section "Building an ERM Program."

Having document management policies that require employees to regularly purge their personal digital stuff and tag documents to keep as business records does a few good things:

- ✔ Spares you from having to go through megabytes of non-records looking for two or three files or e-mails.

- ✔ Protects you against spoliation accusations.

- ✔ Defends you if you inadvertently destroy ESI. Your defense would be something like this:

  "We had reasonable policies and procedures that we followed. Despite our best efforts, our system isn't perfect."

  Taking an honest approach goes a long way with the court.

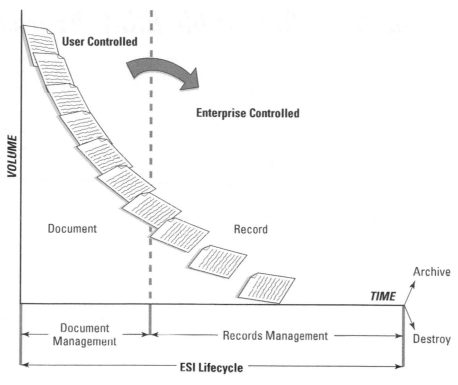

Figure 14-2:
Document
manage-
ment and
records
manage-
ment
programs
defensively
reduce the
volume of
ESI.

Documents that generally don't need to be saved as business records include personal e-mails sent or received on the company's e-mail system, personal files of all types, earlier drafts of documents, memos about company picnics or other events, and items posted on the company's Intranet (such as "free puppies to good home").

At some point, as shown in Figure 14-2, documents that are business records need to be retained, and come under the centralized control of your company. Contracts, financial reports, proprietary information, quality control documentation, project management records, human resource reports, and the like are business records. These records are destroyed when there's no legal or business reason to retain them any longer.

The two primary professional organizations dedicated to records and information management are ARMA International (Association for Records Managers and Administrators), whose Web site is www.arma.org, and AIIM (the Association for Information and Image Management), whose Web site is www.aiim.org. They provide publications, information, and educational programs on records management for both paper and electronic records.

Designing a Defensible ERM Program

Standard out-of-the-box ERM programs simply don't exist anymore than standard off-the-shelf information security programs (firewalls, access control lists, or intrusion detection systems) exist. You start with the basic requirements or functions and then customize from there.

In the following sections, we discuss how to start designing your ERM program. When you have it designed, you can then build it, which we discuss in the "Building an ERM Program" section.

Designing by committee

Your team that's responsible for defining the ERM policies, retention schedules, requirements, and enforcement methods should include IT, legal, human resource, records managers, and business stakeholders. This team may also be the e-discovery response team, or at least some members should be common to both teams. Your company has numerous constraints to take into consideration, such as state and local laws, industry and federal regulations, resource and privacy restraints, information flows, and capabilities of existing systems.

Politics or personal agendas of team members can divert or waste effort. Having a manager with power encourages cooperation and keeps the focus on the overall ERM agenda.

You want an ERM that collects the least amount of ESI that's legally defensible while meeting your business' operational needs and regulatory obligations.

Starting with the basics

Designing a defensible ERM program (also called *records and information management,* or RIM) starts with recognizing a wonderfully binary situation: *keep* or *not keep.* Here's how you start:

1. **Distinguish records from non-records.**

2. **Get rid of the non-records and leave the business records that must be retained.**

Saving everything is never an effective ERM program because the volume of data becomes too overwhelming to control ESI. Hoarding has downsides:

- Hurts your ability to manage business records
- Adds to storage costs unnecessarily because you're keeping non-records
- Exposes records to review costs that you shouldn't have

3. **Categorize the business records and apply retention schedules to records you need to keep.**

   Set retention periods for every category of business record based on federal rules, industry regulation, or other authority.

4. **Dispose of records as scheduled.**

   You face this paradox — ESI can exist on an IT system forever and yet not be accessible when you need it. Records that you don't need to keep any longer need to be cleaned out of your company's digital landfills as soon as possible. If you don't get rid of records as scheduled, you may be forced to keep them. Why? Because once the retention period for records has passed, if a litigation hold is imposed, you're stuck preserving those records. And if that's not enough pain, you may need to produce them if requested.

   You're biggest retention regret is likely to be from over-retained e-mail. E-mail is the number one source of evidence used to compel early settlements and they're the root cause of large sanctions. Destroying e-mail is challenging because it's not truly gone unless every copy of it is gone.

The Department of Defense (DoD) established records management standards that are named DoD 5015. ERM software vendors whose products are certified for DoD 5015 qualify for use by federal government agencies. When evaluating ERM software, look for that certification.

You should set retention and disposition schedules based on legal or other mandates. For example, documents or e-mails that are archived into a financial documents folder may be disposed of in seven years. Environmental or health-related documents get lifetime storage. Any automated system to purge ESI is fine, as long as there's a way to turn it off when a litigation hold is imposed.

Don't write a policy and then forget about it. The courts consider that at least as bad as not having a policy. You can't download a sample policy, slap on the company logo, and think you're protected.

Getting management on board with your ERM program

Most companies don't have well-defined ERM policies and programs in place to control their data growth. That's because their ERM policies/programs aren't updated or executed with e-discovery duties in mind. Companies aren't known to sprint to meet requirements set by what seems like (or actually is) an endless stream of regulations (regs, for short). Privacy, security, anti-terrorism, fraud, the do-not-call registry, bankruptcy, foreign corrupt practices, the environment, and other government regs are very demanding and invariably drop more work on the IT department than is possible to implement properly within the time limits. An ERM policy is just one more thing to do.

When the Sarbanes-Oxley Act was passed in 2002 that gave public companies a compliance deadline for automating strict internal controls over financial reporting (the Act had an anti-manual spirit to it), the series of delays by the companies and extensions by the Securities and Exchange Commission rivaled those of the airlines during bad weather. Managers may be conditioned to expect extensions or reprieves and thus not see any urgency in investing in ERM, particularly in a bad economy.

IT investments tend to be earmarked for profit-generating activities, like increasing sales and new product development. In order for compliance-related items to get their fair share of the budget, you need help from above — top management.

When senior management strongly supports the ERM project by committing to a healthy budget and sufficient resources, it can be successful. Senior management's commitment to success needs to be visible, just like monitoring, to keep employees compliant. The basic principle here is that what's important gets done.

IT managers surveyed on e-discovery

A LiveOffice survey, conducted by Osterman Research in 2007, polled more than 400 IT managers and users across the United States. According to the results, 63 percent of respondents had faced a legal action requiring them to produce e-mail. Fifty three percent said they weren't prepared to meet the amended FRCP, while 30 percent weren't even aware of the FRCP requirements. IT managers felt that responding to e-discovery requests only slightly less painful than dealing with the IRS.

Not ready for prime e-discovery time

In Fall 2008, Kahn Consulting, Inc., in association with ARMA International, BNA Digital Discovery and E-Evidence, Business Trends Quarterly, and the Society of Corporate Compliance and Ethics, surveyed over 400 enterprises on three information management compliance topics. The three topics were governance, risk management, and compliance (GRC); records and information management (RIM); and e-discovery. Key findings of the survey include

✔ Over 90 percent are actively addressing GRC, RIM, and e-discovery issues.

✔ Fewer than 25 percent believe that their employees understand their GRC, RIM, and e-discovery responsibilities and how to fulfill them.

✔ Only 15 percent of employees understand their legal hold and e-discovery responsibilities.

✔ Only 21 percent understand how information should be retained and disposed.

To download the complete survey results, visit www.kahnconsultinginc.com/library/KCI-GRC-RIM-EDD-survey.pdf.

Conversely, without senior management, you're finished. Any unpopular project, such as information security, will fail if users know that it's not a top priority at their company.

Another influencing factor is management's attitude toward risk or risk appetite. *Risk appetite* is the amount of risk — on a broad level — management is willing to accept. The bigger the appetite, the less chance you have of getting all the funding you need.

Emphasize the prelitigation readiness angle when convincing upper management of your ERM. If there's one thing that can capture executive attention, it's litigation. It's no coincidence that companies that have been through e-discovery and litigation at least once are more receptive to implementing ERM, particularly retention and disposition policies.

Some statistics might move the budget in your direction. A company can spend an average of $18 to $19 million to produce and review 1 terabyte (TB) of data. If only 10 percent of that TB should have been cleared out, almost $2 million is spent reviewing ESI that should have been disposed of.

Playing the *cost-reduction card* with IT investments needs to be done with extreme care. You may want to boost your budget by claiming that in addition to mitigating legal risk, ERM can drive down costs and improve operational efficiencies. If that argument is almost threadbare at your company, tread gently on those extras.

Crafting a risk-reducing policy

Your company probably has acceptable use policies (AUP) as well as other types of policies in place. For your ERM policy to withstand scrutiny, it must meet several characteristics that include the following:

- ✓ **Written in language that employees can understand easily:** If the employee needs a law or computer science degree to understand it, it won't pass as a policy.

- ✓ **Recognizes the demands placed on individuals:** If the do's and don'ts are too harsh for employees to comply with, they won't. With overly strict policies, users find ways to outsmart the rules. Anyone who's tried to implement strong password controls knows that creative and lazy employees are quick to figure out workarounds, such as not turning off the computer or writing passwords on sticky notes attached to the monitor.

- ✓ **Circulated to employees:** Employees need to understand what's expected of them. If employees don't see the value of compliance, don't know of any downside to non-compliance, or are not trained to comply, the policy is considered optional, at best. Some employees won't want to part with any of their e-mails.

- ✓ **Available online so everyone knows where they are and you can update them easily.** Make it easy for employees to find the policy and contact information of the point person for questions. Include an FAQ section so they don't need you or the help desk to get answers.

- ✓ **Simple enough to enforce consistently:** If the policy has exceptions and exclusions (like the rules of evidence) and other complexities, they can't be implemented or won't survive for long because they sap productivity.

When drafting policies, remember that everything that you've preserved automatically becomes discoverable in the event of litigation — whether or not you intended it to be.

To claim in court that ESI isn't available because it's been destroyed, you have to back up that claim with a written ERM policy and proof that it's been distributed and agreed to. Keep records that demonstrate how the policy is implemented and how employees are trained in retention and disposal. You also need electronic log files showing that disposal is applied uniformly, on schedule, and according to the written policy. Document all ERM efforts as though you're preparing to testify in court about the policy and how it's enforced.

Punching up your e-mail policy

E-mail plays a big role in creating risk, so e-mail policies play a big role in reducing risk. Yet many companies get that simple relationship wrong. Companies have paid large fines and corporate officers being prosecuted because their employees misused e-mail. According to the market research firm IDC (www.idc.com), 27 percent of Fortune 500 companies have had to deal with harassment claims concerning e-mail. In one case, a major consulting company was sued by one of its former employees for $3.5 million over an alleged defamatory job remark. The employee requested copies of all e-mail records containing his name going back ten years. Of course, the company objected that the request was too burdensome by showing that the retrieval would cost $7.8 million to search 61 backups, and the court agreed.

Issuing policies is like popping diet pills. You need to do more to get lasting and effective results. Here are some things you can do to bolster e-mail policy to reduce the volume of e-mail and risk of misuse:

- **Create a big presence.** Many times, when a company simply announces e-mail monitoring, behavior changes. It's like driving on the highway with a state trooper right behind. Preventing nonsense in the first place saves the most amount of grief.

- **Monitor for compliance and to detect trends.** IT can see behavior patterns and suspicious trends that need a closer look. In order to see what's going on, you need to combine a detection system similar to an intrusion detection system (IDS). You want the system to flag e-mail sent with large attachments or to too many recipients, sending huge volumes of e-mails to free e-mail accounts, and sending confidential files to the sender's personal e-mail account. Basically, you're making potential problems visible so you can investigate and take corrective action.

- **Perform investigations quickly and carefully.** The IT department typically performs the investigations of employee e-mail misuse. But you may want to check with legal or HR first because of employees' right to privacy.

- **Keep it transparent.** Personal e-mail archives complicate e-discovery because they're not under centralized control. Allowing users to save messages on their own, outside of the ERM system and established policies, leads to too many *pocket-archives* whose contents you can see Collecting ESI from pocket archives is time-consuming and has disaster written all over it.

- **Manage the policy and violators.** You can see which policies are being broken and who's breaking them. Violators need to face the consequences listed in the policy, or your policy has a giant gap.

✔ **Keep the capture of e-mail tagged as legal records simple and easy.** Invest in applications that take the guesswork and the work itself out of the hands of the users. Your e-mail archive is only as complete as the users are conscientious, which is alarming. For example, e-mail archiving systems let you define role-based and/or information-based retention policies. Users can tag or drag their e-mail to a folder where it's later classified. Customer e-mail could be dropped into a customer folder, from which the archiving system applies the appropriate retention policy.

Some intelligent (and more expensive) archiving systems offer a wide variety of tagging rules that you can customize to meet your company's retention rules. Tagging rules (that is, actions that are carried out based on the tag) make life easier for you and make retention consistent.

When building or updating your ERM program, here are two universal principles to guide your efforts:

✔ If you can't classify it, you can't manage it.

✔ To produce it, you must preserve it.

Building an ERM Program

Building an ERM program follows a process. The steps in that process are:

1. **Conduct an inventory to determine the kinds of records or information created and used.**

2. **Develop a classification scheme for grouping records into classes.**

   A class consists of similar records that are related as the result of being created, received, or used in the same activity or function.

3. **Prepare a records retention schedule to set retention periods (times) for the various classes of records.**

   A *retention period* is the length of time a given record series is retained for administrative, legal, and historical reasons. A *retention schedule* is a set of policies and procedures that identify and describe how records are treated.

   The records retention schedule needs to take into consideration these four criteria:

- *Business needs:* Your company's future need for records, including who needs access to the records and for how long.

- *Regulatory requirements:* You don't get the option of negotiating time frames under the control of federal, state, and local laws. Consider how agreeable the IRS would be if you choose not to retain records for tax purposes.

- *Documentation for legal purposes:* Your company has more legal documents than you may have thought. There are contracts, agreements, warranties, patents, deeds, and titles. These are legal documents, but they're not required by regulations.

- *Litigation:* Here's the e-discovery reason. You retain and preserve ESI that might be needed to prove or defend a case. Considerations include the cost of accessing, processing, and reviewing documents, even those retained beyond their retention schedule.

4. **Design a prototype or pilot ERM program to test functionality and user acceptance and debug.**

   Your ERM program needs to cover the ESI lifecycle. Stages in that life-cycle are

   - Creation

   - Distribution

   - Retention

   - Protection

   - Discard or destroy

   - Suspension of discard and destroy when there's an anticipated or active investigation, or a litigation hold

5. **Prepare the following written documentation about the policy.**

   You'll notice that it's similar to an insurance policy, which is not riveting reading either.

   - Purpose and scope

   - Responsibilities of officers, managers, and employees

   - Coverage and conditions that create exceptions

   - Retention periods for documents

   - Destruction times, methods, and responsibilities

6. **Implement the ERM program, train employees, monitor compliance, and keep it updated.**

Technology solutions are available for managing e-mail, such as e-mail archiving tools for managing and preserving e-mail and analytic programs for searching archived e-mails. You may want to read The Sedona Conference's *Commentary on E-mail Management: Guidelines for the Selection of Retention Policy* published in April 2007. You can download the publication from the Sedona Conference's Web site at www.thesedonaconference.org.

A 2007 IDG survey reports that the worldwide market for e-mail archiving applications grew by 45 percent in 2006 and is expected to approach $1.4 billion in 2011.

Kicking the keep-it-all habit

Consider your closets or the glove compartment in your vehicle. When you're paying lawyers hundreds of dollars an hour to review e-mail and documents, a smaller pile means a smaller bill. That's your incentive to monitor and enforce policy. Likewise, people will retain many more files and e-mails when there's little incentive to get rid of it.

Doing what you say you are

When a company has a policy that it isn't following, what it has done is define its own standard of care that it's failing to meet. If your opponent can show that you say one thing but do another, you're well on your way to losing your case.

If you explain to the court something such as, "We don't have e-mail messages sent by the employees listed below prior to July 2007," the courts generally accept that situation when it's supported by a statement from someone in IT explaining retention and disposition policies and practices. A court isn't likely to make you prove a negative unless you have done something that put you on the wrong side of the court.

Good recordkeeping that includes archive dates cannot be fully appreciated until you need to defend the loss of ESI. Imagine the difference between being fully prepared with all documentation needed for an IRS audit and having to scramble for documentation.

Getting an A+ in Compliance

When you're producing ESI, you must comply with the rule (specifically with FRCP 34(b)(2)(E)(i)) that deals with producing documents in the usual course of business. You show compliance with that rule by

- ✔ Providing information about where the documents were maintained
- ✔ Identifying who maintained the documents
- ✔ Identifying the sources of the information

When you have to produce e-mails in the usual course of business, you show compliance by

- ✔ Arranging the responsive e-mails by custodian
- ✔ Sorting them in chronological order
- ✔ Including any attachments.

For non–e-mail ESI, you show compliance by

- ✔ Producing the files by custodian
- ✔ Identifying the file's location on the hard drive by identifying each file's
    - • Directory
    - • Subdirectory
    - • Filename

As new mobile applications emerge and social media transform communication, as Twitter and YouTube have done, you need to support a broader range of content types.

Chapter 15

Viewing e-Discovery Law from the Bench

In This Chapter

▶ Judging issues still not settled

▶ Analyzing the role of the judge

ules applicable to discovery are nothing new. What is new is the format of the information sought. The explosion of electronic information has led to an expanding and still-developing area of discovery law. The courts are often faced with the dilemma of deciding whether the old square peg for discovery fits in the new round hole for electronic discovery. They find it usually doesn't. In the world of e-discovery, federal judges have become the darlings of the legal process, the superstars of the legal community, by crafting new decisions that pertain specifically to e-discovery.

In legal cases, judges make determinations of law, and juries make determinations of fact. Electronic discovery involves legal issues and therefore is the province of the judges. In most cases on the federal level, the magistrate judges set the course of e-discovery with the Federal Rules of Civil Procedures (FRCP) for guidance.

Because judges have such an important role in e-discovery, looking to them for insight into the process can be helpful. A judge's insight can aid you in making decisions and set a course during your e-discovery process. In this chapter, you find out about how some influential judges view their role in the process of e-discovery. You gain a valuable perspective on some currently vexing issues that you may get involved with during e-discovery.

Examining Unsettled and Unsettling Issues

The court system is so swamped with e-discovery matters that you may find going to trial is too expensive for what your case is worth. Some of the expense is due to judges who fail to control excessive and expensive e-discovery. In an effort to control costs, judges look to the Federal Rules of Civil Procedure (FRCP) to force a settlement rather than move your case forward. The costs associated with e-discovery can be mind-boggling. In *Oracle Corporation, et al., v. SAP AG, et al.,* the parties were in a dispute over possible discovery of 165 custodians of potentially relevant ESI. The estimated cost of discovery for those 165 was $16.5 million.

The general rule is that if you're responding to the discovery request, you bear the cost of production. You can seek a protective order or ask that your opponent pay some of the cost (which is *cost-shifting*), as discussed in Chapter 12.

In the following sections, we take a look at what you can do to keep your costs down during e-discovery — and stay on the judge's good side at the same time.

Applying a reasonableness standard

FRCP 26(g) requires that you certify that you've made a reasonable inquiry into procuring all the ESI your case requires and that your request and disclosure is complete and correct. Judge Grimm in *Mancia v. Mayflower* warned lawyers not to take this certification too lightly. We discuss this certification in more detail in Chapter 5.

At a minimum, *reasonable inquiry* means your outside counsel interviews both the custodians of ESI and your IT personnel to understand the type of ESI and where it is stored.

If you fail to make a reasonable inquiry, the rule provides for sanctions. You face monetary sanctions, an *adverse inference* ruling (the judge instructs the jury to assume facts about your case — often unfavorable to you), or the judge can throw out your case.

Your failure to engage in effective and efficient discovery can raise your e-discovery costs, and therefore you may find going to court not worth the expense.

In *Qualcomm v. Broadcom,* the court granted significant sanctions against Qualcomm's outside counsel for not making a reasonable inquiry. Judge Major noted that "an adequate investigation should include an analysis of the sufficiency of the document search and, where electronic documents are involved, an analysis of the sufficiency of the search terms and locations."

For a lawyer, a reasonable inquiry isn't just a matter of the FRCP. The ABA Model Rules of Professional Conduct requires that your lawyer not make frivolous discovery requests. It also requires that lawyers make a reasonably diligent effort in attempting to comply with discovery requests. Failure to make a reasonable inquiry could result in sanctions from the court and the Bar Association.

While it is difficult to determine if your lawyer is making a reasonable effort, communication is the key. Long periods without communication from your attorney may indicate that your case is on the back burner. A simple call to your attorney can ease your fears. It is important that from the outset there are open lines of communication between you and your attorney, and you should expect to be kept in the loop at all stages of the case.

Forcing cooperation

Cooperating with your opposing party is key to keeping your e-discovery costs down. If discovery is to be used for the proper purpose, it requires cooperation of all parties involved. Judges rely on you to work out any disputes without them stepping forward to referee.

Judges expect you not to harass your opposing party with unnecessary delays, unreasonable costs and burdens, or create unnecessary expense. You should go to the meet-and-confer session with the expectation that you'll compromise on what ESI you ask for, what ESI you're going to hand over, how you're going to search for ESI (including specific keywords), and in what form you'll hand it over.

Cooperating doesn't mean the courts expect you to always agree with the other side. Of course, don't think the other side will always agree with you, regardless of how right you are.

Cooperation also doesn't mean that you give away everything you have. You can cooperate and still protect your interests. As noted by The Sedona Conference Cooperative Proclamation, advocacy of a position is not the same as adversarial conduct. "It is not in anyone's interest to waste resources on unnecessary disputes." For example, there is no reason not to voluntarily disclose information that you know can and will be discovered or to raise spurious arguments to delay or raise the costs of litigation.

One thing you never want to do is force a judge to step into your case. You can be sanctioned for not cooperating. For example, in *Gross Construction Associates, Inc. v. American Mfrs., Mutual Ins. Co.,* the judge chastised both parties because they couldn't agree on search terms and forced the court to draft a list.

Looking at what's reasonably accessible

You should attempt to deal with any ESI that is not reasonably accessible early in the e-discovery process. Expect to negotiate this standard with your opposing party at the meet-and-confer session. And if you can't come to an agreement, put a plan in place to explain to the court why your ESI is not reasonably accessible. You may need to hire an outside expert to help you convince the judge. This is an added and perhaps unnecessary cost.

If you're producing the ESI, you bear the cost. If you have ESI that is not reasonably accessible due to the cost of retrieving it, you can challenge its production. The court may either issue a protective order (which says you don't have to produce it) or shift the costs of production to your opponent.

The designation of ESI as not reasonably accessible doesn't mean it is not discoverable or that you don't have to produce it. It simply puts your opponent and the court on notice that you can get to the ESI but you can't produce it because of the undue burden or cost. The court may force you produce ESI despite that designation.

ESI that is not reasonably accessible doesn't eliminate or reduce your preservation obligation. It's imperative that you identify any not-reasonably-accessible ESI early in the process and assure that the litigation hold includes that ESI. Failure to do so could and probably will result in sanctions from the court.

Determining who committed misconduct

When the courts are asked to assess sanctions, or if the court thinks sanctions are appropriate, the court makes a two-fold inquiry:

- ✔ Was there misconduct?
- ✔ Who committed the misconduct?

As discussed in Chapter 5, the court has a wide range of sanctions available to deal with misconduct. The misconduct can be by a party, third-party, or counsel. All or some may be sanctioned.

The court may impose sanctions on its own as well as at the request of a party.

Forcing a judge to act

A company filed a lawsuit against one of its former employees and his new employer for illegally obtaining and using its confidential and proprietary information to hire their staff, open new offices, and start a new line of business. The breach of contract case, *Koosharem Corp. v. Spec Personnel, LLC and Kenneth Fuston, Sr.* (2008) was filed in South Carolina in September 2008. The plaintiff Koosharem Corporation was doing business as Select Staffing and Resolve Staffing. Select Staffing is a human resource (HR) outsourcing company in the transportation industry. Select Staffing had purchased Resolve in February 2008.

Defendant Kenneth Fuston, Sr., was a former employee and vice president of Resolve. His employment contract with Resolve included a non-compete agreement. After resigning from Resolve, Fuston became an employee of Spec.

The court granted the plaintiff's motion and ordered the defendants to produce e-mails to or from any current or former employee or customer of the plaintiff found on Fuston's home computer, and documents reflecting communication with the defendant and certain former employees of the plaintiff. In response, the defendants produced 1,936 pages of e-mail. The plaintiff didn't believe that the production was complete, and brought a second motion to compel in July 2008.

Several problems or irregularities the plaintiff identified with the defendants' original production included the following:

✔ All the e-mails produced reflected the date compiled rather than the date received or sent.

✔ Several e-mails allegedly retrieved from Trevor Doyle did not have Doyle listed as a sender or recipient.

✔ Many e-mails were missing their attachments.

✔ Documents were modified even after notice of litigation.

✔ Defendants made no document retention efforts after the lawsuit was filed.

✔ Defendants' new hires were not immediately provided with a company e-mail account and thus conducted work from home computers and personal e-mail accounts.

✔ Former employees e-mailed confidential information to their homes before going to work for defendants.

The defendants argued against the inspection, which the court denied. The court stated that the only issue before it was whether computer forensic analysis should be allowed in light of the defendants' failure to produce documents and because relevant information might be stored on the computers. Finding that forensic analysis was appropriate, the court issued this detailed 20-step protocol:

(continued)

(continued)

1. Defendants will make available for forensic analysis and data recovery to be conducted by an expert forensics firm ("Expert") any business computers and/or any personal computers used to conduct business, correspond in any way regarding business, Spec and/or its current or employees, and/or plaintiffs and/or their current or former employees, for Steve Arnold, Walter Chudowsky, Benita Dillard, Trevor Doyle, Ken Fuston, Kevin Moore, Steve Roberson, and Jude Tallman.

2. The time frame for the forensic analysis and data recovery will encompass the period September 1, 2007, to present.

3. The parties will jointly agree within five (5) calendar days after entry of this order on an Expert that will be used to conduct the data recovery and forensic analysis.

4. Defendants will produce to the Expert within ten (10) calendar days after entry of this order the computers identified in paragraph 1.

5. The Expert will recover only the documents and e-mail account or accounts used by individuals identified in paragraph 1 (or those accounts and documents accessed remotely using another computer).

6. The Expert also will conduct a search or run other appropriate programs to determine whether any e-mails or documents have been deleted, destroyed, altered, or otherwise compromised since January 25, 2008, and whether any programs have been installed that would alter, destroy, erase, modify, or otherwise compromise any portion of each computer or its contents as of January 25, 2008. The Expert also will be permitted to conduct such search efforts as are necessary to form an opinion as to whether any procedures were put into place to preserve e-mails and documents as of January 25, 2008.

   Note: Step 6 looks squarely at whether IT took appropriate affirmative action to preserve ESI.

7. The recovery of e-mails will include all e-mails in any form whatsoever including, but not limited to, deleted e-mails, forwarded e-mails, copied ("cc") and blind-copied ("bcc") e-mails and draft e-mails. The recovery of documents will include all documents including drafts, multiple versions, and final versions.

8. The Expert will securely maintain the original data recovered in order to establish a chain of custody.

9. The Expert will produce a copy of the recovered data to defendants' local counsel of record attorney John Glancy ("defendants' counsel").

10. Defendants' counsel will review the data to identify any privileged or personal e-mails that it seeks to withhold from document production.

11. Within ten (10) business days of obtaining the recovered data from the Expert, defendants' counsel will prepare and provide to counsel for plaintiffs: (I) a log of privileged e-mails ("Privileged E-mail Log") protected against disclosure by a relevant legal privilege and include the identity of the e-mail, the sender and recipient (and any individuals identified in the "cc" and "bcc" fields), the date sent, the nature of the privilege, a general description of the e-mail and the basis for asserting the privilege; and (ii) a log of personal e-mails ("Personal E-mail Log") and include the identity of the e-mail, the sender and recipient (and any individuals

identified in the "cc" and "bcc" fields), the date sent, a general description of the e-mail and the basis for claiming it is a personal e-mail. To the extent that defendants' counsel asserts privilege as to any documents obtained from the forensic analysis, such documents also must be set forth on a document privilege log ("Privileged Document Log") and be produced within ten (10) business days of obtaining the recovered data.

12. Together with the Privileged E-mail Log, Personal E-mail Log, and Privileged Document Log, defendants shall produce (within 10 business days after obtaining the recovered data from the Expert) all e-mails and documents recovered by the Expert, which are not identified on the Logs.

   Note: Step 12 compels IT to produce non-protected e-mails and documents that are recovered by the computer forensics expert. Basically, the outcome of the case falls on IT at this point.

13. For purposes of the procedure described herein, a personal e-mail is one that does not relate to or in any way concern: defendants' employment, whether it deals with past, present, future or prospective employment; plaintiffs' business; plaintiffs' customers and former customers (including contacts at customers and former customers); plaintiffs' employees and former employees; defendants' drivers or plaintiffs' former drivers; plaintiffs and any of its employees; or Spec Personnel and any of its employees, including but not limited to, communications regarding Spec's closing of offices staffed by plaintiffs' former employees or efforts to have anyone take over, purchase or otherwise assume responsibility for any Spec office staffed by plaintiffs' former employees.

14. If any document attachment to an e-mail is identified through the discovery of an e-mail, and such document was opened, saved from, detached or otherwise transferred or reproduced on the hard-drive of defendants' computers, such attachment shall be produced or the Expert shall be given access to defendants' computer to conduct further data recovery in order to obtain such document(s).

15. If any document is identified by the Expert as being opened, saved, altered, transferred or reproduced and it falls within the scope of the request, such document must be produced by the Expert and handled by defendants' counsel in the same manner as though it was an e-mail communication.

16. If plaintiffs disagree with the assertion of any privileges, the parties shall submit to the court the disputed documents and Logs for the court to view in camera and determine whether the documents must be produced.

17. Defendants are responsible for any and all fees, costs and expenses associated with gathering the computers and transmitting them to the Expert.

18. At this time, the parties will share equally the fees, costs and expenses charged by the Expert. When the Expert is retained, the Expert will be jointly informed that any billing or retainer must be split evenly between the parties. If any retainer is required, the parties are obligated to provide the retainer within three (3) business days of the Expert's request so that the process is not delayed in any way. Neither party waives its right to seek reimbursement or payment of any fees, costs and expenses charged by the Expert if it is determined that award of such is appropriate pursuant to the Federal Rules of Civil Procedure, Local Rules or case law.

(continued)

(continued)

19. By agreeing to this order, no party waives its rights or objections to the discovery sought herein.

20. The parties understand and agree that this order addresses the preliminary scope for the computer production and forensic analysis. If the initial production and analysis determines that additional searches are necessary, either party may petition the court to revisit the scope of this order. This lengthy order was preliminary and the scope of the investigation might expand.

This court also ordered that the parties share equally the fees, costs, and expenses charged by the expert.

Then in September 2008, the plaintiff filed a motion for sanctions [pursuant to Rule 37(b)(2)], claiming that the court should infer that the reason the defendants' didn't produce all relevant ESI was that it was harmful to them in the case. The court denied this extreme motion for sanctions, but also said that if the defendants didn't comply with the order (all 20 steps of it), then the plaintiff could resubmit their motion for sanctions. Basically, the defendants were out of options and IT had a lot of work to do.

Exploring the Role of the Judge

The judge can play an active or passive role in e-discovery. Judges differ on the exact nature of the involvement a judge should have. Some prefer to be a bystander unless you ask for their intervention. Others see themselves as part of the process from the initial conference.

Judges have little patience if you procrastinate. The courts are always looking at fairness and reasonability. If you cause a delay, you had better have a good reason — one the court will find reasonable and not unfair to your opponent. For example, in *Ford Motor Co v. Edgewood Props.*, there was an eight-month delay before the requesting party objected to the form of production. The court found the delay to be unreasonable. Judge Salas noted, "it is without question unduly burdensome to a party months after production to require that party to reconstitute their entire production to appease a late objection."

Actively participating

Judges prefer for you to cooperate and agree with your opponent on all aspects of e-discovery. The reality is that cooperation is a wonderful goal but generally not feasible, and judges have to step in at some point.

The FRCP anticipates some judicial involvement in the e-discovery process. Judges are first involved in e-discovering issues at the initial Rule 16 conference.

This initial conference is held after the meet-and-confer session and usually results in an order that establishes the case management, including initial discovery time frames and any agreements among the parties.

The court also has the inherent power and duty to make sure the case is proceeding appropriately by doing the following:

- ✔ **Overseeing agreements:** The scheduling order may include agreements of the parties such as clawback agreements or other agreements on the discovery issues. A *clawback agreement* allows discovery to proceed and any inadvertently disclosed privileged or protected communication to be returned or "clawed back" by the disclosing party.

- ✔ **Issuing orders of protection, orders to produce or sanctions:** Judges may be involved in determining what's accessible to the form or production to developing search terms for the parties. You might seek an order to produce if you believe your opponent is not disclosing all relevant ESI. You may also seek a protective order limiting the ESI you have to produce (if you have privileged, protected, or not reasonably accessible ESI).

Scheduling conferences

Judges are expected to take an active role in pretrial/scheduling conferences under Rule 16. Judges generally establish case management orders to force you to keep the case actively progressing.

FRCP Rule 16(c)(2)(C) specifically provides for the court's role in controlling and scheduling discovery. Judges hope that the meet-and-confer session results in as many agreements as possible, which allows them to keep the case moving forward. Usually the judge incorporates these agreements into his or her *scheduling order* (a document outlining how the case will proceed).

The court has the power under Rule 16 to control discovery but also under its inherent power to control the judicial process of a case.

Appointing experts

Sometimes the IT professionals don't agree with the lawyers. The lawyers want certain e-discovery, but your IT expert says it's not possible or may cost too much money to get it out of the archive.

So in that case, the court may bring in an expert to help settle your e-discovery issues (called a *Special Master*). FRCP Rule 53 provides for the appointment of a Special Master to

- ✔ Perform duties consented to by you and your opposing party

- ✔ Hold trial proceedings and make or recommend findings of fact on issues to be decided without a jury

The powers and duties of the Special Master are set forth in an *appointing order* (appoints the person to serve as Master and establishes what the Master will do). In general, the Special Master may have the power to

- ✔ Regulate the process of discovery.

- ✔ Exercise authority to compel or protect evidence.

- ✔ Provide advice and guidance to the court.

- ✔ Invoke sanctions. The sanction power doesn't include Contempt of Court, but the Special Master may make that recommendation to the court.

In *Peskoff v. Faber,* the judge found that the ESI sought by the plaintiff from the defendant couldn't be obtained without the aid of a forensic examination; the court decided to bring in a computer forensic expert.

The use of Special Masters is growing with the evolution of e-discovery. The judge in *In re Seroquel Products Liability* noted that a familiarity with The Sedona Principles is important for e-discovery cases. From the candidates agreeable to both parties, the judge selected the person with the most hands-on experience in e-discovery.

Judge Scheindlin makes the case for the use of Special Masters in e-discovery disputes. In a co-authored article at 30 Cardozo Law Review347, the judge investigated various uses of Special Masters in aiding the court in the complex area of e-discovery. He set out four common uses for Masters in e-discovery:

- ✔ Facilitating the process of e-discovery.

- ✔ Monitoring discovery compliance as it relates to ESI.

- ✔ Adjudicating legal disputes related to ESI.

- ✔ Adjudicating technical disputes and assisting with compliance on technical matters, such as system inspections.

- ✔ Adjudicating claims of privilege or protection. In fact, the Federal Judicial Center's *Managing Discovery of Electronic Information: A Pocket Guide for Judges* indicates that this is a good use of a Special Master. See Chapter 10 for a discussion of privilege and protection.

A case of an active judge

The case of *Sheila El-Amin, et al., v. George Washington University* is an excellent example of how a judge may be of assistance to the parties in moving a case forward. The court doesn't want a truckload of boxes filled with hard-copy documents to be brought to the courthouse and used in a trial. No judge wants to have to canvas thousands of documents when making decisions on motions. In this case, Judge Facciola became an active participant in assisting the parties. The judge noted that the primary goal was to "create a system whereby all existing documents are hyperlinked to fields in a database that will permit the instantaneous retrieval from within the database of information offered by plaintiffs in support of any factual proposition." The secondary goals are identified as coming up with a system that is "capable of being easily used by counsel and by the Court."

The judge noted that the court must be provided with the software. Furthermore, the system must be self-contained so that its use isn't contingent on outside information. In other words, everything is there that will be needed to handle production and deal with objections. The court noted: that it would like to see a database that allows for the parties to hyperlink proposed evidence. The system should allow the opposing party to review and state its objection and hyperlink any evidence it would offer in opposition. This would also be available to the Court for its review and ruling of the issue. A seamless flow of e-discovery.

The court then established requirements for the selection of a vendor for this system. The judge indicated that all existing ESI must be subject to being captured by Optical Character Recognition (OCR) for integration, all handwritten information coded for integration, all information provided to the vendor will be returned and must be preserved by the party information, and the system must provide protection so that information inputted by counsel stating why evidence is or is not sufficient must preclude disclosure of earlier drafts. Judge Facciola seemed to favor a Web-based database for ease of meeting the goals. However, the judge acknowledged that there may be valid concerns over Web-based security. If a non–Web-based system is used, then the parties and the court must have access.

Judge Facciola took the unusual step of providing the parties with a database example that might be appropriate. The following minitable is Judge Facciola's chart.

Claim No.	Dr.	Date	Plaintiff's Evidence in Support	Defendant's Objection and Any Countering Evidence	Court's Ruling
23	Smith	10/02/01	Document of testimony	Counter argument why evidence is insufficient; tender of countering evidence with explanation	Claim sustained or denied with reason

For example, if you've determined that your ESI is not reasonably accessible, the Special Master can determine whether your search results were adequate or other technical matters. Because judges, like lawyers, often lack the technical skill or background, the use of Special Masters can help resolve discovery disputes. This Special Master is not just facilitating or overseeing the e-discovery process but actually dealing with the technology. As a result, the Special Master should have appropriate technology credentials.

The use of Special Masters can alleviate significant burdens on the time and resources of the court system. They are discretionary and should have clearly defined tasks. They can be effective in promoting efficiency and economy in the legal process. If you have a case, don't be shy about asking for the appointment of a Special Master.

A Special Master may be appointed by the court at your request or at the request of your opponent. The appointment is totally in the judge's discretion. Or the court can decide on its own to appoint a Master. You then share the costs.

Determining the scope of costs

Cost-shifting (asking your opponent to pay for some of your production costs) may also be appropriate as a sanction for misconduct. The courts have little or no patience for misconduct. Although adverse inference or termination sanctions aren't the norm, the court is generally amenable to shifting the cost. Cost-shifting is done under either the FRCP or the court's-inherent power. The costs can be significant as the court seeks fairness in the process.

In determining if cost shifting is appropriate, the court attempts to determine the additional costs you're forced to incur as a result of the misconduct of your opponent. This includes not only the costs associated with discovery of the ESI but includes your attorney and expert fees. Of course, the judge has the ultimate say in the amount and type of sanction, but you must consider this when planning for e-discovery.

Chapter 16

e-Discovery for Large-Scale and Complex Litigation

In This Chapter

▶ Getting ready for complex litigation

▶ Using ESI to win your case

▶ Informing the judge of your ESI issues

▶ Going to court for e-discovery resolution

▶ Assessing accessibility

▶ Bringing in others

*T*he expediential growth of ESI has been a nightmare for some and a boon for others. Companies are now faced with the potential of significant time, effort, and costs in complying with e-discovery. This is especially true in large multi-party and complex litigation and other types of matters, such as governmental investigations. Any litigation where the dollar amounts are $100,000 or more is considered a large case.

Knowing how to deal with these ESI discovery issues and proper preparation can significantly reduce your burdens. It might also mean the difference in the outcome of a case. Additionally, it might avoid unnecessary and costly sanctions.

In this chapter, you see the special issues applicable to e-discovery in large-scale and complex cases, the approach of the courts, and dealing with outside vendors. Also discussed is the important role that cost-shifting plays in these types of cases.

Preparing for Complex Litigation

Quite possibly, the outcome of a case might be determined by one e-mail. Finding that one e-mail might be like finding the proverbial "needle in a hay-stack" because that one e-mail might be among hundreds of thousands of documents relevant to the case. In fact, it might not be found at all. There is also the problem of the other side playing "hide and seek" with that very relevant ESI. They hide; you seek and hope you find.

Seven Network Ltd. v. News Ltd. took five years to conclude at an estimated cost in excess of $200 million. Discovery resulted in ESI containing 85,653 documents or 589,392 pages. Of those, 12,849 documents or 115,586 pages were admitted into court. The plaintiff lost the suit.

Complex ESI matters might be encountered in any types of case. ESI may be present in all types of litigation. The following examples are considered large cases either because of the complexity of the issues or the large amounts in controversy. Some examples are

- ✓ **Anti-trust:** The government claims that a company has engaged in behavior that reduces competition in the marketplace. For example, *United States v. Microsoft.*

- ✓ **Sexual harassment/retaliation:** A party claims they were subject to harassment or a hostile work environment based on gender or that the company retaliated against them for making a claim of sexual harassment. For example, *Zubulake v. UBS Warburg LLC.*

- ✓ **Securities fraud:** This is where a company or persons engaged in behavior that defrauded or mislead investors. This is a civil case. For example, *Coleman (Parent) Holdings, Inc. v. Morgan.*

- ✓ **Criminal fraud:** Where a party engaged in any type of criminal fraud relating to financial transactions. For example, *United States v Bernard Madoff.*

Complex litigation often involves multiple parties and complex legal issues. You should start preparation well in advance of litigation or investigation. Your company should have an overall document retention and identification plan in place that assumes you will be involved in e-discovery. Preparing before the lawyers come knocking on the door may save both time and money. Preparation is your secret weapon in e-discovery. Your document retention plan should include the following:

- ✓ An archive policy that ties into the document retention policy

- ✓ A regular plan to survey the location of potentially privileged or protected ESI

- ✓ An indexing system to identify protected and privileged ESI

Make sure that employees are aware of the policy and how to implement it. Regularly monitor them to assure compliance. Regularly test that the system is working effectively and efficiently.

Ensuring quality control

In the e-discovery process, you will soon find that there is no one best way to negotiate the e-discovery process. Each case has its own unique issues and problems that cannot be solved by a cookie-cutter approach.

Often, large-scale cases involve voluminous ESI located in multiple venues with large numbers of people having potential access. This creates major challenges for quality control assurance, such as

- ✔ The more people with access and the more remote the locations of the ESI, the more difficult it is to both preserve and produce the relevant ESI.

- ✔ The volume creates a problem of locating and culling privileged and protected ESI. This may be further complicated by multiple parties (defendants or plaintiffs) and numerous legal issues.

Complex litigation is characterized by the legal difficulty of the issues involved. A result of more complex issues is a need for more evidence, which usually translates into more ESI and more potential for problems associated with e-discovery. A well-thought-out project management approach is the best way to deal with these challenges.

The Sedona Principles, Second Edition: Best Practices, Recommendations & Principles for Addressing Electronic Document Production (2007) and *The Sedona Conference Best Practices Commentary on the Use of Search and Information Retrieval Methods in E-Discovery* at www.thesedonaconference. org are good places to start your preparing for litigation.

Quality can be viewed in two ways:

- ✔ **The need for quality control over the process:** The specific procedures and tools you use in the e-discovery process.

- ✔ **Quality assurance:** The results are complete and accurate. The court can impose numerous sanctions for your e-discovery misconduct.

According to The Sedona Conference, quality assurance is also important for at least four other reasons:

- ✔ Without a quality process, you can affect the outcome of your case by not discovering or uncovering relevant ESI.

- ✔ You may inadvertently disclose privileged or protected ESI and the court may refuse to provide you relief. (See Chapter 10.)

- ✔ Taking the time to measure quality assures your results are accurate and allows you to correct any mistakes you've made.

- ✔ You may have to repeat the entire e-discovery process again if your first effort was poorly planned, costing more money than doing it right the first time.

Quality control impacted the outcome of *Victor Stanley, Inc. v. Creative Pipe.* Judge Grimm held that the privilege claim on inadvertently produced documents was waived because of a lack of quality control to show they were truly inadvertent. The judge noted that Creative Pipe had a number of failures in quality control: failure to prove the keyword search was reasonable, failure to provide the qualifications of the person who came up with the search terms, failure to explain how what they did was sufficient in the context, and failure to show any quality assurance testing.

Getting a project management process in place

Having a project management process in place is important from the start of e-discovery.

This process involves both IT and lawyers. *The Sedona Conference Best Practices Commentary on Achieving Quality in the E-Discovery Process* recognizes that no matter what tools you use, you won't get a successful outcome unless you do the following:

- ✔ Your team understands the circumstances and requirements of your case.
- ✔ You use thoughtful and well-defined methods.
- ✔ You measure your results for accuracy.

Proper preparation before the meet-and-confer session could be a deciding moment in the litigation. Being prepared and understanding the ESI issues is essential to an effective meet-and-confer session.

We discuss putting a project management process in place in Chapter 3.

Proving the merits of a case by using ESI

Because more than 90 percent of all business documents are electronically generated and the use of electronic communication (such as e-mail, texting, or social networking sites) is growing, ESI is essential to almost any case. As we discuss in Chapter 12, once authenticated, ESI may be introduced as evidence in court. Therefore, it is not only essential to a case to know what ESI you have but also what else might be out there.

Because complex and large-scale cases generally have a number of complicated legal issues and voluminous ESI, proving the merits of the case become more difficult. Locating the relevant ESI from numerous locations and preserving it can be a challenge for any company. Adding to this complexity is the discovery and protection of privileged and protected ESI that may on a hard drive of an employee's computer. Determining what relevant ESI the other party or a third party has that is needed to prove your case and how to get it is only multiplied when the issues become more complex. It can become even more burdensome when there are multiple parties as the challenges grow exponentially.

Educating the Court about Your ESI

The court is responsible for overseeing your conduct — and your opposing party's conduct, as well — during the course of your case. The court rules on the admissibility of evidence, may sanction you or grant summary judgment on your pleadings, and can even take the case out of the jury's hands.

The importance of educating the judge about the issues of the case and the ESI is so the court can adequately manage the process of the case. If you're in federal court, check out *Manual for Complex Litigation, Fourth (Manual)* at `www.fjc.gov/public/pdf.nsf/lookup/mcl4.pdf/$file/mcl4.pdf`. This manual describes methods that federal judges may employ in complex cases and addresses ESI discovery issues directly.

Your initial conference with the court addresses litigation management and most likely results in a *case management order*. The case management order establishes benchmarks to keep the case moving forward. If your case somehow gets off track from the case management order, you need to discuss with your opponent new timelines, and then submit a proposed order to the court incorporating what you've agreed to. The initial conference under FRCP Rule 16 takes place no later than 120 days after the defendant has been served or 90 days after the defendant has appeared, whichever is earlier.

You must keep the court informed on the progress of your case — either formally (through a written status report) or informally (by phone).

During the initial conference, the judge questions your attorney to focus the issues and relevant facts of your case. Topics will include:

- ✔ The nature and potential dimensions of the case
- ✔ The procedural and substantive problems that are likely to be encountered
- ✔ Procedures for the efficient management of the case

Using summary judgment and other tools

A *summary judgment* is a decision on the outcome of the case made by the judge based upon the evidence available to the court at the time. It is a matter of law. If you feel that your opponent hasn't stated a legal cause of action or has no legal defense, you can ask the judge for a summary judgment. Judges are reluctant to take cases out of the jury's hands or to rule without a trial on the merits, so it's unlikely the judge will grant you a summary judgment. Nevertheless, it's a good tactic to take because it can force your opponent to provide additional, more-focused discovery to address the issues raised in your motion. This can help to move the case forward and ultimately reduce costs.

If the judge doesn't grant your summary judgment, and you can't come to an agreement of the facts about your case, you can try the following things:

- ✔ **Force your opponent to stipulate to facts:** Judges frequently force you to stipulate certain facts in an attempt to determine what facts are at issue. The courts are encouraged in the *Manual* to have you participate because clients often take the admit-nothing approach. There may be strategic disadvantages to denying matters on which the other side clearly will prevail at trial or denying something that should not have been disputed. That may bring into question your denials of things that really do matter if you deny matters where you are clearly wrong.

- ✔ **Request for admissions from your opponent:** In this request, you list the facts that you're requesting the other party to admit. If he admits the fact, then it is no longer an issue before the court. Your opponent will probably deny your requested admission on some trivial disagreement with the statement to be admitted. However, their response goes in the court document. If your opponent fails to answer in good faith, they can be sanctioned and you might recover your costs in proving something they denied.

- ✔ **Draft a series of numbered narrative statements of the objective facts:** These should not be conclusion of law and avoid being argumentative. Your opponent must then address each of these facts and indicate those that are admitted or will not be contested and those that are contested and the basis for the position. He can make additional narrative fact statements to be answered by you. The result should be a consolidated statement reflecting what you've agreed to and what you haven't.

Employing an identification system

The court often requires you to use a uniform identification system for documents that you're producing. With paper discovery, this is *Bates stamping* or *Bates numbering* (named for the Bates Manufacturing Company that held the original patent on the stamping machine). With ESI, the court can order a system of identification that complements or integrates a paper-based system.

However, databases containing millions of data elements, none of which is meaningful alone, can be difficult or impossible to break down and organize in a way directly analogous to conventional documents. An identification system might make use of hash values to develop a numbering system for identification. If you've properly prepared for the meet-and-confer session, you can come up with an agreeable production system that you can then propose to the court.

A production log helps you later if you get into a dispute with your opponent about production.

Form of production

In complex litigation, the courts want to avoid trucks backing up to the court-house to unload boxes of documents. The *Manual* favors production of ESI in electronic form rather than paper. It recognizes many benefits from this, including:

- ✔ The ability to search, retrieve, and organize large amounts of data quickly
- ✔ The ease of performing computer-sophisticated analysis on the ESI
- ✔ Cost and time savings in storage, duplication, and transmittal of information
- ✔ The ability to preserve ESI links and attachments
- ✔ The ease of presentation in the courtroom when using technology

We talk more about production in Chapter 11.

Creating document depositories

When you're dealing with a lot of ESI, you might want to create a central document depository to keep ESI production efficient and economical. Require that your team produces all discovery materials in common, computer-readable formats and insist that these materials be made available on computer-readable media (such as CD-ROMs or DVDs) produced at a central location, through a secure Web site or a dial-in computer network. Doing so reduces the expense and burden of document production and inspections. A depository also helps you keep track of what documents you've produced and the information in them, which can help minimize later disputes with your opponent. Part of the process of establishing a central depository is setting up uniform procedures for acquiring, formatting, numbering, indexing, maintaining, accessing, and copying the stored ESI.

The cost of establishing and maintaining a central depository may be substantial. The court can consider whether the costs are justified by the cost savings and other benefits derived from the depository's use. If you find the expense to be too great, you can do the following:

- **Ask the court to allocate some of the costs to your opponent.** The judge could order your opponent to pay the setup and maintenance costs of the depository.

- **Use a pay-as-you-use system.** The costs are set at an amount to cover the costs of the depository. You only incur costs to the extent that you access the central depository. If there are multiple parties, a pay-as-you-go system may be a great savings to you if you don't have the same ESI issues as others.

- **If you can't pay any of the costs, ask the judge for special arrangements.** If there's a depository already set up for a case that has similar issues as yours, the judge can simply grant you access, which can reduce duplicative production costs and the cost of maintaining the central depository.

If you're involved in a case that involves multiple lawyers in several locations, consider establishing your own depository, whether the courts advise one or not. If Internet-based, it can be a virtual 24/7 discovery management system that allows attorneys at various locations to access, review, search, make notes, and provide comments on the ESI. Responsive ESI can be indexed and privileged, and protected ESI can be identified and tagged as privileged or protected. But you must be careful to limit access only to what each individual needs so you don't compromise any privilege you might want to claim later.

Many vendors can create (or assist in creating) these depositories (which we talk about later in this chapter). Vendors are helpful in litigation because, if needed, you have an expert to verify the collection processes and procedures. Additionally, many law firms use litigation support and production software for storage and retrieval, which serve the same function as depositories.

Avoiding Judicial Resolution

You face sanctions if you don't meet and confer in good faith. The courts expect you to settle most disputes with cooperation. If you don't come to the meet-and-confer session ready to work with your opponent, you can lose your case. You can agree to protocols that are costly yet might not protect information you want to keep privileged or confidential. Or you can put the issue before a judge who may not look favorably upon your case.

It is imperative that you come to the meet-and-confer session with a full understanding of what ESI you have, what you want from your opponent, and what you don't want to give to your opponent.

You won't always get what you want, but with proper planning, understanding, and negotiation, you can usually get what you need.

When dealing with large-scale litigation, getting everything in order for the meet-and-confer session is a huge task. Here are some methods that can help you:

- ✔ **Discuss an informal production of documents and search protocols.** Clearly the best way to reduce costs is for you to turn over ESI voluntarily. Of course, there are legal considerations and constraints that your lawyer will consider before deciding whether to hand it over. Another way to save time and costs is agreeing to search protocols for relevant ESI and to cull privileged or protected ESI.

- ✔ **Consider a rolling discovery schedule.** Rolling discovery is like climbing a hill and then coasting down the other side. You start with a small initial request to test the search terms and criteria. This can provide you with a more realistic view of the scope and costs of ESI before proceeding further. It can focus your e-discovery requests and if you ask the court for an order of protection to protect against burdensome e-discovery.

- ✔ **Agree to clawback and or quick peek agreements.** Both of these reduce some of the cost and time burden. Clawback agreements allow you to exchange ESI freely with your opponent; if you accidentally disclose privileged or protected ESI, you can get it back, and your opponent can't use the ESI against you. In a quick peek agreement, you provide a snapshot of ESI for the purpose of establishing what you may have and the format it is in; you then can determine to a greater extent what you want to see in full discovery. If there is any privileged or protected ESI, you can't use it and must return it to your opponent.

- ✔ **Agree to statistical sampling.** Properly structured search protocols with appropriate quality control and assurance allow you to perform software-based searches instead of reviewing hundreds of thousands of pages by hand.

You can set up your software to allow documents that are tagged as responsive or privileged to be put into folders for appropriate review while not touching other documents. Privilege and redaction logs can be created. This does not eliminate the need for a legal review, but will reduce the manpower and man-hours needed.

Determining the Scope of Accessibility

The drafters of the Federal Rules of Civil Procedure (FRCP) provided that practical limits should be placed on discovery. Any nonprivileged matter that is relevant to your claim or defense is subject to discovery; but you may not have to submit it to the court if you reasonably calculate it may lead to the discovery of admissible evidence. Under Rule 26 (b)(2)(C), the court may place limits on discovery if:

- ✔ The burden or expense of the proposed discovery outweighs its likely benefit (considering the needs of your case), the amount in controversy, your resources, the importance of the issues at stake, and the importance of the discovery in resolving the issues.

- ✔ The discovery sought is unreasonably cumulative or duplicative, or you can obtain it from some other source that is more convenient, less burdensome, or less expensive.

- ✔ You've had ample opportunity to obtain the information by discovery in the action.

In ESI related matters, the FRCP limits the requirement to preserve and produce if you've identified the ESI as not reasonably accessible because of undue burden or cost. The court can order discovery subject to certain conditions, one of which is asking your opponent to bear some of the costs.

You're responsible for any costs associated with preserving and producing your own ESI. The court can shift, in limited circumstances, all or part of those costs to your opponent.

Not reasonably accessible is not the same as *inaccessible*. Very little ESI is actually inaccessible. With the right technology and financial resources, almost all existing ESI is accessible. The focus of the courts is on any undue burden or cost. There is no definition in the FRCP of what is not reasonably accessible. This has become a much-litigated area. This concept is discussed in greater detail in Chapter 6.

Doing a good-cause inquiry

When you've shown that the requested ESI is not reasonably accessible, then your opponent can attempt to show good cause for the court to order that it be produced. The court looks at the following factors when determining good cause:

- ✔ The specificity of the discovery request

- ✔ The quantity of information available from other and more readily accessible sources

- ✔ Your failure to produce the relevant information that is likely to exist or have existed and is not available on more easily accessible sources

- ✔ The likelihood that relevant ESI will be produced that cannot be obtained through other more readily accessible sources

- ✔ The importance of the information sought

✔ The importance of the issue that the ESI is expected to address to the outcome of the case

✔ Your resources

If your opponent requests ESI that you believe is not reasonably accessible, make an offer to produce it if the other party pays all or part of the costs of production. If you make a reasonable offer of cost-sharing and the other party rejects it, then that might indicate to the court that the other party does not find the requested ESI to be that important to the case; certainly, a factor the court might consider.

Cost-shifting

The court has the inherent power to oversee and manage the discovery process. In looking at the good cause issue, the court can set conditions on allowing the discovery of not reasonably accessible ESI. Among those conditions is cost-shifting to reduce or eliminate your undue cost burden. If your opponent really wants ESI you believe to be not reasonably accessible, he can pay for it.

In *Rowe Entertainment, Inc. v. The William Morris Agency, Inc.* the court applied an eight-factor test for allocating costs. In *Zubulake,* Judge Scheindlin modified the factors and applied a seven-factor test:

✔ The extent to which the request is specifically tailored to discover relevant information

✔ The availability of such information from other sources

✔ The total cost of production, compared to the amount in controversy

✔ The total cost of production, compared to the resources available to each party

✔ The relative ability of each party to control costs and its incentive to do so

✔ The importance of the issues at stake in the litigation

✔ The relative benefits to the party of obtaining the information

The *Zubulake* factors apply at the federal level. Many states pattern their approaches to the example set by the federal courts. Some states take an absolute approach. That is, if ESI is not reasonably accessible and you want it, then you pay to get it.

The court is not likely to shift costs after they've been incurred. If you are seeking cost-shifting, make sure you do it before incurring the costs.

Getting Help

Electronic discovery–related services have become a cottage industry. Vendors offer solutions to lawyers and companies alike. Outside vendors might serve as document depositories (as discussed earlier) and consultants, or provide a wide range of search and other e-discovery solutions. Many law firms either do not have a dedicated e-discovery group or do not have the resources for a particular project. As the litigation becomes larger and the ESI issues more complex, there is a greater need for outside assistance.

Some firms have both dedicated in-house e-discovery teams and software tools. Software solutions are available for searching, processing, documenting, and reviewing ESI.

Partnering with vendors or service providers

Vendors can provide services that assist in two areas of e-discovery: add needed expertise and control costs. Some vendors offer a one-stop-shop approach to e-discovery. Others offer specialized legal or IT expertise. They might provide valuable assistance in the collection, processing production, and storage of ESI. They might add a second set of eyes for consulting or data forensics that require independent experts to authenticate and establish a chain of custody.

The costs must be weighed against the benefits they can provide. Some solutions can be very costly. The expenses are front-loaded in the litigation process, but they may end up being a savings. Much of this is a matter of what services are needed. For example, it is not unusual for a law firm to hire contract lawyers for document review. The downside to outside vendors or consultants is a loss of some control and less communication than having it done in house.

Selecting experts or consulting companies

You bear the ultimate responsibility for the actions of your attorney and other vendors and consultants. The courts show little sympathy for a sloppy, late, or ill-conceived discovery search protocol simply because an outside vendor did it.

All cases are not the same and involve unique issues. An outside vendor must be able to tailor the services to the needs of the case. That also requires the ability to adjust midstream to changes as the case unfolds. Experience cannot be understated. State of the art technology can improve vendor performance, but ultimately, a human element comes into play.

It is important that you get to know your vendors or consultants to develop a good working relationship. You may want to consider the following process to select a vendor:

1. **Submit a request for information (RFI).**

   An RFI allows you to ask for information about the skill level, staff, experience, software, and services offered. Ask for references and consider interviewing vendors that submit RFIs so you can get a better feel for a possible working relationship.

2. **Submit a request for proposal (RFP).**

   The RFP sets forth the services that you require and asks for a proposal for those services. You should include a series of measurements of vendor performance. These will include assurances of timely performance and quality assurance. You may also want to include assurance that the most up-to-date technology will be used in your project.

3. **Negotiate a contract.**

   After you focus on a vendor, you will negotiate the final terms of the contract. Be sure to include performance metrics.

Many law firms use litigation and production support software. Your attorney should have someone who is well versed in the technology assigned to the e-discovery aspects of the action. Smaller firms may not have this luxury and may rely more on manpower or outside vendors or consultants. You should know this up front. This should not be a disqualifying point but you should make sure that you know whom the vendor is and what will be done. You may wish to be involved in the selection of an outside firm that will be doing the e-discovery work. This is more often a problem in a small case where the attorneys may not be large firms. In most complex litigation, you will find larger firms with full litigation support within the firm.

Chapter 17

e-Discovery for Small Cases

In This Chapter

▶ Profiling small cases

▶ Hunting and gathering e-evidence

▶ Keeping a lid on costs

▶ Looking at e-evidence in small cases

▶ Figuring out whether it's real or fake

*E*lectronic discovery is not always extensive, complex, or wildly expensive. It's used in many types of legal actions where the dollar amount in dispute isn't great (less than $100,000), there's not a large quantity of ESI to go through, or there's only one or a few data custodians who also might be one of the parties in the lawsuit. Small-matter litigation are common occurrences in both state and federal courts. Breach of contract, Internet defamation, divorce, or custody disputes, which fall under state law, and theft of intellectual property or trade secrets, personal bankruptcy, employment discrimination, and harassment heard in federal courts are examples. Much of small litigation is *person-vs-person,* in contrast to *enterprise-vs-enterprise,* litigation. People operate their lives from their digital devices, leaving histories that, if properly handled, may be admissible in court.

In this chapter, you find out how e-discovery can be affordable and critical to discovering the truth in small cases. These cases don't require a full arsenal of litigation support services or a fully stocked e-discovery team. The price tag for cases that are *e-discovery light* can come in under $2,000. You also read about the rule on proportionality, which keeps e-discovery within the scale of the value at issue. Establishing and protecting the integrity of the e-evidence plays a big role because often opponents know each other and have access to each other's laptops and cellphones. And you also read how IT policies that allow personal use of company-owned laptops or cellphone devices make those devices subject to forensic search in domestic and other personal cases.

Defining Small Cases that Can Benefit from e-Discovery

Harassment or discrimination cases can result from ill-fated relationships between an employee and non-employee (or two employees) who text, tweet, e-mail, or send compromising photos via your company's networks or devices. Other types of small cases that can implicate your company or its computer and cellular resources are labor disputes, wrongful terminations, corporate espionage, or trademark or intellectual property disputes. All of these cases can land one or more of your company's hard drives or flash drives in court. The hard or flash drive can come from work computers, personal laptops, or personal and business cellphones.

Theft of proprietary data and breaches of contract

You work for a small to medium enterprise (SME), and you're concerned that an employee who's leaving is sending privileged information via the company's e-mail system to the new employer. Certainly leaving such obvious clues is outright dumb, yet it's widespread — in part, because some people take the path of least effort. The departing employee may mistakenly believe that by deleting the sent messages, the evidence is gone. Theft of intellectual property or breach of contracts leave obvious trails and details that you can use to recover losses due to the theft.

Some terminated employees may steal customer or product data to improve their job opportunities with a new employer. In addition to traditional state remedies, such as misappropriation of trade secrets, you can take advantage of the federal Computer Fraud and Abuse Act's (CFAA) civil remedies to sue former employees and their new companies to get compensated for your losses.

Marital matters

E-mail, GPS, and cellphone logs; Web photo albums (such as Google's Picasa Web Albums, at `http://picasa.google.com`); and postings on social networks give divorce lawyers many avenues of proof of misconduct.

If you have evidence that at any relevant e-evidence is stored on your spouse's hard drive, you can file an e-discovery request seeking complete access to the hard drive. You may even be granted access to password-protected files if there's a reasonable possibility that such files contain relevant evidence.

Your company can become a third party to divorce cases. For example, in a divorce case brought against an executive vice president (EVP) on the grounds of adultery, the plaintiff may seek to discover the defendant's texts, e-mails, and incoming and outgoing phone records from the company-issued BlackBerry. The plaintiff may subpoena the EVP's employer for access to the defendant's desktop and laptop computers. The EVP's messages may contain references to corporate trade secrets and to attorney-client-privileged matters with corporate counsel that are unrelated to the divorce action. You may need to hire forensic computer experts and lawyers to preserve and remove all privileged ESI. If you're in this situation, see Chapter 13, where we talk about computer forensics specialists.

When parties are emotionally embroiled, that volcanic situation has the power to interfere with the e-discovery process and even make cost concerns secondary or irrelevant to a personal agenda. Nowhere is that more true than in bitter divorce cases. As you can find out in the later section, "Characterizing Small Matters," your company computers and handhelds may become discoverable in marital cases.

Defamation and Internet defamation

Defamation can lead to a lawsuit. Defamation is a false statement that damages a person's reputation and exposes that person to public contempt, hatred, ridicule, or condemnation. If the false statement is published in print or through broadcast media, such as radio or TV, it's *libel*. If the defamation is spoken, it's *slander*.

You must usually prove these three things for defamation:

- ✔ The statement was published. Someone had to see or hear the statement.
- ✔ The statement is false. The statement that's made about the person has to be more than only an opinion.
- ✔ A person or company's reputation was damaged in some way.

Defamatory statements made in blogs or text messages (including those on Twitter) are leading to lawsuits. The first libel suit against a Twitter user was filed in a United States court in March 2009. Singer Courtney Love was sued for libel for her allegedly defaming remarks about fashion designer Dawn Simorangkir on Twitter and MySpace. This lawsuit is one of a growing class of suits against bloggers, posters, tweeters, and social media users. You can't hide if you've posted something that is defamatory.

In 2009, the Media Law Resource Center (`www.medialaw.org`) tracked 258 Web-related U.S. lawsuits. That number was a steep increase from 110 cases in 2008. The lawsuits included defamation, copyright infringement, and fake profiles on social network sites such as MySpace and Facebook. Blog postings made up the majority of Internet-related lawsuits.

Characterizing Small Matters

Electronic discovery may be the only method that allows you to easily find evidence and win your case. Electronic evidence in the form of e-mail messages of secret relationships or attachments with stolen client lists are pretty much irrefutable.

Keeping ESI out of evidence

One of the most common defense methods in small-matter cases is to file a motion arguing that the e-evidence is inadmissible because the device was illegally accessed and/or the e-evidence was improperly obtained. It's tempting for cost reasons to underestimate the importance of retaining a computer forensics expert to create a forensic image the hard drive and to later attest to the e-mails' authenticity. The risks you face for giving in to that temptation are not being able to defend yourself in court because the opponent shot down your unauthenticated e-mail evidence. Without any chance of a do-over, your case may be doomed.

Here are some motions to have ESI excluded from the case, along with the conditions under which they're effective or the reasons why they fail:

- ✔ **Wiretap violation:** A wiretap is a device attached to a communication system to listen in on what's being sent over the wire, so to speak. Wireless communication can also be wiretapped to eavesdrop. Wiretapping is illegal because it violates our right to privacy. The wiretap statute only covers messages that are intercepted while in transit. The statute does not cover messages that are stored on a hard drive or flash drive after the transmission has ended. Arguments that you've accessed either sent or received e-mail or text messages illegally because of the wiretap statute won't succeed because those messages are *at rest*, and not *in transit*.

- ✔ **Privacy invasion:** Privacy is the right to be left alone. Privacy protection requires that reasonable efforts were made to actually protect privacy. You can't expect to have privacy if you've not taken or implemented security defenses to ensure privacy-protected conditions. Here are a couple of scenarios where privacy wasn't protected:

  - • When a computer is in a kitchen, family room, or other shared space where it is (or can be) used by both spouses, a claim of invasion of privacy has no foundation, even if the computer is employer-owned.

  - • When access to a computer is not password protected and files are not password protected or encrypted, you haven't got a prayer in an expectation of privacy motion.

For example, in a 2004 Connecticut divorce case, the husband wanted to search his wife's laptop to help his case. (In Connecticut, it's legally relevant if one partner is responsible for the marriage collapse.) Stamford Superior Court Judge Kevin Tierney ordered the wife to stop using her laptop and turn it over immediately to the court clerk's office.

Shared characteristics with large cases

Cases of all sizes share common characteristics. You use e-discovery in small or personal cases to learn the truth of the matter and to win your case, just as you do in complex litigation. Arguments about privilege to keep some e-evidence inadmissible are common to both. However, e-discovery in small matters has unique characteristics and would not be (or would not need to be) managed as a scaled-down version of large or complex e-discovery. Using the full strength of complex litigation support could amount to using a bulldozer to pick violets.

Companies involved in occasional small matters may choose to manage those cases as they do large cases if they have litigation support services available, or as a matter of policy. Chapter 16 covers how to handle large cases, if that's how you choose to conduct your small case.

No matter what the type of case, several issues are essentially the same. Here are nine characteristics that large and small cases tend to have in common:

- The outcome or resolution may be based on budget constraints instead of the merits of the case.
- You file motions and counter-motions to include or exclude ESI to be resolved by the court or a Special Master. A Special Master is a neutral expert appointed by the court to act as a referee for the parties and to advise the judge. The Special Master may be a lawyer with technical expertise or an IT expert appointed by the court to help resolve e-discovery disputes.
- Disputes arise over what's protected and what's not.
- Electronic evidence can be hidden or fabricated.
- ESI of third parties may be subject to e-discovery.
- Electronic evidence needs to be authenticated in order to be admissible.
- Cutthroat tactics can be the norm.
- The proportionality rule applies in that courts will not compel you to pay more for e-discovery than the value of the case, unless there's good cause. You read more on this topic in the upcoming "Curbing e-Discovery with Proportionality" section.

✔ **Federal or state rules of civil procedure and evidence apply.** The typical small matter is tried in state courts and, therefore, isn't subject to the amended federal rules, but your state may have adopted comparable rules. As of mid-2009, 21 states have added e-discovery amendments to their civil rules. Check with your lawyer about specific state laws.

Unique characteristics and dynamics

Small cases have several unique characteristics and dynamics that affect the handling of ESI or the e-discovery process. Small cases have one or more of the following characteristics:

✔ ***Individual vs. Individual, (20##):*** A big difference is who's suing whom. Both parties in the case may be individuals, such as in defamation, certain types of contracts, negligence, divorces, or child custody cases. Even if a case is a personal matter between individuals who may be business partners, co-workers, worker and supervisor, former friends, or soon-to-be former spouses, companies may become involved if responsive e-mail, photos, or text messages are sent via company-owned equipment.

✔ ***Employee vs. Employer (20##):*** The plaintiff is an employee filing a suit against the company or another employee, who could be the supervisor.

✔ **Low case value:** Value of the case is $100,000 or less, assuming that the plaintiff has valued the case realistically.

This upper-bound is not a hard and fast amount that separates all cases into small-case or large-case categories. The value of the case may be much lower.

We've seen cases where the plaintiff sues for a ridiculously high and round number, like a million dollars. That's not grounded in reality. Baseless valuations may be an attempt to intimidate the defendant into settling the case. Settlement can consist of a series of pretrial maneuvers that may lead to a resolution of the case by a monetary or some other nonfinancial agreement. Cases may be settled with an apology, granted a big monetary award, or the defendant publicly admitting a wrong against the plaintiff.

Some lawsuits are filed by parties even though they know the case has no merit or justification. Courts refer to them as *frivolous litigation.*

✔ **Low cost of e-discovery or computer forensics:** Cost of the e-discovery, including the forensics work, may be as low as $2,000, but likely under $20,000. The circumstances of the case may require only an expert who can review and analyze the e-evidence and provide an opinion.

✔ **Few data repositories:** Electronic evidence can be found on one or two computers or digital devices; or the data may need to be provided by an Internet service provider (ISP), for which a subpoena or court order would be needed.

✔ **Instant onset:** There may not be a prelitigation or litigation-readiness stage. In domestic disputes, future defendants would be concerned with trying to eradicate ESI and not preserve it. That is, if the individual even thinks about it at all.

The frequency with which indiscretions are caught because of personal collections of reveal-all messages shows that people don't learn from the destroyed careers and messed-up lives of others.

Putting aside ethical or moral issues, the chances of indiscreet messages being exposed are darn high. But then, the over-the-top lavishness of Las Vegas exists because people refuse to believe that the laws of probability apply to them.

✔ **Emotional decisions:** What a case lacks in value it can more than make up for in passion and drama. One or both of the parties may make decisions that are driven by a strong emotion (such as payback) or by the attitude that "it's the principle of the thing," which may not make economic sense.

Even if a company is not one of the litigating parties, company-issued laptops, PDAs, and cellphones may be targeted for evidence. As you read in the nearby sidebar, e-discovery may not involve a litigation team or support services.

Proceeding in Small Cases

Procedures to follow in e-discovery for small cases can amount to a single step. You hire a computer forensics expert who performs the investigation live in court.

But that approach would be unusual. Lawyers ask judges for court orders to seize computers and cellphones and copy the drives, particularly if there is an opportunity to glimpse a couple's full financial picture, or whether a person is suitable to be a child's custodian.

You retain your own computer forensic or e-discovery expert to investigate, review, and give an opinion about the e-evidence and IT issues. We cover computer forensic methods in Chapter 13.

A computer is a filing cabinet without e-discovery immunity

In 2007, a wife (the plaintiff) filed for divorce, citing cruel and inhumane treatment and her husband's extramarital relationship with a woman he met in an online chat room. The plaintiff had found several hundred pages of incriminating instant messages (IMs) on a laptop that her husband, a retired IT consultant, left in the trunk of a car. The sole issue being disputed was the ownership of the laptop, and not the specifics of the IMs. If the wife had no right to access the laptop, the IMs would not be admissible evidence, and she could not use them to support her position.

The wife claimed the laptop was used by the family. The husband argued that the laptop was issued by his employer for his use. The defendant's lawyer filed a motion to suppress the contents of the laptop on the grounds that the wife had improperly seized his personal, work-issued computer. The wife's lawyer contested the motion, citing, among other precedents, *Byrne v. Byrne* (2002) in which Brooklyn Supreme Court Justice William Rigler compared a home computer to a filing cabinet. Justice Rigler wrote

"Clearly, plaintiff could have access to the contents of a file cabinet left in the marital residence. In the same fashion she should have access to the contents of the computer."

New York Supreme Court Justice Saralee Evans ruled that the wife's actions did not constitute computer trespass nor had she used a computer without authorization because the files were on a readily accessible computer. In her ruling, the judge also cited the filing cabinet analogy. Justice Evans denied the husband's motion to suppress, stating

"Defendant states that only he was authorized to log on and that his password was a 'strong one.' Plaintiff's expert [attests] that no files on the computer were encrypted and no passwords were required."

The judge ruled that the company-issued laptop was subject to e-discovery because, in effect, it was a mixed-use laptop — for both business and personal use.

When a computer is shared by the family, or couples have revealed their passwords to each other, reading a spouse's e-mail messages and introducing them as evidence in a divorce case is often allowed. Authenticity may or may not become a challenging issue, depending on whether the person whose e-mail is revealed denies sending them or that they were accurate.

Here are the key steps for managing e-discovery in small matters:

1. **Find out what access or contact the other party has had with the devices, storing potentially relevant ESI, as well as the ESI itself.**

   Prior to the filing of a case, the other party may have close proximity to the devices or ESI, or may own them. She's had the opportunity to snoop around e-mail, spreadsheets, financial programs, Internet histories, and so on. She may have conducted a do-it-yourself type of search and already seen or collected the ESI. Suspicious individuals, in an effort to find the truth, may have installed keystroke loggers to computers, obtained cellphone logs, or snooped through computers and handhelds, opening files and messages. Possibly the other party has already seen the e-evidence and knows exactly where it is, or has made a copy of the files or messages.

Opening files puts a big dent in their integrity and compromises their use as evidence. Stay away from using any compromised ESI that could weaken your case. Do-it-yourself e-discovery tactics — such as hacking a computer or installing spyware on it — most likely are illegal or could compromise the ESI. Spyware programs may violate federal and state wiretap laws, leading to large-scale lawsuits over their use.

2. **Send a preservation letter.**

   The next step is to compose and send a preservation letter notifying the other party not to delete responsive ESI or destroy the hardware on which it's stored. The letter informs him to stop using, accessing, turning on, powering, copying, deleting, removing, or uninstalling any programs, files, or folders; or booting up. You can find examples of preservation letters in Chapter 7.

3. **Retain a computer or mobile forensics expert.**

   In many cases, you'll need a forensics expert. Your expert might refute your opponent's expert on the interpretation of the ESI.

   Hiring a computer forensics expert is necessary when you've made a motion to have the other party turn over a computer or cell device to have hard drives copied. If the court grants the motion, she has to turn the computer or device over to your computer forensics expert or the court clerk immediately. The expert makes a forensics copy of each hard drive and places those copies with the court clerk. Most likely, those files are not accessed or reviewed until stipulation by both you and your opponent or on further order from the court. The holdup on the review of the ESI is due to privilege and confidentiality issues. Unlike complex litigation, where ESI is reviewed for privilege before producing it, all ESI is produced when the hard drive is surrendered.

If you have confidential or privileged e-mails or documents on a hard drive, prepare a privilege log listing any documents that should be exempt from discovery. We talk about privilege logs in Chapter 10.

4. **Review and analyze the reports of both forensic experts.**

   After the forensics expert has examined the drives for responsive ESI, she prepares a report detailing the facts about what was found, interprets those facts, and draws inferences and opinions. The expert's report is given to your opposing party, whose expert reviews the facts, interpretations, and inferences — and most likely reports another opinion. Both opinions are then reviewed and used in negotiations to reach a settlement or proceed to trial.

Forensic accountants follow financial scents

In fraud, dissipation of assets, embezzlement, or financial legal matters involving small amounts, you need the specialized knowledge of a forensic accountant. The forensic accountant gathers evidence from accounting programs for personal or small-business use, such as QuickBooks or Quicken, and other records from hard drives and e-mail. Those records or transactions are then carefully traced back to the source of fraud. In addition, forensic accountants assist in bankruptcy cases. Evidence is gathered to check for suspicious financial activity surrounding the case. Copywriting and patent infringement, insurance fraud, personal injury, and construction audits are among the kinds of cases when a forensic accountant is called in to investigate. Hiring both a computer forensic expert and forensic accountant may be necessary if opinions are needed on password-protected files or Internet activities.

Curbing e-Discovery with Proportionality

Federal or state rules put a limit on e-discovery costs. Judges decide when discovery cost is proportional to measures of value of the case. Decisions are based on estimates of these two values:

- **Case value:** The lawsuit specifies an amount being sought by the plaintiff from the defendant.

- **Probative value of the evidence:** This value is a measure of how worthwhile the evidence is to the elements of the case. The evidence value looks at the significance or how likely the evidence affects the outcome of the case from the perspective of the judge or jury.

The *proportionality rule* (it's FRCP 26(b)(2)) requires that discovery be limited by the court if

the burden or expense of the proposed discovery outweighs its likely benefit, considering the needs of the case, the amount in controversy, the parties' resources, the importance of the issues at stake in the litigation, and the importance of the proposed discovery in resolving the issues.

Sleuthing Personal Correspondence and Files

Authenticating e-evidence is potentially the thorniest question in e-discovery, but it's one that has received very little attention in the courts. Authenticating digital evidence in civil trials has not gotten a lot of judicial attention, in part because most civil cases never go to trial, but also because lawyers and judges tend to treat it no different than paper evidence.

The question of the foundation and authentication of electronic records is a complicated problem. Anyone with editing software such as Adobe Photoshop can create fakes of almost any type of file or photo. Courts have to figure out what's real and what's not.

Magistrate Judge Paul Grimm addressed authenticating e-evidence in his ruling in *Lorraine v. Markel Am. Ins. Co.* Both parties tried to enter copies of e-mails in support of their motions for summary judgment in a $36,000 insurance claim. Grimm ordered both parties to resubmit their evidence because neither had made an attempt to authenticate the messages.

Problems are best avoided by asking for or acquiring the original, electronic version of a file, or making a forensic copy of the original. You read about forensic copies in Chapter 1.

For the most part, courts have interpreted the rules for authenticating ESI as simply as possible. For example, in *United States v. Tank* (2000), the court allowed chat room records entered into evidence when the government

> presented evidence sufficient to allow a reasonable juror to find that the chat room log printouts were authenticated.

In this case, sufficient evidence consisted of testimony of another chat room member. In most cases, courts have ruled that as long as the party introducing e-evidence can produce an expert or witness who can claim that the records appear to be authentic, it's generally entered into evidence.

Part VII
The Part of Tens

The 5th Wave   By Rich Tennant

What's the chance of settling this without getting attorneys involved?

HARVARD LAW SCHOOL ALUMNI PICNIC

ANTS, GNATS AND BEES

In this part . . .

This seventh part of the book addresses three top questions about e-discovery: what are the top rules ruling e-discovery (Chapter 18), how do I keep an edge on my opponents (Chapter 19), and the #1 self-help chapter, what do judges expect me to know walking into an e-discovery case (Chapter 20).

In Chapter 18, you have the top ten e-discovery rules explained to you. You'll find this chapter has exactly what you need to know. And we can verify that you can't find a listing of ten rules so perfectly explained anywhere else.

In Chapter 19, we give you a roadmap to e-discovery resources and commentary to keep you informed and dangerously armed to win. You'll want to leverage and advance your legal and technical e-discovery knowledge, which we help you with. If you see either of us at any of these conferences or vendor events, come over and say hi.

In Chapter 20, we provide lessons from those who suffered terrible fates and the wrath of judges to bring them to you. Unless you were born on the sun, you'll want to know about these incredibly hot legal spots to avoid.

Chapter 18

Ten Most Important e-Discovery Rules

In This Chapter

▶ Mastering the most critical procedural rules

▶ Sticking to the rules of evidence

. . . .

*I*n this chapter, we briefly present the top-ranked rules of procedure and rules of evidence around which to build your e-discovery strategy. These rules potentially determine your e-discovery success, so think of them as the top ten things you want to know to stay in control. They're guides to help you dodge debilitating blows, such as getting hit with a sanction, adverse inference, loss of privilege protection, or the full costs of e-discovery.

You also hope your opponents are clueless about these rules so that when they make a mistake, you can turn it into your advantage. Whatever your preferred perspective, here's your handy reference for the biggest rules.

FRCP 26 (b) (2) (B) Specific Limitations on ESI

Rule 26(b)(2)(B) debuted the concept of *not reasonably accessible (NRA)* electronically stored information. The concept of *not reasonably accessible paper* had not existed, or at least it wasn't recognized in discovery in the past. Traditionally, the responding party paid the expenses of complying with discovery requests. But that was before the world shifted from paper to digital copy. This rule provides procedures for shifting the cost of accessing NRA to the requesting party.

With this rule, ESI is broken into two classes (or tiers) based on how attainable it is. Table 18-1 shows the two tiers.

Table 18-1	Accessibility of ESI
Reasonably Accessible	*Not Reasonably Accessible*
E-mail, data, and files on hard drives or actively used devices and networks	Data or files that need to be retrieved using computer forensics methods
Data on flash drives, CDs, DVDs	Un-indexed, hard-to-search backup tapes
ESI on backup tapes in use	ESI stored on obsolete media
ESI routinely accessed through the normal course of operations.	ESI that was automatically deleted according to a good faith data retention/ disposal policy

You're being thrown a lifeline, which is avoiding the cost of getting the old or legacy storage media and their contents into searchable condition, but you have to be prepared to grab onto it. You must know where your ESI is so you can convince the judge that it's NRA. This rule turns on the judge's decision. It's literally a judgment call. Courts may demand detailed descriptions of the precise burdens and costs associated with the collection and production of ESI, which in itself can be a big pain to prepare.

You also need to grab this lifeline while it's there for you because the rule is protective and only protective. It's not a rebate. That means its intent is to protect you from undue costs. In the case of *Cason-Merenda v. Detroit Medical Center (2008)*, Detroit Medical asked for cost shifting under FRCP 26(b)(2)(B) after it had produced the requested ESI. The court refused. FRCP 26(b)(2)(B) is intended to provide protective relief before you bear the undue burden or cost.

Include the word *reasonably* instead of taking a shortcut. Use the entire term *not reasonably accessible* because the term *inaccessible* has a much narrower meaning. Your opponent may try to argue that your ESI is not inaccessible. Spare yourself having to defend against that argument by not opening that door.

Rule 26(b)(2)(C) factors may weigh strongly in favor of e-discovery of not reasonably accessible ESI if the information sought is highly relevant, not duplicative, and cannot be obtained from other sources.

FRCP 26 (b) (5) (B) Protecting Trial-Preparation Materials and Clawback

You have a duty to disclose responsive ESI, but some things are sacred. The duty does not apply to protected material, such as your secret recipe or formula, trade secrets, intellectual property, or materials prepared in preparation for the possible trial. The duty to disclose also does not apply to privileged material (between you and an attorney, for example).

However, mistakes happen. Too many (or not enough) people are involved, there isn't enough time to purge the privileged content from the ESI you're producing, or documents are redacted superficially or incompletely. The point is, you inadvertently gave away protected materials and you want them back.

FRCP 26(b)(5)(B) gives courts a clear (or at least a clearer) procedure for settling claims if you hand over ESI to the requesting party that you shouldn't have. Typically, when privileged ESI is inadvertently sent to the requesting party, you may get the privileged material returned or destroyed if a clawback agreement exists between the parties and you move fast. For privileged attorney-client and work product–protected ESI, FRE 502 bolsters FRCP 26(b)(5)(B) by maintaining the privilege or protection for inadvertently disclosed ESI. The carpenter's principle of *measure twice, cut once* applies here.

Specify the scope of your right to clawback inadvertently produced privileged information with your opponent and exercise that right as soon as you make an inadvertent disclosure. A clawback agreement enables you to get back inadvertently disclosed ESI, or have it destroyed, or at least not be used by the opposing party. Clawback allows for more liberal and timely e-discovery while still protecting your privilege, confidentiality, or work product protection. But local rules may have different procedures and timelines.

Rule 16(b)(6) permits inclusion of your agreements regarding non-waiver and clawback of privilege material in case management and scheduling orders.

FRCP 26 (a) (1) (C) Time for Pretrial Disclosures; Objections

FRCP 26(a)(1)(C) states that you must make any initial disclosures no later than 14 days after the Rule 26(f) meet-and-confer session unless there's an objection or another time is set by stipulation or court order. If you have an objection, now is the time to voice it. If you don't recognize your objection soon enough, you may have missed your chance.

In ruling on the objection, the court must determine what ESI disclosures, if any, are to be made and must set the time for disclosure.

FRCP 26 (f) Conference of the Parties; Planning for Discovery

Rule 26(f) is the meet-and-confer session. This rule forces all parties to meet within 99 days of the filing of the lawsuit and at least 21 days before a scheduled conference. At this get-together, you're supposed to play nice to discuss the nature of the claims and the ESI to back them up. The intent of this rule is to speed up or increase the possibility of a quick settlement. Judges expect you to resolve any disputes between yourselves — or at least attempt to do so.

Before you meet and confer, your attorney has a duty to become familiar with your ESI. He should meet with IT personnel to identify where and how ESI is stored, how accessible it is, and the estimated cost of retrieval. He needs to arrive armed with this intelligence to strike a good deal (or at least avoid being duped into a bad one).

Your attorney should also have a good idea of the relevant ESI that the other side may have in its possession. Further, he should make an initial determination of any relevant ESI that a third party may possess. You should also know who's going to be your company's FRCP 30(b)(6) witness, also known as a deposition designate. Rule 30(b)(6) requires you to designate one or more individuals to prepare for and testify on behalf of your company during deposition. You read about witnesses later in "FRCP 30(b)(6) Designation of a Witness" section.

In complex civil litigation or those involving huge volumes of ESI, a single meet-and-confer session is not enough. You may need to investigate your ESI more thoroughly and even come back with consultants to help understand technical issues.

FRCP 26 (g) Signing Disclosures and Discovery Requests, Responses, and Objections

A favorite e-discovery enforcement tool of the federal bench is Rule 26(g). Judges use Rule 26(g) as a stick to deal with e-discovery abuses. In *Mancia v. Mayflower Textile Services Co.* (2008), Magistrate Judge Grimm explained:

"The rule aspires to eliminate one of the most prevalent of all discovery abuses: kneejerk discovery requests served without consideration of cost or burden to the responding party as well as ending the equally abusive practice of objecting to discovery requests reflexively — but not reflectively — and without a factual basis."

Rule 26(g) is not subtle. It demands that an attorney sign every e-discovery request, response, or objection. The signing attorney is certifying that, to the best of his or her knowledge and belief formed after a reasonable inquiry, the request, response, or objection is genuine and not an attempt to undermine the system.

Rule 26(g) imposes mandatory sanctions on lawyers for violations that are not substantially justified. The sanction may include an order to pay the reasonable expenses, including attorney's fees, caused by the violation. The signature of the attorney also serves as yours.

FRCP 30(b)(6) Designation of a Witness

The responding party has to designate at least one witness who can testify on behalf of an enterprise. That witness is cleverly referred to as the 30(b)(6) witness, and that person has a duty to be knowledgeable enough to testify.

The 30(b)(6) witness's role is to explain your company's operations, such as IT infrastructure, data retention policies, or accounting practices, that relate to the case as well as how and where responsive ESI is stored and managed. Often, the witness needs to testify on the steps taken to find and produce requested documents to ensure that efforts were done in good faith. This witness does not actually testify on the facts of the case.

The role of the witness is most critical if you don't produce all the requested ESI or fail to produce meaningful documents. In those situations, the witness needs to present a convincing explanation for what appears to be the lack of good faith cooperation.

For large or complex cases, you may need more than one witness. If a witness cannot answer the questions, you're in trouble because you've failed to comply with the rule and may have to either produce another witness or face a sanction. Using an unprepared or panic-stricken witness is like failing to appear, which may also lead to a sanction, and risks losing the court's confidence, which is never a smart move. Conversely, a 30(b)(6) witness can persuade a judge you did everything you could to produce the ESI.

Be careful what you share with your witnesses because witness preparation is discoverable. If you show privileged documents to your witness, you may find them suddenly unprivileged and have to hand them over to the other party.

FRCP 34 (b) Form of Production

To stop arguments about the form of production, FRCP 34(b) establishes protocols for how documents are produced to requesting parties.

As the requesting party, you get to choose the form of production. Typically, you want to request native files because they could have potentially damaging metadata or show the history of track changes.

Don't forget to specify a format for ESI, because you might not otherwise like what you get from the responding party. The other party can choose a form of ESI production that's as they ordinarily maintain it. You might not have the equipment or expertise to read the ESI easily if it's not in a form you pick.

As the responding party, you produce the ESI in the form that's been requested. You can object to the requesting party's form of production and state your own format. If the requesting party opposes the suggested format, that party has to take action. But if you drag your feet in producing, the court may find that the delay wipes out your objection and then you have to hand over the ESI in the form the requesting party wants.

Ford Motor Co. v. Edgewood Props. (2009) stemmed from allegations about contaminated concrete following the demolition of a Ford plant in New Jersey. Edgewood's initial document request called for ESI production in native format, which implies *with metadata*. Ford responded by informing Edgewood that it intended to produce TIFF (tagged image file format) files with accompanying searchable text instead of producing in native format. Edgewood left this disagreement over format unresolved. As such, Ford proceeded to produce its documents as TIFFs in March 2008, August 2008, and November 2008. Again, Edgewood did not disagree with the production format at these times. In January 2009, Edgewood sought to compel reproduction of Ford's documents in native format, as originally requested. The court denied the motion. Edgewood lost its chance to control the form of production by its non-response, and the court allowed Ford to use the form they wanted. Ford counted on Edgewood's non-response — and it worked.

Rule 34(b) also requires that the documents that you produce to your opponent be reasonably usable. Case law has further defined that to mean that you should organize, index, and identify your ESI so the documents can be read or used by the other party. What that long statement is saying is that you can't data dump: You can't dump a mess of documents on your opponent and expect him to figure out how to extract the data he needs. Some parties have tested this principle, and reconfirmed the rule was not merely a suggestion. *In re Payment Card Interchange Fee & Merchant Discount Antitrust Litigation* (2007), the judge ruled that producing documents in non-searchable form violates Rule 34(b). In *3M Company v. Kanbar* (2007), the judge found that producing 170 boxes of unorganized data did not meet the requirements imposed by the rule.

Choosing hard copy production waives production in electronic format.

FRCP 37 (e) Safe Harbor from Sanctions for Loss of ESI

It's not possible to retain all ESI that's created or generated. Companies reuse backup tapes, which overwrite older data and files. Servers crash. New systems are implemented and older ones retired. ESI loss will happen in any of those examples. ESI that you cannot produce because you have lost it exposes you to spoliation sanctions, which are deliberately harsh to act as a deterrent.

Rule 37(e) creates a safe harbor from sanctions if you did not preserve, and therefore no longer have, ESI that's requested provided that certain conditions and circumstances are met.

Rule 37(e), of course, doesn't apply if you deliberately destroyed the ESI. Your chance of a safe harbor is zero.

A key to falling within the safety of Rule 37(e) is having a written electronic records management policy and routine procedures, and following them consistently.

Once your duty to preserve kicks in, you need to take affirmative action to stop routine procedures that could destroy the responsive ESI. Forgetting to stop the destruction or waiting a while before stopping is negligence. Negligence, ironically, destroys your safe harbor.

Rule 37(e) is like the rule of last resort. You're required to meet and confer to limit scope of discovery and discuss the forms of production, among other things, before judges are required to get involved. Failing to work through those rules in good faith may result in sanctions under Rule 37(e).

Federal Rules of Evidence 502(b) Inadvertent Disclosure

We switch now from rules of procedure to Federal Rules of Evidence. Rule 502(b) Inadvertent Disclosure may give you protection when attorney-client privileged– or work product–protected material is inadvertently disclosed. By now, you know that nothing comes easy. There are always strings attached. Here are three of the strings needed to be covered by the rule:

✔ The disclosure had to be inadvertent.

✔ You (as the holder of the privilege or protection) took reasonable steps to prevent disclosure.

✔ You noticed and responded promptly to your error and took reasonable steps to fix the error.

Federal Rule of Evidence 901 Requirement of Authentication or Identification

In e-discovery, so much attention is grabbed by what is and is not reasonably accessible, meeting schedules and deadlines, and motions to compel or resist being compelled, that one serious issue is largely ignored: ESI being used as evidence. Evidence has to be admissible. One requirement of admissibility is that the evidence is what it claims to be; that is, it must be authenticated.

Magistrate Judge Paul Grimm discussed admissibility of ESI as evidence in *Lorraine v. Markel* (2007), stating

> "Considering the significant costs associated with discovery of ESI, it makes little sense to go to all the bother and expense to get electronic information only to have it excluded from evidence or rejected from consideration during summary judgment because the proponent cannot lay a sufficient foundation to get it admitted. The process is complicated by the fact that ESI comes in multiple evidentiary 'flavors,' including e-mail, Web site ESI, Internet postings, digital photographs, and computer-generated documents and data files."

Under Federal Rule of Evidence 901, the authentication requirement needed for admissibility is met rather simply. ESI may be authenticated by testimony that a matter is what it is claimed to be. Whether the ESI evidence is authentic is a fact question for the jury to decide. Metadata may be used to authenticate an ESI.

Chapter 19

Ten Ways to Keep an Edge on Your e-Discovery Expertise

In This Chapter

▶ Bookmarking e-discovery favorites

▶ Finding brief and lengthy commentary from e-discovery leaders

▶ Checking out case summaries

▶ Making use of government and university sites

*E*lectronic-discovery is an exciting, evolving, and at times exasperating practice field. Every new IT gadget and communication method adds to the volume of ESI, necessitates updates in retention policies, and causes a bear of a time trying to throw a legal hold around it. Corporate and personal blogging and text messaging can sink cases just as easily as e-mail. With new tech toys rolling in continually, you want to top off your knowledge periodically.

Keeping up with the riveting action — the scores, fumbles, and judgment calls — can be a snap. In this chapter, we cover ten resources worth bookmarking on ESI, case law, judicial opinions, and news and commentary on everything e-discovery related. Some are brief, some are lengthy, and some offer interactive search.

We present these resources in groups that hail from organizations (.org), commercial sites (.com), government (.gov), and university (.edu) sites. All are free resources, but face it; someone has to be paying the bills. There may be some vendor influence.

The Sedona Conference and Working Group Series

www.thesedonaconference.org

Staying informed about e-discovery would not be complete without The Sedona Conference at the top of your reading list. It's the undisputed thought leader in this field. The Sedona Conference is a nonprofit educational organization founded in 1997 that exists to provide a place for judges, lawyers, academics, and other legal experts in e-discovery, complex litigation, intellectual property, and antitrust law to collaborate on cutting-edge issues. It is highly influential in creating the standards of e-discovery.

E-discovery pioneer and attorney Kenneth Withers (www.kenwithers.com) is the director of judicial education at The Sedona Conference. Ken was greatly involved in the federal rules amendment process.

In 2008, The Sedona Conference launched a multi-year, multi-pronged effort to promote greater cooperation in e-discovery and to restore sanity to pre-trial practice. A document called the *Cooperation Proclamation* outlines its call for action and lists federal and state judges who have signed on to its principles.

The Sedona Conference has various components and special committees:

- ✔ The Working Group Series (WGS) launched in 2002. Each working group is a mini think tank that works through challenging issues facing the legal system. The WGS receives financial support from private sponsors. You see the list of working groups, their charges, and links to the publications at www.thesedonaconference.org/wgs. Publications are copyrighted, but free and downloadable from the site.

- ✔ The Sedona Conference Institute (TSCI) is the continuing legal education extension of The Sedona Conference WGS that offers programs once or twice per year. You see their list of topics at www.thesedona conference.org/tsci_html.

- ✔ The *Voices from the Desert* WGS Audio Update Series gets the word out about the efforts of the working groups. Each series is recorded onto a CD and can be ordered from www.thesedonaconference.org/wgsa_html.

- ✔ *The Sedona Conference Journal* is published annually and contains materials from the conferences and their authors. Journal issues can be ordered from www.thesedonaconference.org/thejournal_html.

Discovery Resources

www.discoveryresources.org

Discovery Resources is a composite Web site intended for legal professionals interested in learning about e-discovery's technological and legal challenges.

Posts are relatively brief and made by those in the industry or Fios, Inc (the Web site sponsor). You find sections on standards and best practices, a library, and archived Webcasts and podcasts. The *Views from the Bench* section provides the latest judicial opinions and judicial advice to counsel. The library offers selected news and references from various trusted sources.

Two blogs are linked to the site. Mary Mack, Esq., who is corporate technology counsel for Fios, Inc. posts brief comments in the *Sound Evidence* blog. One of the intentions is to raise issues and offer ways to contain costs when complying with ESI requests.

Discerning e-Discovery is a collaborative blog where readers and their own contributors get to post comments.

You also find links to other e-discovery blogs. You can follow them on Twitter.

Law Technology News

www.lawtechnews.com

Law Technology News (LTN) is a media publication that's available online and in print. The LegalTech trade show is an intensive learning opportunity with continuing legal education (CLE) accredited educational tracks on e-discovery.

LTN provides a wide range of materials in large volume.

You can follow LTN on Twitter. Resources offered are podcasts and links to a variety of blogs. Attorney Craig Ball is a featured contributing author at LTN whose lengthy articles are clever and informative. He brings a unique perspective from serving as a Special Master. His Web site is www.craigball.com.

Electronic Discovery Law

www.ediscoverylaw.com

Electronic Discovery Law is a blog providing up-to-date e-discovery legal issues and best practices published by the e-Discovery Analysis and Technology (e-DAT) Group of K&L Gates law firm.

A unique resource is the *Electronic Discovery Case Database* containing more than 1,000 federal and state cases. K&L Gates maintains and continually updates the database. The database is searchable by keywords, 29 case attributes (cost shifting and preservation, for example), rules, motions, and more. You can access and search the database free. Search results include a list of relevant cases, brief descriptions of the nature and disposition of cases, the e-evidence involved, and a link to a more detailed case summary if available.

The posts are well written, brief, and clearly for the benefit of lawyers. Case summaries, news, and updates are also valuable features.

E-Discovery Team Blog

http://ralphlosey.wordpress.com

E-discovery blogger and attorney Ralph C. Losey offers up-to-the-moment critiques, interviews, explanations, views, and opinions on law and IT. Archives extend back to November 2006, just prior to the December 1, 2006 effective date of the FRCP amendments. The blog provides content for a wide audience of legal and IT professionals who are new to e-discovery or seasoned experts.

His commentary is lengthy, witty, and candid. In one post, he quotes Oliver Wendell Holmes, saying, "Lawyers spend a great deal of their time shoveling smoke." With lots of good one-liners, he presents the good, the bad, and the ugly of every facet of e-discovery. The artwork and diagrams are informative, and history buffs will love the photos.

You find podcasts (if you prefer listening to updates) and the transcripts. Being digitally multi-lingual, he offers Tech Twitters.

LexisNexis Applied Discovery Online Law Library

www.applieddiscovery.com

In 2000, Applied Discovery developed the first online law library featuring case summaries devoted to the topic of e-discovery. The LexisNexis Applied Discovery Online Law Library (click the Online Law Library tab on the home page) offers a remarkable set of resources, but you need to be a registered user. Registration is free with a standard form to fill to create your account.

The resources likely to be most valuable on this site are

- **Case summaries:** Quick links to case summaries, which are sufficient to understand the issues. But if you want to view the entire case, the link takes you to Lexis.com access, which requires a paid subscription. If you're already a subscriber, then this connecting link saves you time.

- **Court rules:** This section offers a summary of ESI state codes and federal local rules.

- **Ethics opinions:** For bar association ethics opinions related to e-discovery, this is your resource. For premium content, you need to be a subscriber, which is free. Copies of the opinions that you download are also free.

American Bar Association Journal

www.abajournal.com

The *American Bar Association (ABA) Journal* is dedicated to the full spectrum of law. You can guess from the name that this is the Web site of the ABA's flagship publication.

The online resource has many features and conveniences including:

- Legal news that is updated frequently throughout business days.

- Analysis from more than 2,500 legal blawgs (they use a less traditional spelling of blog).

- Legal affairs stories.

- iPhone and iPod touch applications. Breaking news can be read from these popular handhelds.

✔ Mobile edition to BlackBerry or other wireless device that connects to the Internet available at `http://mobile.abajournal.com`. If you don't have wireless access, there's a free AvantGo mobile content service.

✔ Twitter and RSS feeds. You can access the news with Twitter, via instant messaging, or with RSS feeds. If it's digital or deliverable, the *ABAJournal.com* has you covered.

The extensive site has common newspaper features — stories, archives, and classifieds.

Legal Technology's Electronic Data Discovery

`www.law.com/jsp/legaltechnology/edd.jsp`

Electronic Data Discovery (EDD) is a specialized section of Legal Technology. Consider this Web site a consolidator of news from other legal sources. On their main page are four or five article titles and brief summaries. Each article title links to the full version on the original source.

In addition to the articles, the *EDD Update* blog collects and consolidates other blogs' posts. You view brief blog posts, whose titles are hyperlinks to the source blog.

The third feature is the e-discovery road map based on an electronic digital rights model (EDRM). The road map is interactive explaining the process that you click. You can continue to drill down to more detailed descriptions of rules, cases, case laws, records management, and much more.

Supreme Court of the United States

`www.supremecourtus.gov`

You can go right to the source, the Supreme Court of the United States. Don't overlook or underestimate the value of this Web site. You can search the Supreme Court files for documents containing terms that are of interest to you. Results are portable data format (PDF) documents and available for download. Having a law degree may be necessary to understand the cases.

Under the Recent Decisions heading are links to various other pages including Docket, Oral Arguments, and Opinions. What you may find useful from the Docket page are reports from Special Masters at `www.supremecourtus.gov/SpecMastRpt/SpecMastRpt.html`.

The docket system is the court's automated case-tracking system for information about pending and decided cases. You can do a search for cases using docket numbers or case names. The format for Supreme Court docket numbers is *Term Year-Number* (for example, 08-100). Clearly, this feature is not for techies.

Cornell Law School Legal Information Institute and Wex

`www.law.cornell.edu`

Legal Information Institute (LII) is the research and online publishing branch of the Cornell Law School. Full texts of the following collections are available and searchable.

- ✔ **The bailout bill:** Yes, The U.S. House of Representatives bill to purchase and insure certain types of troubled assets for providing economic stability. Lawsuits stemming from violations of this bill will surely involve ESI discovery.

- ✔ **Federal Rules:** You can read the Federal Rules of Civil Procedure, Criminal Procedure, and Evidence.

- ✔ **Court opinions:** You can read opinions of the Supreme Court, Federal Courts, and various state courts.

- ✔ **Law by source of jurisdiction:** They provide federal law, state law, and world law.

Wex (`http://topics.law.cornell.edu/wex`) is a wiki-like (collaboratively built) legal dictionary and encyclopedia run by LII and the Cornell Law School. This free resource is intended for a broad audience of law novices, which applies to seasoned lawyers entering new areas of law.

Chapter 20

Ten e-Discovery Cases with Really Good Lessons

In This Chapter

▶ Learning from the experience of others

▶ Tracking opinions of the e-discovery judges

▶ Finding the *but* (exception) in every rule

▶ Steering clear of hot spots

*I*f you're irresistibly drawn to learning from legal blunders and unwise e-discovery tactics, you're in luck. Most legal cases have a winner and loser, but the outcome (verdict or decision) doesn't necessarily reflect who took the biggest financial hit. Although it's impossible to estimate how much money is spent because of ignorance of e-discovery case law, stupidity, or poor planning, our safe guess is a lot. The discovery rules have actually increased the costs of litigation. In this chapter, we compile cases whose lessons can help prepare you to win or spare you from an expensive experience.

These ten cases illustrate a lesson in e-discovery. Although other cases might be more glamorous, paying attention to the cases in this chapter can help you efficiently, effectively, and competently deal with ESI discovery.

Zubulake v. UBS Warburg, 2003–2005; Employment Discrimination

The opinions of Judge Shira A. Scheindlin in *Zubulake v. UBS Warburg* LLC (*Zubulake I, II, III, IV, and V*) have become iconic e-discovery rulings, so we have to include them at the very beginning of this chapter. The series of five decisions, spanning 2003 to 2005, made this employment discrimination lawsuit arguably the most referenced and definitive case on e-discovery. The test established by the court in *Zubulake I* is the leading standard for determining cost-shifting.

Top lessons from the Zubulake decisions are

- **You don't need to preserve ESI on backup tapes that are not reasonably accessible and beyond the normal retention times established by your company policy.** Two possible exceptions are

    - If you can identify backup tapes where specific employee ESI is stored, then you must preserve those tapes, whether the tapes are reasonably accessible or not.

    - If backup tapes are actively being used for information retrieval, then the tapes would likely be subject to a litigation hold.

- **Your lawyer has a duty to affirmatively monitor your compliance with ESI preservation and production.** Simply notifying you and your employees about a litigation hold is not sufficient. Lawyers need to review your documentation of preservation efforts and send reminders to employees of their obligations during the hold.

- **If you ask that your opponent pay for production costs (*cost-shifting*), your request should be reasonable.** Analysis of the work and costs involved should be grounded in fact, for example based on the results of ESI data sampling rather than guesswork. You should be able to back up your request with specifics of what you need, with a specific dollar amount.

- **At the end of the day, the duty rests with the party.** In other words, you're the one held responsible for anything that goes wrong.

You should be familiar with Zubulake decisions and be prepared to craft arguments and responses accordingly. If you don't, you risk the wrath of the judge.

Qualcomm v. Broadcom, 2008; Patent Dispute

Fiery disputes about the failure to produce relevant e-mails were non-stop in *Qualcomm v. Broadcom*. The judge found that Qualcomm's lawyers misrepresented (legalese for "lied about") the existence of certain electronic documents pertaining to video compression technology. The court pointed to Qualcomm's lawyers adamantly maintaining that no Qualcomm employee had sent e-mail to the Joint Video Team (JVT) standards-setting organization (SSO). On one of the last days of the trial, one of Qualcomm's own witnesses testified that she had e-mails that Qualcomm had claimed did not exist. Like the *Titanic*, Qualcomm's case started sinking. The trial ended, but Broadcom's lawyers were able to force the production of those e-mails four months later plus another 200,000 relevant e-mails and documents. In addition to losing its case, the very angry court invalidated Qualcomm's video-related patents and ordered them to pay Broadcom's attorney fees, court fees, expert witness fees, and other litigation costs — roughly $8.6 million. The court then ordered Qualcomm's lawyers to give convincing arguments as to why additional sanctions shouldn't be imposed. Then the judge in a never-seen-before-move sanctioned Qualcomm's six outside lawyers and recommended that the California State Bar take disciplinary actions against them.

Three warnings made clear by this case are

- Electronic discovery misconduct is extremely expensive and stupid.

- Electronic discovery can change the outcome of a case.

- Electronic discovery misconduct by attorneys might subject them to discipline affecting their license to practice.

Top lessons from the *Qualcomm v. Broadcom* case are

- Prepare your expert witness and make sure your expert can answer questions.

- Know what your expert witness knows. Hearing it for the first time in court is dangerous.

- Design, validate, and make sure you understand the data map to minimize the risk of failing to identify and search storage media containing responsive ESI.

- Don't lie.

- Consult external and objective IT experts for their opinions and help in explaining technical issues.

Victor Stanley, Inc. v. Creative Pipe, Inc., 2008; Copyright Infringement

A defendant's poorly executed ESI and document review handed the opponent a win in *Victor Stanley, Inc. v. Creative Pipe, Inc.* Creative Pipe initially had requested a clawback agreement because it had inadvertently handed over privileged documents that it wanted back. Later, to get more time to review documents, Creative Pipe traded off that clawback request. Then, without the clawback protection, Creative Pipe mistakenly turned over 165 documents to its opponent. The documents included communications between the company and its lawyers, which typically are protected by privilege.

Adding to their unfortunate handling of ESI review, Creative Pipe did not identify the keywords used to search, used an "expert" to select the keywords and perform the search whose qualifications were never revealed, and failed to demonstrate quality-assurance testing. When Victor Stanley challenged the search and production, Creative Pipe did not have a reasonable explanation of what they'd done and why it was sufficient.

U.S. Chief Magistrate Judge Paul Grimm ruled that defendant Creative Pipe had no attorney-client privilege in those documents.

Lessons from Grimm's opinions are

- ✔ Be able to show your work.
- ✔ Use a reasonable, transparent, and defensible ESI review methodology.
- ✔ Find and fix your inadvertent disclosures promptly.
- ✔ Your counsel should cooperate in attempting to reach non-waiver agreements.

Doe v. Norwalk Community College, 2007; the Safe Harbor of FRCP Rule 37(e)

We included *Doe v. Norwalk Community College* for a couple of reasons: the use of an adverse inference sanction for spoliation and the application of the FRCP Rule 37(e) safe harbor. A *safe harbor* is a potential safety net against sanctions if you lose or inadvertently destroy ESI provided that you acted in good faith.

Doe claimed that the hard drives of key witnesses were scrubbed of data based upon the conclusion of a forensic computer expert. In determining if an adverse inference instruction could be given to the jury, the court looked at:

- ✔ Did Norwalk have a duty to preserve? The court found that Norwalk had a duty to preserve the ESI (because of rules set forth from *Zubulake*). The college tried to assert that the destruction was the result of the normal operation of the system.

   The court took exception to this assertion on two grounds: a duty to intervene in the normal operation once the litigation hold took effect and the college did not have one consistent routine system in place and did not follow the policies in place. As a result, the safe harbor does not apply.

✔ Was Norwalk behind the spoliation? After the court found a duty to preserve the evidence and that the safe harbor did not apply, it turned its attention to the adverse inference ruling. The court found that failure to properly implement a litigation hold to be at least grossly negligent if not reckless. The judge also found evidence that Norwalk selectively destroyed the evidence. This shows intent.

✔ Was the destroyed evidence relevant? Lastly, the court addressed the issue of relevance. The court held that the fact that, at a minimum, there was gross negligence present was enough for an adverse inference. An adverse inference is an instruction by a judge to a jury that they can assume the worse about a situation. The court also indicated that if it were mere negligence, then Doe would have to show the destroyed evidence would have been favorable to her case.

Lessons pertaining to Safe Harbor Rule 37(e) and adverse inferences:

✔ You can't complain about an adverse inference ruling against you if you hadn't implemented a litigation hold.

✔ You must be sure to halt any destruction of evidence as soon as there's a litigation hold.

✔ You must follow your policy on routine document retention consistently.

✔ You must avoid any grossly negligent action.

✔ You're only protected when your e-evidence is lost as a result of the routine, good faith operation of your IT system.

You should always develop and maintain a workable document retention policy that is regularly reviewed and revised as needed. This can avoid problems later and be very helpful in litigation.

United States v. O'Keefe, 2008; Criminal Case Involving e-Discovery

U.S. v. O'Keefe (2008) is an influential case because it addresses ESI in criminal matters. There is no rule in the Federal Rules of Criminal Procedure (FRCrimP) related to presenting documents or ESI to the defendant in an organized fashion. No rule says the government cannot just dump documents on the defendant.

In *O'Keefe*, Magistrate Judge Facciola referred to the e-discovery civil rules as guidance and authority in this criminal case. The Judge noted that the Federal Rules of Civil Procedure (FRCP) was already in place and could be used as a guideline. The Judge recognized that the FRCP is not perfect but has been amended to take into account electronic documents. For example,

FRCP Rule 34 requires that you produce ESI in the same way you keep them or you must organize and label them according to the way the requesting party asks for the ESI. Accordingly, the government could not hand over a box of documents without file folders or labels, because those files are not ordinarily maintained in that manner.

Lessons for criminal law cases involving ESI for which no rules of criminal procedure exist are

- ✔ When e-discovery is too technical and complex for attorneys to assess adequately, experts might be necessary to determine whether an e-discovery search is adequate.
- ✔ Where Federal Rules of Criminal Procedure don't provide guidance on the handling of large quantities of ESI in a criminal case, the FRCP should be looked to for guidance.

The FRCrimP are slowly developing in this area as ESI becomes more prevalent in criminal prosecutions. The FRCP and best practices are important guides down this path.

Lorraine v. Markel American Insurance Co., 2007; Insurance Dispute

Lorraine v. Markel American Insurance Co. was a lawsuit over insurance coverage for a boat damaged by lightning. The insurance company paid a claim for damage, but later Lorraine found additional damage and claimed an additional $36,000 to fix the boat. The matter went to arbitration, and the arbiter gave Lorraine an award of $14,000. Lorraine filed this action claiming the arbiter did not have authority to reduce the amount, but could only determine if the damage occurred as a result of the lightning. Both parties filed motions for *summary judgment* (to end the case in their favor) and attached copies of e-mails.

In this case, Judge Grimm goes to great lengths to discuss the differences between the Federal Rules of Civil Procedure and Federal Rules of Evidence. The case is a primer on how proffered ESI can also be admissible into evidence at the trial. It doesn't do any good to have it if you can't use it.

Lessons learned from *Lorraine v. Markel American Insurance Co.* are

- ✔ Because both sides in this case failed to offer e-evidence to support their motions, Judge Grimm denied a motion for summary judgment.

> ✔ ESI that is discoverable might not be admissible.
>
> ✔ Authentication is key to admissibility.
>
> ✔ There is very little case law on admissibility of ESI but best practices applied to e-discovery can be applied to admissibility in court.
>
> ✔ A comprehensive document retention policy can help ensure admissibility under the self-authentication rules of FRE 901 or as an exception to the hearsay rule under Rule 803(6).

You can help yourself by implementing a comprehensive document retention policy. For e-discovery issues the importance can't be understated. You could establish arguments under the safe harbor rule and admissibility rules. Just because it is discoverable does not mean it will be admitted in court.

Mancia v. Mayflower Textile Services Co., et al., 2008; the Duty of Cooperate and FRCP Rule 26 (g)

Mancia v. Mayflower Textile Services Co., was a collective action against several Mayflower companies for violating the Fair Labor Standards Act (FLSA). The plaintiffs' claim was that they had not been paid for overtime work, and illegal deductions were being made from their wages. Despite warnings, the parties didn't cooperate or communicate as they were obligated to do.

In *Mancia v. Mayflower Textile Services Co.*, Magistrate Judge Paul W. Grimm's 30-page opinion created case law mandating greater cooperation and communication between opposing lawyers during discovery. The judge was annoyed with the requesting lawyer's use of the words "any and all" and the responding lawyer's equally foot-dragging objections that included the words "overbroad" or "burdensome." In his opinion, Grimm focused on FRCP Rule 26(g), which he considered the most violated discovery rule.

Rule 26(g) is an interesting rule in that it requires the parties and their lawyers to comply with the purposes of Rules 26 through 37. How? By requiring lawyers to certify (by signature) that each and every discovery request, response to a request, and objection to a request is legitimate — not meant to drive up costs or cause delays. The certification is critical to ensure that parties cooperate in good faith during e-discovery to control costs and avoid delays. To motivate cooperation, the rule also encourages judges to impose sanctions for any attempts to abuse discovery.

Top lessons to be learned from Judge Grimm in this case are

- ✓ If you or your attorney violates the certification rules, you'll be sanctioned.
- ✓ Attorneys have an affirmative duty to behave responsibly during discovery.
- ✓ You should consider the needs of your case, the importance of the issue, and the amount in controversy in discovery.
- ✓ Discovery should be conducted so that the costs are proportional to what is a stake in the case.
- ✓ Your attorney needs to cooperate in the discovery process.

The cautions are both legal under the FRCP and ethical under the professional rules of conduct.

Mikron Industries Inc. v. Hurd Windows & Doors Inc., 2008; Duty to Confer

In *Mikron Industries Inc. v. Hurd Windows & Doors Inc.*, a breach of contract case, the defendant sought both a protective order and cost-shifting. However, Hurd didn't show that it had met its obligation under Rule 26(c), which requires that you confer in good faith with your opponent. The judge ruled against the defendants because if you want a protective order or cost-shifting, you must in good faith meet and confer with your opponent. The judge found that the defendants didn't comply with Rule 26(c) because they didn't respond to plaintiff's counsel when it:

> "identified specific 'gaps' in production and reasonably asked defendants to articulate the foundation for their assertion that unsearched ESI would produce "little additional responsive information."

The judge added:

> "A conversation with opposing counsel does not become a "meet-and-confer" conference simply because a party has attached that label to the discussion."

You should always get a protective order before responding to an e-discovery request in case you make a mistake and inadvertently (unintentionally) produce privileged information. A protective order, as the name implies, helps protect your claim of privilege if you make that mistake because it's possible to waive privilege of documents if you produce them. When you attempt to get the opponent to pay for e-discovery costs, that's known as cost-shifting.

The court denied the motion for a protective order and cost-shifting.

Lessons to be learned from this case are

- ✔ **Failure to meet and confer in good faith and work with the opposing party can increase your costs and even destroy your case.** Even though shifting the burden of cost from one party to another is an accepted practice, Judge Robert S. Lasnik denied a motion to do so because the requesting party failed to meet and confer in good faith.

- ✔ **Complying with the good-faith rule entails a substantive discussion with your opposing party.** Specifically, your difficulty in producing responsive ESI, the extent to which you've searched ESI to date, and the foundation for your belief that a more thorough search of ESI, including backup tapes, would yield only information that has already been produced.

- ✔ **You need to demonstrate why the requested ESI is not reasonably accessible.** You provide sufficient detail to allow the requesting party to evaluate the costs and benefits of searching the requested sources.

Some courts are more willing to sanction parties for failing to participate in e-discovery in good faith. Always be prepared to actively and effectively participate in the discovery process.

Gross Construction Associates, Inc., v. American Mfrs. Mutual Ins. Co., 2009; Keyword Searches

Gross Construction Associates, Inc., v. American Mfrs. Mutual Ins. Co., (2009) was a multi-million dollar dispute over alleged defects and delays in the construction of the Bronx Criminal Court Complex. The construction management company, a non-party to the litigation, sought to produce relevant ESI (as required), but without producing its entire e-mail database. Both of the parties had suggested such overly common construction terms as "sidewalk", "driveway", and "budget", which were unreasonable search terms. The non-party had an obligation to suggest reasonable search terms based upon its knowledge of employee classifications and abbreviations.

Magistrate Judge Peck warned lawyers of their responsibility to use e-discovery practices that are reasonably designed to retrieve responsive ESI. Not performing basic e-discovery tasks, such as interviewing key custodians about their communication practices, is inexcusable.

Lessons from this case are

✔ Select keywords and search terms with input from the custodians of that ESI to learn the words and abbreviations they use. You need to consult them to be able to reasonably identify and retrieve responsive ESI. Without substantive knowledge, you're unable to engage in a meaningful Rule 26 meet-and-confer process.

✔ Test the proposed methodology to verify its accuracy in retrieving responsive ESI and eliminating false positives.

✔ Don't force the court to draft keyword searches.

✔ Be sure to cooperate with your opponent.

✔ Hire an expert if you need one.

Seminal decisions discussing the critical importance of transparency and agreement on search methodology, including: *Victor Stanley, Inc. v. Creative Pipe, Inc., United States v. O'Keefe,* and *Equity Analytics, LLC v. Lundin,* provide guidance on the minimum expectations for reasonable and effective e-discovery representation.

Check out *The Sedona Conference Cooperation Proclamation* at www.the sedonaconference.org for more information.

Gutman v. Klein, 2008; Termination Sanction and Spoliation

Gutman v. Klein serves as a warning to everyone involved in e-discovery of the seriousness of misconduct. It's also one of the funniest cases to read because of the fumbling testimony of the defendant's "computer guy" (who was a relative of the defendant hired to give testimony about the electronic evidence) and the glaringly obvious signs of attempts to destroy electronic evidence from a laptop. The unprepared relative's reply when asked what he was told to do with the laptop said.

"I don't remember the exact wording. Whatever. I told him whatever. I did whatever I felt right to do, whatever."

The court didn't find the witness' comments comical. When the defendant finally turned over the laptop as they were required to do, the case was hot to the touch, and one of the screws from the hard drive casing was missing — red flags of tampering with the contents.

Klein was put on notice about a litigation hold. Klein failed to notify employees of that hold. The failure to notify employees didn't change his obligation to preserve evidence. The forensic examiner found among other things backdating of files, tampering with the computer, backdating of the system clock, backdating of the operating system installation, use of a scrubbing program, unrecoverable file deletion, thousands of files with the same create date, and a so-called "stolen" laptop.

The court indicated that this was such an intolerable case of misconduct that an adverse inference to the jury was not sufficient to compensate for the prejudice (harm) to the plaintiff. The court granted a default judgment in favor of the plaintiff, basically deciding the outcome based on the misconduct of the defendant.

This case goes another step. The sanction recommendations of Magistrate Judge Levy were adopted by Judge Cogan, and ordered that the court clerk send a copy of the order and the magistrate's recommendations to the United States Attorney for possible criminal action.

The many lessons to be learned in this case are

- ✔ The court can terminate your case in favor of the other side for misconduct.
- ✔ Sanctions are cumulative.
- ✔ Electronic discovery misconduct in a civil case could lead to a possible criminal case.
- ✔ The computer maintains information that can detect misconduct.
- ✔ You had better have a good explanation for your actions.
- ✔ Think twice before using a relative as a witness.

Although this case is one of extremes, it goes to prove that you can't always outsmart the forensic experts. Misconduct can have wide-reaching implications.

Glossary

30(b)(6) witness: An employee who's designated to testify on behalf of your company. The 30(b)(6) witness testifies about the company's computer and e-mail systems, storage locations, electronic records management policies, and both the formal and informal (actual) practices. You witness does not testify about the facts of the case. Your witness must prepare for the testimony by learning enough about computer operations to respond to the questions and categories identified in the notice. Also called *Rule 30(b)(6) witness*.

accessible: Data that's stored in a ready-to-use format. Although the time it takes to actually access the data ranges from milliseconds to days, the big issue is that the data doesn't need to be restored or worked on in order to be usable.

acquisition: The process of creating a forensic copy of a hard drive or device using specialized tools or software.

active data: Online data that's accessible, such as word processing documents, spreadsheets, databases, e-mails, and electronic calendars. Generally, active data is simple to access through the computer's file manager program. See also *accessible* and *replicant data*.

active file: A file that's accessible via the operating system.

admissible evidence: Relevant evidence that's presented at trial and allowed by the judge.

adverse inference: An instruction to a jury by a judge that they can assume the worst about a situation. For example, when a judge instructs a jury to assume an adverse inference about the loss of ESI, the judge is telling the jury they can assume that the party got rid of the ESI deliberately because they had something to hide.

affirmative act: Being proactive or deliberately taking action.

ambient data: See *residual data*.

analysis: The phase in e-discovery when the content of ESI is evaluated, including key patterns, topics, people, and discussion.

archival data: See *replicant data*.

archive: Organized long-term ESI storage. Archives differ from backup copies in that backups can be unsearchable data dumps.

archiving: Retaining e-mail, data, or records in an organized way and with an index (typically using a specialized archiving system) so that you can manage the archive centrally. Archiving is not the same as preserving because archiving is done as a routing operation while preserving is done for legal purposes.

authenticate: To provide sufficient proof that something is what it claims to be.

authentication: Ensures that the forensic image and the original computer media are identical.

back up the truck requests: Slang for requests for huge volumes of data. The phrase is a carryover from paper discovery days. Expect these types of requests to be denied.

backup data: Data that's not actively in use by a company and that's copied and stored separately on portable (removable) media. The purpose of backup is to free up space and for disaster recovery in the event of a system failure. Backups are usually stored offsite.

backup tape recycling: Reusing backup tapes by overwriting them with new backup data, usually on a fixed schedule, such as every month or every three months. Because backup tapes contain large amounts of data, restoring this data to review the material relevant to a case is expensive and can take a long time.

Best Evidence rule: A rule stating that you need to submit the original evidence, and not a copy of the original evidence.

bit-stream image: An exact bit-by-bit duplicate of a hard drive using non-invasive procedures. Also called a forensic copy. All active, inactive, deleted, and residual data and files are captured in the image. This read-only evidence file is also called a forensics or *sector-by-sector image*. It's not the same as a mirror copy or mirror image, which contains only the active files. See also *mirror image*.

Brook's Law: States "adding manpower to a late software project makes it later." See also *mythical man month*.

burdensome: When doing something is too much work or too disruptive or expensive given the circumstances. Also referred to as *undue burden*.

cache: A type of memory that temporarily stores frequently used information.

case law: Body of law or precedents created by judges' written opinions and decisions.

chain of custody: The care, control, and accountability of evidence at every step of an investigation to verify the integrity of the evidence. The chain shows how the e-evidence was gathered, tracked, and protected on its way to court. If you don't have a chain of custody, you don't have evidence.

civil case: A case that begins when a person, company, or the government (the plaintiff) claims that another person (the defendant) has failed to carry out a legal duty owed to the plaintiff. Civil cases are brought in state or federal courts. See also *criminal case.*

clawback: An agreement that enables a party who has inadvertently disclosed ESI to get it back, or have it destroyed, or at least not be used by the opposing party. Clawback gives the responding party some slack (in terms of time and precision) when producing ESI while still protecting the ability to claim privilege, confidentiality, or work product protection.

cloud computing: Computing services that are rented via the Internet (the cloud) from a vendor's servers without owning the IT infrastructure that supports them. The cloud model is also called utility computing because, like electricity and gas, you pay for the service on a per-volume basis.

collection: A phase in e-discovery during which ESI is collected in a secure manner.

computer forensics: The use of specialized techniques by trained experts to find and recover electronic evidence; and then preserve, authenticate, and analyze it.

concept searching: A search method that uses the meaning of words to find responsive documents. This search technique doesn't just match words, but uses something similar to a thesaurus to find synonyms.

criminal case: A case that's brought by the government, on behalf of the people of the United States, against a person accused of a crime. The United States Attorney's Office prosecutes the case if the person is charged with a federal crime. A state's Attorney's Office prosecutes state crimes.

critical path: In project management, the critical path is the longest path made up of activities that must be completed on time or the project's deadline is not met.

dashboard: Like a dashboard of a car, a (computer) dashboard provides the litigation team with real-time information to track the status, timelines, and completion of e-discovery activities.

data custodian: Person who knows how ESI is kept, where it's kept, and whether it's accessible. Also called a *record custodian*.

data map: Diagram or list defining the ways that ESI moves through a company from its creation through storage or disposal. The map can be used to explain to outside counsel where data is stored and who has access to it.

Daubert test: In order for an expert's testimony about scientific evidence to be admissible, the expert must meet certain criteria. The criteria form what's called the Daubert test.

dedupe (deduplication): Process of comparing electronic documents or ESI and removing the duplicates.

defamation: A statement that injures someone's reputation and exposes that person to public contempt, hatred, ridicule, or condemnation. If the false statement is published in print or through broadcast media, such as radio or TV, it's libel. If it's only spoken, it's slander.

defendant: The person or party who's accused. The defendant is listed on the right side of the *v.*, as in *Plaintiff v. Defendant*.

delete: To hide a file or its filename. Deleted files are recoverable because a computer system never truly deletes (gets rid of) files.

deposition (also known as a *depo*): Testimony given by a witness under oath that's recorded by a court reporter. Depositions are made before the trial begins, but not in court. A deposition can be the most painful and mentally exhausting activity you perform during the case.

discoverable: Subject to discovery.

discovery: The pretrial process during which each party has the right to learn about, or discover, as much as possible about the opponent's case.

drilldown: Finding the details of summary data. For example, summary data are linked to the data that they summarize. When summary data is clicked, you see the details.

duty to preserve: Your company's pre-discovery obligation to preserve potential sources of discoverable ESI.

e-discovery: Part of the legal system that allows parties involved in a lawsuit to request ESI from their opponent in preparation for trial.

e-discovery extortion: The process of threatening a party with expensive e-discovery to force that party to settle a lawsuit or case.

e-discovery request: An official request for access to or the production of ESI that may be used as evidence. Also called *production request.*

Electronic Discovery Reference Model (EDRM): Organization that develops guidelines and standards for e-discovery consumers and providers. The model provides a framework for e-discovery that's widely accepted.

electronic evidence (e-evidence): Evidence in digital or electronic form, such as e-mail, computer files, instant messages, PDA calendars, and BlackBerry phone lists.

electronic records management (ERM): The plan and procedures for retaining, disposing, and destroying documents and data. Also called *records and information management (RIM).*

electronically stored information (ESI): Digital content; a term introduced and used in the 2006 amendments to the Federal Rules of Civil Procedure.

ESI lifecycle: The period from when ESI, such as a record or document, is created until it is destroyed.

evidence law: A long list of rules about evidence that have exclusions, which in turn have exceptions. *Rules* state which evidence is admissible. See also *exception; exclusion.*

exception: A rule that contradicts exclusions and makes evidence admissible. See also *exclusion; evidence law.*

exclusion: A rule that makes evidence inadmissible. See also *exception.*

external counsel: Lawyers who specialize in litigation or trial lawyers who are retained by a company as needed. They have the most extensive knowledge of the rules of procedure, rules of evidence, and recent case law. Also called *outside counsel.*

false negative: When filtering ESI to identify what's relevant, a false negative is a file that's incorrectly (falsely) marked as non-relevant, when in fact it is relevant. The result is not including ESI that you should, or under-inclusiveness. False negatives are marked as *discards.* False negatives increase the risk of being accused or sanctioned for not producing all responsive ESI. See also *false positive.*

false positive: When filtering ESI to identify what's relevant, a false positive is a file that is incorrectly (falsely) marked as relevant, when in fact it isn't relevant. False positives result in including too much ESI, or over-inclusiveness. These errors increase the amount of ESI to be reviewed, thereby increasing the time and cost of review. See also *false negative.*

FAT (File Allocation Table): A system of keeping track of where files are stored on a hard drive, which is formatted as a FAT volume or file system.

Federal Rules of Civil Procedure (FRCP): The rules that federal courts use to determine proper procedure for civil cases, including what material is subject to discovery or e-discovery.

Federal Rules of Criminal Procedure (FRCrimP): Rules that control the conduct of all criminal proceedings brought in federal courts to protect a defendant's rights.

Federal Rules of Evidence (FRE): The rules that federal courts use to determine what evidence is relevant in civil or criminal cases. Includes 67 individual rules divided into 11 articles. Articles IX and X address authentication and identification of evidence and specific rules regarding writings, recordings, and photos.

forensic accounting: Investigating accounting practices to find evidence of fraud, embezzlement, and other financial crimes.

forensic copy: A technical term for the copy of a hard drive that's created when the ESI on that drive is acquired using computer forensics. See also *bit-stream image*.

forensic tool: A program that applies computer science operations to establish facts in accordance with strict legal evidentiary standards.

form of production: The form in which responsive ESI is handed over to the requesting party. Typically, native form is the form of production.

Fourth Amendment: This amendment to the United States Constitution generally protects against unreasonable search and seizures without a warrant. However, the United States also has warrantless searches for national security purposes, which can defeat the protection provided by the Fourth Amendment.

fragmented data: Active data that's been broken into fragments and stored in various locations on a single hard drive or disk.

general counsel (GC): The company's legal advisors who begin identifying the ESI with the help of IT. Other terms for GC are *in-house counsel* or *corporate counsel*.

good faith: Acting ethically and making informed decisions that are not motivated by self-interest.

hash: A computer-based mathematical process of calculating a unique ID to authenticate e-evidence.

hash value: A digital fingerprint that uniquely identifies the image just as a human fingerprint uniquely identifies an individual. The hash value is used to verify and authenticate a file or forensic copy.

headerless encrypted files: Files that are encrypted and invisible because they don't have a header for the operating system to detect. Files don't get tougher than this to find and open.

hot docs: Slang for documents, e-mail, text messages, or the like that contain relevant content that may affect the outcome of the case. Also referred to as *smoking gun documents or e-mails.*

identification: The phase in e-discovery during which you learn the location of all ESI that you may have a duty to preserve and disclose.

image: A short term for *bitstream image* or *forensic image.* The evidence file created by using forensic software that contains all files from the hard drive or other storage media.

inactive data: Data no longer routinely accessed, but retained because of regulatory or reporting requirements.

inadvertent disclosure: Producing (and therefore disclosing) ESI that should not have been produced. See also *clawback.*

intentional disclosure: ESI that's produced and that's not protected by privilege.

interrogatories: Questions asked prior to trial to find facts about the opposing party's case. The party receiving the interrogatory must answer the questions

keyword search: Search for specific ESI that contains one or more keywords.

legacy: Old or outdated; that is, legacy data or legacy systems are based on older technology and may no longer be in use.

litigation hold: A red alert and a notice to preserve ESI that may be requested as part of e-discovery. You need to take affirmative action to prevent the destruction of physical or digital documents relevant to a lawsuit or government investigation. The purpose of the litigation hold is to stop routine (or any other) destruction of potentially responsive ESI and to make sure it stays safe until the hold is released. Failed litigation holds have gotten some of the biggest headlines in e-discovery because a failed litigation hold is the most likely path to a spoliation sanction.

meet and confer (meet-and-confer conference): Within 99 days of a lawsuit being filed, litigants have a duty to participate in a meet-and-confer conference to negotiate an e-discovery plan.

metadata: Data describing a file or its properties, such as creation date, author, or last access date.

mirror image: Generally, it's a copy of only the active files on a hard drive of a computer, and doesn't include deleted or residual data. See *bitstream image*.

mythical man month: A principle predicting that when you add another member to a team, you may increase the time to complete the project delaying its completion. New members take up the time of current members who need to stop what they're doing to train the newbies. See also *Brook's Law*.

native format: A file in the format in which was created, such as .doc or .docx for Microsoft Word, and that preserves its metadata.

near-line: Near-line data is stored on removable media, like a DVD or flash drive, that's relatively quick and easy to access. A contraction of *near-online*.

near-line storage: Refers primarily to removable media that store files randomly, such as DVDs or flash drives.

non-party: Neither of the litigants (plaintiff or defendant) in a lawsuit, but a party somehow involved because of an ESI connection. Non-parties have the same obligations when served with a subpoena to produce ESI. Also referred to as a *third party*.

not reasonably accessible: ESI that's not easily or readily usable. Backup tapes must be restored, fragmented data must be de-fragmented, and erased data must be reconstructed, all before the data is usable.

offline: Not readily available. With offline storage, files typically are stored on magnetic tape, which requires restoring the tape to read it.

offline storage and archives: Data storage outside the network, such as on backup tapes. This category is either magnetic tape or optical disks and is referred to as *JBOD* — just a bunch of disks.

online: Connected and accessible.

online media: Random access media. *Random access,* also known as *direct access,* means that a stored file can be accessed directly regardless of its location on the storage medium.

online storage: ESI that's immediately available and most accessible.

operating system (OS): A master control program that runs a computer; an interface between hardware and software. Examples are Windows, DOS, Mac OS, Unix, and Linux.

petabyte: Measure of data storage capacity that's roughly 1,000 terabytes.

plaintiff: The party bringing the charge; the requesting party in e-discovery. See also *defendant.*

prelitigation readiness: Preparing for e-discovery, for example by implementing an electronic records management (ERM) program to ensure ESI is being preserved according to litigation and regulatory requirements.

preservation: The phrase in e-discovery following identification during which ESI is protected from destruction and alteration. Preserving ESI is archiving that's motivated by a strong sense of urgency. There's a duty to preserve ESI, but no duty to archive. See *archiving.*

preservation order: A court order that clearly states what to preserve. Complying with a preservation order is mandatory or you risk being sanctioned by the court.

privilege: Communications protected from being used as evidence.

probative value: A standard used to judge whether evidence is useful to the issues of the case.

processing: The phase in e-discovery that reduces the volume of ESI and converts it, as necessary, to forms more suitable for review and analysis.

production: The phase in e-discovery when ESI is delivered to others.

proportionality: A standard used to balance the value of the case with the cost of producing different kinds of ESI. Proportionality is based on the subject matter of the dispute, the rules, and the judges.

protection (or protected): Refers to the status of ESI. If ESI is protected, such as by privilege or privacy, it doesn't have to be disclosed.

PST: A personal folder file in Microsoft Outlook.

quick peek: An agreement that allows the requesting party to look at the ESI subject to certain agreements. The parties agree that providing the ESI for this quick peek is not a waiver of privilege or protection.

RAM (random access memory): A computer's short-term memory (storage). Provides memory space for the computer to work with data. Data stored in RAM is lost (ceases to exist) when the computer is turned off.

random access: An access method in which a stored file can be accessed directly (as opposed to sequentially) regardless of its physical location on the storage medium. Also cleverly called *direct access.*

reasonableness: A standard of reasonable behavior that's very tough to define.

reasonably accessible: See *accessible.*

record retention: Length of time a given record is kept according to policy or ERM procedures.

records managers: Experts who are important to e-discovery because of their knowledge of how electronic and non-electronic records are retained, stored, and destroyed.

redact: To remove or obscure text from a document so that the obscured parts remain confidential and protected.

replicant data: Data or documents stored on a hard drive when a computer automatically backs up while you work on a file. These backed-up files are created and saved to recover data that may be lost because of a malfunction or power loss.

residual data: Data that remains on a hard drive after a file is deleted. Also called *ambient data.*

restore: Process of transferring data from backup storage, such as tape, to an online system to make it accessible.

review: The phase in e-discovery when ESI is evaluated for relevance and privilege.

rolling production: Producing batches of ESI as they become available. Rolling production can occur over a short time or a year or more.

Rule 16(f): Requires opposing parties to meet and discuss a discovery plan and evaluate the protection and production of ESI within 120 days of a complaint being served. See *scheduling (and planning) conference.*

Rule 26: Each company has the duty to preserve documents that may be relevant in a case.

Rule 26(a): Parties must identify all sources of ESI that may be relevant by category and location.

Rule 26(b)(2)(B): Introduced the concept of *not reasonably accessible* ESI.

Rule 26(b)(5)(B): Established a uniform procedure among the United States district courts for claims about inadvertent production.

Rule 26(f): The meet and confer rule that requires attorneys to be prepared to discuss e-discovery issues in-depth within 99 day of a complaint being served.

Rule 34: Electronic records and communications are subject to subpoena and discovery for use in legal proceedings.

Rule 34(b): Addressed form of production of ESI.

Rule 37(e): Created a safe harbor from sanctions for loss of ESI under certain circumstances.

Rule 702: Federal Rule of Evidence that governs the admissibility of expert testimony. The witness must be qualified as an expert to provide testimony.

rules of evidence: Rules that control which material the judge and jury can consider (what's in) and cannot consider (what's out).

safe harbor: A safety net against sanctions if you lose or inadvertently destroy ESI in certain cases. The safe harbor only applies to ESI that's destroyed by routine, good-faith operations of an information system.

sampling: Statistically testing or searching stored ESI to estimate the likelihood of finding relevant ESI. Sampling is basically a test or an audit.

sanction: Punishment imposed by the court for violating a rule, failing to comply with a court order, or attempting to deceive the court.

scheduling (and planning) conference: A hearing attended by the prosecuting attorneys, defendants, defendant's attorneys, and the judge to schedule certain dates and deadlines for the case. This meeting is generally the first time the litigants and their attorneys come before the court. It takes place after the court has received the parties' meet-and-confer report.

Sedona Conference: An influential e-discovery research and educational organization that presents conferences and mini-think tanks (Working Groups) that provide e-discovery guidelines that courts and litigants refer to.

sequential access: The method used to access files stored on tape. To be able to access any particular file, the tape must be read from the beginning, just like with an old-fashioned tape recorder. See also *random access.*

social media: Refers to the "many-people-to-many-people" content created and published online by anyone with the desire to do so. Social media is made of personal conversations that contain a staggering amount of content that's typically stored and available for e-discovery.

social networking: Web sites created by anyone and shared with others, such as blogs, wikis, podcasts, and RSS feeds.

Software-as-a-Service (SaaS): SaaS is basically a rental or an on-demand computing service. Rather than buy an ESI review software package, you rent those capabilities when you need them. Also referred to as *hosted applications*.

Special Master: A neutral lawyer with technical expertise or an IT expert appointed by the court to manage and resolve e-discovery disputes in such areas as forms of production, keywords, and protocols. Courts appoint Special Masters when the parties need a referee, usually when they won't cooperate.

spoliation: The destruction or extreme alteration of evidence. Spoliation is an obstruction of justice crime.

subpoena: A legal document telling the receiver of it to appear in court or face a penalty for not showing up.

summary judgment: Decisions made by the court based on the evidence presented for the record. Summary judgment would take place prior to settlements agree to by the parties.

system data: Data that's generated automatically and maintained by the computer itself. The operating system records routine transactions and functions, such as password access requests, the creation and deletion of files.

third party: See *non-party*.

triers of fact: Judges and juries. These people consider and weigh the evidence to reach verdicts or decisions.

tweet: A short message or post of 140 characters or fewer that is sent via Twitter.

two-tiered test: A distinction between ESI found on sources that are reasonably accessible and sources that are not reasonably accessible because of undue burden or cost.

Web 2.0: The social side on the Internet comprised of social networks and social media.

WG1: This first working group of The Sedona Conference is the *Working Group on Electronic Document Retention and Production*.

work product: The materials that a lawyer develops, including research notes, memos, minutes of conversations with the client or witness, while preparing the case. Work product is protected from subpoena by the opposing party because they're considered confidential.

Index

• A •

access logs, litigation service provider, 184
accessibility, *Zubulake I*, 30–34
accessibility scope, 271–273
accountant-client privilege, 169
accounting personnel, 103
acquisition, 36, 321
active data stage, 32, 34
admissibility
  experts, 214–215
  Federal Rules of Evidence (FRE), 71–73
  Lorraine v. Markel American Ins. Co., 204
  rules, 204–208
Adobe Acrobat, redaction editing, 183
Advanced Micro Devices (AMD), 14
adverse influence ruling, 252
affirmative steps, 45
algorithms, hash, 223–224
American Bar Association (ABA)
  civil discovery standards, 80
  Formal Opinion 06-442, 95
  Model Rules of Professional Conduct,
    83, 253
American Bar Association Journal, 305–306
and not operator, Boolean search, 227
and operator, Boolean search, 226
anti-trust, large case litigation, 264
Applied Discovery, online law library, 305
appointing order, Special Master, 261
archive policy, 264
archives, 33, 46–47
Association for Information and Image
    Management (AIIM), 239
Association for Records Managers and
    Administrators (ARMA), 239
attorney-client privilege, 168
attorney-eyes-only agreements, 178
authentication
  chain of custody, 206–207
  ESI admissibility hurdle, 205–206
  hash values, 223–224

Lorraine v. Markel Am. Ins., 287, 298–299
rules of evidence, 72
self-authenticating ESI, 206
United States v. Tank, 287
authenticity, *Lorraine v. Markel Am.
    Ins. Co.*, 46
automatic deletion systems, 123
automatic systems, 205–206

• B •

backup tapes, 33–34, 123
bad faith, inherent power behavior, 89–90
bankruptcy, 35
Bates stamping, identification, 268–269
best evidence, 72, 210
best practices search, keywords, 158
bit-stream copy, 222–223
blogs, 52, 303–306
Boolean operators, 226–227
breach of contract, 258, 278
business records, 206, 238–239

• C •

California, Civil Discovery Act, 36
CAM time/date stamps, 226
carved files, searches, 227
case law, 13, 323
case management order, 267
CDs, near-line storage media, 29
certifications, 86–87
chain of custody, 192–193, 206–207
chief information officer (CIO), 102
circumstantial evidence, 205
clawback agreements, 23, 178, 259, 271
cloud computing, 162, 323
collaboration platforms, Web 2.0, 54
collaborative search, 158
collect to preserve protocol, 124
communications, 22, 171. *See also*
    privileged communications
company-issued laptop, 284

complaint served, deadlines, 18–19
complaints, litigation hold trigger, 121
complete review, rolling production, 185
complex litigation. *See also* litigation
  anti-trust, 264
  case management order, 267
  clawback agreements, 271
  consulting companies, 274–275
  cost-shifting, 273
  criminal fraud, 264
  document depositories, 269–270
  document retention plan, 264
  educating the judge, 267
  experts, 274–275
  form of production, 269
  good-cause inquiry, 272–273
  identification systems, 268–269
  judicial resolution, 270–271
  meet and confer session, 270–271
  project management process, 266
  proving the merits of the case, 266–267
  quality control issues, 265–266
  quick peek agreements, 271
  rolling discovery schedule, 271
  scope of accessibility, 271–273
  securities fraud, 264
  service providers, 274
  sexual harassment, retaliation, 264
  statistical sampling, 271
  summary judgement, 268
  vendor partnering, 274
computer forensics. *See also* forensics
  assurances, 218
  authentication, 223–224
  Boolean searches, 226–227
  carved files, 227
  consent to search electronic media, 221
  data sampling, 216–218
  defensible approach elements, 231
  deleted ESI, 213, 224–225
  disguised ESI, 213
  e-discovery support, 229
  encrypted ESI, 213
  expert functions, 214
  experts admissibility, 214–215
  fishing expeditions, 229–230
  hash authentication, 223–224
  headerless encrypted files, 213
  image acquisition/preservation, 222–223
  investigation preparation, 220–222
  National Institute of Standards and
    Technology, 211
  password protected ESI, 213
  Peskoff v. Faber, 261
  planted ESI, 213
  process steps, 218–219
  reports, 228
  reverse engineering concerns, 218
  scientific method, 215–216
  search-broadening methods, 225
  search-limiting methods, 226
  small case litigation, 282, 285
  tampered ESI, 213
  when to hire an expert, 212–213
  withheld ESI, 212
Computer Fraud and Abuse Act (CFAA),
    278
computer systems, 36–37, 284
concepts, search method, 158
Conference of Chief Justices, 79
conference scheduling, judge's role, 259
confidential information, 170–171
confidentiality, avoiding waivers, 173
consent to search, electronic media, 221
consultants, data mapping services, 111
consulting companies, 274–275
cooperation
  judicial intervention, 73–74
  Mancia v. Mayflower Textile Services Co.,
    315–316
Cooperation Proclamation, Sedona
    Conference, 302
copyrights
  *Drew Heriot & Drew Pictures Pty LTD v.
    Byrne*, 196
  Victor Stanley, Inc. v. Creative Pipe, Inc.,
    311–312
Cornell Law School, Legal Information
    Institute and Wex, 307
corporate strategic plans, 171
corrupted ESI, 33–34, 161
cost of discovery, *Oracle Corporation, et
    al., v. SAP AG, et al*, 252, 273
cost-shifting, 273
court orders, ESI agreements, 178–179
criminal case, 313–314, 323

criminal e-discovery, 313–314
criminal fraud, 264
critical path method (CPM), 57

• D •

dashboard, 162, 323
data carving tools, file searches, 227
data compilation, authentication, 205
data custodian, 104–105, 324
data extractions, ESI processing, 154
data librarians, 103
data map, 108–111, 324
data ranges, 105
data repositories, 283
data safeguarding, *Kevin Keithley v. The Home Store.com*, 45
data sampling, 216–218
data sets, 183–193
database administrator, 102
data-driven search, keywords, 158
date range, search-limiting method, 226
Daubert test, 203, 214–215, 324
deduping, duplicate documents, 103
defamation, 279, 324
defendant objects, *Johnson v. Kraft Foods N.A.*, 27
defensive strategies, judicial advice, 45–46
delays, 121–122
deleted ESI, 213, 224–225
demands, 13, 40–41
Department of Defense (DoD), 241
deposition, 140–141, 324
destructive changes, 17
destructive process, 123–125
Digital Intelligence, 223
digital release, 183–184
direct evidence, authentication, 205
disaster recovery personnel, 103
Discerning e-Discovery, blog, 303
disclosures, 65, 293–295, 298
discovery abuses, *Mancia v. Mayflower Textile Services Co*, 294–295
discovery limits, 272
discovery orders, 87–88
discovery requests, 294–295
Discovery Resources, 303
discovery timetable, 139

disguised ESI, 213
distinctive characteristics, 205
document history, 15–16
documentation, 191–193
documents
  bit-stream copy, 222–223
  versus business records, 238–239
  deduping, 103
  depositories, 269–270
  descriptions, 85
  identification techniques, 149–150
  improper redaction examples, 188–189
  metadata extractions, 194–195
  proper redaction examples, 189–190
  redaction editing, 183, 187–190
  scheduling order, 259
  self-authenticating ESI, 206
downsizing, litigation hold, 122–123
drilldown, 162, 324
due diligence, 84–87
duty to confer, *Mikron Industries Inc. v. Hurd Windows & Doors Inc.*, 316–317
duty to preserve
  litigation deadlines, 18–19, 21–22
  versus preservation, 116
  Zubulake VI, 22
DVDs, near-line storage media, 29

• E •

e-discovery
  Federal Rules of Civil Procedure (FRCP) amendments, 9–13
  FRCP boundaries, 75
  limiting conditions, 167
e-discovery scope, 104–106
E-Discovery Team, blog, 304
e-discovery teams, 102–103
Electronic Data Discovery (EDD), 306
Electronic Digital Rights Management (EDRM), 194–195, 237
Electronic Discovery Case Database, K&L Gates, 304
Electronic Discovery Law, blog, 304
Electronic Discovery Reference Model (EDRM), 80, 191–192, 325
electronic media, consent to search, 221

electronic records management (ERM).
  designing by committee, 240
  developing/implementing, 20–21
  DoD 5015 standards, 241
  doing what you say, 248
  e-mail policy, 244–246
  keeping-it-all, 247
  manager commitment, 241–243
  policies, 236, 243–244
  process steps, 246–247
  record identification, 240–241
  retention period, 246
  retention schedule, 246
  risk appetite, 242
electronically stored information (ESI)
  accessible versus inaccessible
    categories, 33
  acquisitions, 36
  active data stage, 32
  admissibility rules, 204–208
  analyzing for privilege, 22
  archives, 33
  authentication rules, 207–208
  backup tapes, 33
  bankruptcy, 35
  best evidence rule, 210
  chain of custody, 192–193
  cherry-picking content concerns, 37
  clawback agreements, 23, 178
  complexity, 15–16
  corrupted files, 33
  cost reduction methods, 12
  court orders, 178–179
  data retention, 112–113
  data search methods, 12
  data sets, 182–190
  deduping, 103
  demand cost cutting methods, 40–41
  destructive changes, 17
  digital release method, 183–184
  disclosure response, 175
  dispute types, 26
  document forms, 11–12
  documentation production, 190–192
  duty to preserve, 21–22
  duty to preserve versus preservation, 116
  early case assessment tools, 152–154

electronic records management
    (ERM), 20–21
e-mail lifecycles, 29–30
erased files, 33
exponential growth, 166
false negatives, 150
false positives, 150
filtering, 22, 146–151, 156–157
forensically sound acquisition, 219
fragility, 16–17
fragility/persistence paradox, 17
fragmented files, 33
FRCP amendments, 9–13
good cause production, 35
hard costs, 39
hashing method, 207
hearsay rule, 208–210
hidden costs, 39
identification techniques, 149–150
inadvertent disclosure, 23
legal review costs, 38–39
limiting conditions, 167
litigation cost examples, 37–38
litigation holds, 36–37, 48–51
litigation services platform, 183–184
media types/accessibility degree, 27–29
meet-and-confer session topics, 26
mergers, 36
metadata, 15–16
near-line, 29
non-party responsibilities, 47
obstruction of justice matters, 96–97
offline, 29
offline storage, 33
online media, 28–29
overlooking sources, 111–112
versus paper documents, 14–18
physical delivery method, 183–184
post-production reviews, 12
pre-production reviews, 12
presentation at trial, 24
preservation factors, 36–37
preservation protocols, 124
privilege logs, 173–174
probative value, 167, 210
processing, 22, 146–151, 154–155
production cost shifting, 35
production forms, 23

proportionality negotiations, 108
proportionality of scale, 107
proprietary systems, 36
reasonable accessibility, 113
reasonably accessible negotiations, 254
replicant data, 17
review platforms, 161–162
reviewing, 146–151, 161
sampling, 159–160
searches, 147–149
self-authenticating, 206
self-replication, 15
small case exclusion conditions, 280
software/hardware dependency, 18
spoliation defense, 50–51
subject matter waivers, 172–177
transaction databases, 36
trial and error search process, 151–152
two-tier test, 34–36
Web 2.0 platforms, 51–54
e-mail, 29–30, 195, 216–217, 244–246
e-mail threads, ESI processing, 155
embedded tables, redaction issues, 190
employee departures, 122–123
Employee Retirement Income Security Act
     (ERISA), 230
employee versus employer, 282
employment discrimination, *Zubulake v.*
     UBS Warburg LLC, 13, 309–310
EnCase, forensics software, 223
encrypted ESI, 161, 213
erased files, 33–34
ESI costs, 38
ESI export, ESI processing, 155
ESI locations, 105–106
ESI retention
   Doe v. Norwalk, 124
   Gippetti v. United Parcel Service, Inc.,
      123–124
ESI withholding, 85
evidence admissibility, rules, 204–208
evidence preservation, 45, 136–137
evidence searches, lawyer's effort, 85
exception, 72, 325
exclusion, 72, 325
expert appointment, *In Re Seroquel*
     Products Liability, 261

expert testimony
   Daubert v. Merrel Dow Pharms, Inc., 203
   Galaxy Computer Services, Inc.
      v. Baker, 203
experts
   admissibility issues, 214–215
   appointing order, 261
   complex litigation, 274–275
   computer forensics, 212–215
   e-discovery team member, 103
   judge's appointments, 259, 261–262
   qualifying, 202–203
eXtensible Markup Language (XML), 228
external counsel, 102, 107–08, 325

• F •

Facebook, social media, 53
failure to appear, 88
failure to disclose, 88
failure to participate, 88
failure to provide ESI, 88
false negative, 150, 325
false positive, 150, 325
Federal Rules Advisory Committee, 81
Federal Rules of Civil Procedure (FRCP).
      See also rules
   e-discovery amendments, 9–13
   e-discovery boundaries, 74–75
   e-discovery comparisons, 62–63
   litigation timelines/deadlines, 18–19
   judge's guidance, 251
   Rule 1, 63
   Rule 16, 63–64, 169, 259
   Rule 26, 65, 77–78, 85–87, 119, 169, 171,
      179, 272, 286, 291–295, 315–316
   Rule 30, 295–296
   Rule 30(b)(6) witness, 140–141
   Rule 33, 65
   Rule 34, 65, 77–78, 137, 248, 296–297
   Rule 34(b)(ii), 23
   Rule 37, 64, 76–78, 87–88, 297, 312–313
   Rule 45, 76, 169
   Rule 53, 172, 259
   sanctions, 87–89
Sedona Conference Cooperation
      Proclamation, 74

Federal Rules of Criminal Procedure
(*continued*)
e-discovery comparisons, 62–63
Rule 16, 71
Rule 17, 71
Rule 17.1, 71
Rule 41, 71
Federal Rules of Evidence (FRE).
See also rules
admissibility, 71–73
e-discovery comparisons, 62–63
irrelevancy, 72–73
relevancy, 72–73
Rule 104, 202
Rule 401, 167
Rule 501, 168
Rule 502, 172, 175–177, 298
Rule 702, 203, 215
Rule 803, 209
Rule 807, 209
Rule 901, 205, 298–299
Rule 902, 206
Rule 1002, 72
federal search and seizure return, 70
federal search and seizure warrant, 69
federal search warrant, 68
file formats, ESI processing, 154
file size, search-limiting method, 226
files
best practices search, 158
carved, 227
collaborative search, 158
concept search, 158
corrupted, 33
custodian filtering, 156–157
data range filtering, 157
data validity testing, 159–160
data-driven search, 158
deduping, 157
erased, 33
file-level chain of custody, 193
forms of production, 193–194
fragmented, 33
keyword search, 157
near-line storage, 29
offline storage, 29
phrase search, 157
production history tracking, 184

random versus sequential storage, 28–29
size/type filtering, 156
small case litigation, 286–287
filter cost, *Rowe Entertainment v. Williams
Morris et al.*, 166
filters, ESI search protocols, 156–157
first-pass reviews, ESI processing, 161
first-tier data, 34–35
fishing expeditions, 229–230
flash drives, near-line storage media, 29
forced cooperation
*Gross Construction Associates, Inc. v
American Mfrs. Mutual Ins. Co.*, 254
judge's decision, 253–254
forensic accountants, 286
forensics, 220, 222. *See also* computer
forensics
Form 35, Report of Parties Planning
Meeting, 134–135
form of production
3M Company v. Kanbar, 297
complex litigation, 269
D'Onofrio v. SFX Sports Group, Inc., 137
ESI, 23
Ford Motor Co. v. Edgewood Props., 296
*In re Payment Card Interchange Fee &
Merchant Discount Antitrust
Litigation*, 297
meet-and-confer sessions, 137
native format, 193–194
near-native format, 194
near-paper format, 194
paper (hard copy), 194
Fourth Amendment, 67, 326
fragility, ESI versus paper, 16–17
fragmented files, 33–34
frivolous litigation, 282
FTK, forensics software, 223
fuzziness, search-broadening method, 225

• *G* •

general counsel (GC), 102, 326
good cause, 35, 272–273
good faith, 136, 326
good faith ideal, 116
Google Desktop, search software, 147
Google Docs, collaboration platform, 54

government agencies, 169
granular level, IT architecture, 108
graphs, redaction issues, 190

• H •

hard copy (paper), file production, 194
hard costs, ESI, 39
hard drives, 32, 123–124
hardware
  chain of custody, 192–193
  ESI versus paper documents, 18
hash values, 223–224
hashing method, ESI numbering, 207
headerless encrypted files, 213
hearsay rule, exceptions, 208–210
hidden costs, ESI, 39
history logs, EDRM, 191–192
hold notice, *re eBay Seller Antitrust Litigation*, 126
homonyms, search-broadening method, 225
hosted applications, Software-as-a-Service (SaaS), 162
hot ESI, first-pass review, 161
human resource (HR) personnel, 103
husband-wife privilege, 168
HyperText Markup Language (HTML) reports, 228
hypotheses, 215–216

• I •

identification, evidence, 298–299
identification systems, 268–269
image acquisition, 222–223
image files, 194
improper redaction, *Schaefer v. GE*, 188
inadvertent disclosure, clawback agreements, 23, 178
incompetence defense, *Garcia v. Berkshire Life Ins. Co. of America*, 86
indexes, ESI processing, 155
indexing system, 264
individual versus individual, small case litigation, 282
information management, 237
information security (infosec), 103
information technology (IT), 10, 13, 236–237
inherent power, sanctions, 89–90

in-house counsel. *See* general counsel (GC)
instant onset, small case litigation, 283
insurance, 314–315
Intel, Advanced Micro Devices (AMD) lawsuit, 14
Internet defamation, 279
interrogatories, 66
inventory, ESI processing, 154
inventory logs, Web 2.0, 52
investigation threats, 121
Irrelevant ESI, first-pass review, 161
IT architecture, 108–113
IT personnel, 102

• J •

judges
  active participation, 258–259
  admissibility determinations, 202
  adverse influence ruling, 252
  appointing order, 261
  case management order, 267
  complex litigation education, 267
  conference scheduling, 259
  expert appointments, 259, 261–262
  Federal Rules of Civil Procedures (FRCP) guidance, 251
  forcing cooperation, 253–254
  misconduct determinations, 254
  orders to produce, 259
  overseeing agreements, 259
  protection orders, 259
  reasonableness standard, 252–253
  reasonably accessible ESI, 254
  sanctions, 259
  scheduling order, 259
  scope of cost determinations, 262
  Sheila El-Amin, et al. v. George Washington University, 260
  summary judgement, 268
  tiers of fact, 214–215
  unreasonable delay rulings, 258
judicial advice, defensive strategies, 45–46
juries
  adverse inference instructions, 115
  adverse influence ruling, 252
  evidence weight determinations, 202
  tiers of fact, 214–215
just a bunch of disks (JBOD), 33

• K •

K&L Gates, *Electronic Discovery Case Database*, 304
Kahn Consulting, Inc, 243
Kazeon, forensics software, 223
key players, 104–105
keyword search
  Equity Analytics v. Lundin, 13
  Gross Construction Associates, Inc. v. American Mfrs. Mutual Ins. Co., 317–318
  U.S. v. O'Keefe, 13, 149
  Victor Stanley, Inc. v. Creative Pipe, Inc., 13, 158
  William A. Gross Const. Assoc., Inc. v. Am. Mfg.Mutual Ins. Co., 74
keywords, 157

• L •

Law Technology News (LTN), 303
lawyer misconduct, *Qualcomm Inc. v. Broadcom, Inc.*, 92
lawyer oversight, *Bratka v. Anheuser-Busch Co.*, 94
lawyers
  ABA Model Rules of Professional Conduct, 253
  certifications, 86–87
  due diligence, 84–87
  ESI production, 86
  evidence searches, 85
  FRCP sanctions, 87–89
  frivolous discovery requests, 253
  inherent power sanctions, 89–90
  IT (information technology), 10, 13
  misconduct, 91–93
  Model Rules of Professional Conduct, 83, 93–94
  Rules of Professional Responsibility, 83
  Special Master, 12, 74
Legal Information Institute (LII), Cornell Law School, 1307
legal reviews, ESI costs, 38–39
Legal Technology, 306
LegalTech, trade show, 303
Lexis Nexis, 305
libel, small case litigation, 279

limitations on ESI, 291–292
limitless scope of discovery, 87
LinkedIn, social media, 53
litigation. *See also* complex litigation; small case litigation
  e-discovery timeline, 10–11, 18–20
  ESI cost, 12, 37–38
  meet-and-confer meeting, 133–134
litigation holds
  Arteria Property Pty Ltd. v. Universal Funding V.T.O., Inc., 46
  buying in strategies, 49–50
  custodial compliance documentation, 126–127
  defensive strategies, 48–51
  digital recycling issues, 123–125
  downsizing protections, 122–123
  employee departures, 122–123
  ESI, 36–37
  forensics-level preservation, 130–132
  implementation steps, 125–126
  preservation letters, 127–132
  purpose, 119
  sanction events, 121–122
  self-interest delay, 122
  termination sanction concerns, 119
  trigger events, 120–121
  when to issue, 121
litigation services platform, 183–184
litigation threats, 121
low case value, 282

• M •

magnetic disks, online storage, 32
magnetic tape, 29, 33
Manual for Complex Litigation, Fourth, 267
marital matters, 278–279
Media Law Resource Center, 279
meet-and-confer sessions, 133–134
  clawback agreements, 23, 178
  complex litigation, 270–271
  data maps, 108–111
  discovery timetables, 139
  ESI accessibility issues, 139
  ESI discussions, 26
  evidence preservation, 136–137
  Form 35, 134–135

forms of production, 137
good faith sanctions, 88
inaccessible ESI restoration costs, 139
litigation deadlines, 18–19
mutual interest discovery, 141
privileged ESI, 138
production file formats, 186
protected ESI, 138
quick peek agreement, 138
reasonably accessible negotiations, 254
search protocols, 139
mergers, ESI accessibility, 36
merits of the case, 266–267
Message Digest 5 (MD5), 223–224
metadata
    *Autotech Techs Ltd. P'ship v.
        Automationdirect.com,* 137
    document extractions, 194–195
    document history, 15–16
    e-mail extractions, 195
    ESI processing, 155
    file production forms, 193–194
    native format, 77
    rules, 77–78
metadata standards, *Williams v. Sprint,* 16
Microsoft Office Live Workspace, 54
Microsoft Windows, search utility, 147
misconduct, rules, 91–93
Model Rules of Professional Conduct, ABA,
    83, 93–94
MySpace, social media, 53

• *N* •

National Conference of Commissioners on
    Uniform State Laws, 80
National Institute of Standards and
    Technology (NIST), 211
National Software Reference Library
    (NSRL), 146
native format
    computer forensics reports, 228
    file production form, 193–194
    metadata, 77
native production, 186
native production motions, 185–187
near-line media, 29, 32, 34
near-native format, 194

near-paper format, 194
negligent management, 115
network administrator, 102
newspapers, self-authenticating ESI, 206
non-cooperation, *In Re Seroquel Products
        Liability Litigation,* 136
non-duplicate review, 185
non-party
    ESI responsibilities, 47
    *United States ex rel. Prikh v.
        Premera Blue Cross,* 47
nonpriviliged matter discovery, 65
non-repetitive review, 185
not reasonably accessible (NRA) ESI,
    291–292
Nuix, forensics software, 223

• *O* •

offline media, 29, 33–34
online media, 28–29
oppression, protective order reason, 75
optical character recognition (OCR), 190
optical disks, 32–33
or operator, Boolean search, 227
orders to produce, judge's decision, 259
Osterman Research, 242
outside counsel, 252–253

• *P* •

paper (hard copy), 194
paper documents, versus ESI, 14–18
Paraben, forensics software, 223
password protected ESI, 161, 213
patent dispute, *Qualcomm v. Broadcom,*
    310–311
patents
    *Kucala Enterprises, Ltd. v. Auto Wax Co.,
        Inc.,* 224
    Qualcomm v. Broadcom, 310–311
periodicals, self-authenticating ESI, 206
personal correspondence, 286–287
personally identifiable information (PII), 171
physician-client privilege, 168
pilot tests, rolling productions, 184
planted ESI, 213
pocket-archives, e-mail issues, 245

podcasts, social networking, 52
policies
  data retention, 112–113
  electronic records management (ERM),
      20–21, 236, 243–244
  e-mail management, 244–246
Portable Document Format (PDF)
    reports, 228
post-production reviews, ESI, 12
pre-investigation, 220–222
prelitigation practices
  affirmative steps, 45
  archiving, 46–47
  critical path method (CPM), 57
  defensive strategies, 44–47
  ethical conduct/credibility maintenance, 57
  litigation holds, 48–51
  project management, 55–57
  response teams, 54–55
  spoliation defense, 50–51
  triple constraints, 56–57
  Web 2.0 platforms, 51–54
pre-production reviews, ESI, 12
preservation
  versus duty to preserve, 116
  ESI factors, 36–37
  good faith ideal, 116
  WG1's 2008 guidelines, 117–119
preservation letters, 121, 127–132, 285
preservation order, 64
preservation protocols, ESI, 124
preserve in place protocol, 124
pretiral disclosures/objects, 293
priority order, rolling productions, 185
privacy invasion, ESI exclusion, 280–281
private, ESI first-pass review, 161
privilege, avoiding waiver, 173, 329
privilege logs, ESI, 173–174
privileged communications. *See also*
    communications
  accountant-client, 169
  attorney-client, 23, 168
  clawback agreements, 23
  husband-wife, 168
  Mira Inc. v. O'Brien, 95
  physician-client, 168
  psychotherapist-client, 168
  religious leader-follower, 168
  self-incrimination, 169

privileged documents, *Rico v. Mitsubishi
    Motor Corp.*, 95
privileged ESI
  first-pass review, 161
  meet-and-confer sessions, 138
probative value, ESI, 167
procedures, data retention, 112–113
production form, 66
production history logs, 191–192
production logs, 127
project management, 55–57, 266
proportionality of scale, 107
proportionality rule, 286
proportionality test, 119
proprietary data theft, 278
proprietary research, 171
proprietary systems, ESI accessibility, 36
protected ESI, 138
protected materials, 292–293
protective order, 64, 75, 259
psychotherapist-client, 168
Public Access to Court Electronic Records
    (PACER), e-discovery opinions, 13
public documents, 206
public records, 205–206

• *Q* •

quality controls, 265–266
queries, Boolean operators, 226–227
quick peek agreement, 138, 177–178, 271

• *R* •

random access, online media, 28–29
Really Simple Syndication (RSS), 53
reasonable accessibility, 113
reasonable inquiry, 252–253
reasonableness ideal, ESI, 116
reasonableness standard, 252–253
reckless conduct, power behavior, 89
records. *See* electronic records
    management (ERM)
records, documents versus business
    records, 238–239
records managers, 103, 330
recycling, litigation hold issues, 123–125
redact ESI, 161, 330

redaction
  electronic versus standard, 187
  human oversight requirements, 190
  improper examples, 188–189
  Magnatrax Litigation Trust, Plaintiff v. Onex Corporation, 191
  proper examples, 189–190
  redacting without cause, 191
  Schaefer v. GE, 188
Redax, document redaction software, 183
Reference Data Set (RDS), 146
relevance, 204, 214–215
relevancy, Federal Rules of Evidence (FRE), 72–73
relevant evidence, 167
religious leader-follower privilege, 168
repetitive files, 154
replicant data, 17, 330
reports, 205, 228, 285
reproduction, *White v. Graceland College Center for Professional Development & Lifelong Learning, Inc.*, 195
request for information (RFI), 275
request for proposal (RFP), 275
resources, 302–307
response teams, 54–55
responsive ESI, 105, 161
retention period, 246
retention schedule, 246
reviews
  consistent redaction, 163
  duplicate file links, 163
  ESI processing, 161
  link/relationship preservation, 163
  metadata preservation, 163
  rolling production, 185
  small case litigation, 285
  tag verification, 163
  Web-based platforms, 161–162
Rich Text Format (RTF) reports, 228
risk appetite, ERM, 242
robotic storage systems, 32
rolling discovery schedule, 271
rolling production, data sets, 184–185
rules. *See also* Federal Rules of Civil Procedure (FRCP); Federal Rules of Criminal Procedure (FRCrimP); Federal Rules of Evidence (FRE)
  attorney misconduct, 91–93

authentication, 72, 207–208
best evidence, 72, 210
case law interpretations, 13
Conference of Chief Justices, 79
e-discovery comparisons, 62–63
Electronic Discovery Reference Model (EDRM) Project, 80
electronic records management (ERM) compliance, 248–249
evidence admissibility, 204–208
exceptions, 72
exclusions, 72
Federal Rules Advisory Committee, 81
hearsay, 208–210
litigation timelines/deadlines, 18–19
metadata, 77–78
National Conference of Commissioners on Uniform State Laws, 80
not reasonably accessible ESI, 113
proportionality of scale, 107
sanction, avoiding, 75–77
Sedona Principles, 79
rules of evidence, 331

• *S* •

safe harbor, *Doe v. Norwalk Community College*, 76, 312–313
sampling, ESI validation, 159–160
sanctions
  Ajaxo, Inc. et al. v. Bank of America Technology and Operations, Inc., 95
  Atlantic Recoding Corp. v. Howell, 90
  avoidance methods, 75–77
  Bray & Gillespie Mgmt. v. Lexington and Lexington Insurance Company, 90
  inherent power behaviors, 89–90
  judge's decision, 259
  Keithley et al. v. The Home Store.com, Inc., 90
  Nursing Home Pension Fund v. Oracle Corp., 90
  Padgett v. City of Monte Sereno, 50
  Phoenix Four, Inc. v. Strategic Red. Corp., 90
scanned images, redaction issues, 190
scheduling conference, 18–19, 259
scheduling order, judge's decision, 259
scientific method, 215–216

scope of accessibility, 271–273
scope of cost determinations, 262
search protocols, 139
searches
  best practices, 158
  Boolean operators, 226–227
  collaborative, 158
  computer forensics, 225–226
  concepts, 158
  data carving tools, 227
  data sampling, 216–217
  data validity testing, 159–160
  data-driven, 158
  ESI, 147–149
  false negatives, 150
  false positives, 150
  filters, 156–157
  Google Desktop, 147
  keyword, 157
  phrase, 157
  trial and error process, 151–152
second-tier data, 34–35
Secure Hash Algorithm 1 (SHA-1), 223–224
Secure Hash Algorithm 256 (SHA-256), 223
securities fraud, 264
security, 183–184
Sedona Conference, 74, 117–119, 265, 302
Sedona Principles, 79
self-authentication, 206
self-incrimination privilege, 169
sequential access, online media, 28–29
service providers, 274
sexual harassment, 264
simple negligence, power behavior, 89
slander, 279
small case litigation. *See also* litigation
  breach of contract, 278
  computer forensics, 282, 285
  data repositories, 283
  defamation, 279
  e-discovery benefits, 278–279
  emotional decisions, 283
  employee versus employer, 282
  ESI exclusion conditions, 280–281
  files, 286–287
  forensic accountants, 286
  individual versus individual, 282

instant onset, 283
Internet defamation, 279
large case characteristics, 281–282
low case value, 282
low e-discovery cost, 282
management procedures, 283–285
marital matters, 278–279
personal correspondence, 286–287
preservation letters, 285
proportionality rule, 286
proprietary data theft, 278
reports, 285
reviews, 285
smoking gun, *Ernst v. Merck & Co., Inc.*, 85
social media, Web 2.0 platform, 53–54
social networking
  Biegel v. Norberg, 52
  Web 2.0 platform, 52–53
software
  computer forensics, 223
  data mapping, 111
  ESI processing, 155
  ESI versus paper documents, 18
  litigation holds, 123
  Web-based review platforms, 161–162
Software-as-a-Service (SaaS), 162
Sound Evidence, blog, 303
Special Master
  appointing order, 261
  e-discovery dispute resolution, 12, 74
  e-discovery tasks, 261
  ESI dispute resolution, 172
specimen comparisons, 205
spoliation
  Coleman (Parent) Holdings, Inc. v. Morgan Stanley & Co., 90
  Gutman v. Kelin, 318–319
  Phillip M. Adams and Associates v. Dell, Fujitsu, Sony, ASUS Computer International, et al, 50–51
  United States v. Philip Morris, 95
statistical sampling, 271
stemming, search-broadening method, 225
subject matter waivers, 172–177
summary judgement, 268
Supreme Court of the United States, 306–307
synonyms, search-broadening method, 225

system files, ESI processing, 154
system upgrades, litigation holds, 123

• *T* •

tables, redaction issues, 190
Tagged Image File Format (TIFF) reports, 228
tampered ESI, 213
termination sanctions
  failed litigation holds, 119
  Gutman v. Klein, 318–319
The Sedona Conference Institute (TSCI), 302
third-party vendors, 88–89
tiers of fact, Daubert standard, 214–215
time frames, 105–106
timetables, meet and confer sessions, 139
trade inscriptions, 206
trade secrets
  Ameriwood Ind., Inc. v. Liberman, 230
  confidential information, 171
trade shows, LegalTech, 303
trademarks, *Koninklijke Philips Electronics N.V. v. KXD Technology*, 220
transaction databases, 36
trial lawyers. *See* external counsel
triple constraints, prelitigation, 56–57
Twitter, social media, 53
two-tier test, 34–36, 119

• *U* •

undue burden, protective order reason, 75
undue cost, *Cason-Merenda v. Detroit Medical Center*, 292
unreasonable delay, *Ford Motor Co v. Edgewood Props*, 258

• *V* •

validation, ESI sampling, 159–160
vendor errors, *In re Seroquel Products Liability Litigation*, 89
vendors
  complex litigation partnering, 274
  contract negotiations, 275
    data mapping services, 111
    document depositories, 270
    e-discovery sources, 152
    e-discovery team member, 103
    request for information (RFI), 275
    request for proposal (RFP), 275
    selection guidelines, 153–154
    third-party protections, 170–171
virtual private network (VPN), 183
volume, ESI versus paper documents, 15

• *W* •

waivers, subject matter, 172–177
Web 2.0 platforms, prelitigation, 51–54
Web sites
  American Bar Association (ABA), 80
  American Bar Association Journal, 305–306
  Association for Information and Image Management (AIIM), 239
  Association for Records Managers and Administrators (ARMA), 239
  Citizen Media Law, 52
  Conference of Chief Justices, 79
  Cornell Law School, 307
  Craig Ball, 303
  current time, 226
  Discovery Resources, 303
  E-Discovery Team blog, 304
  Electronic Data Discovery, 306
  Electronic Discovery Law, 304
  federal rulemaking process, 10
  FRCP (Federal Rules of Civil Procedure), 10
  Kahn Consulting, 243
  Kenneth Withers, 302
  Law Technology News, 303
  LexisNexis Applied Discovery, 152, 305
  Media Law Resource Center, 279
  National Conference of Commissioners on Uniform State Laws, 80
  National Security Agency (NSA), 190
  National Software Reference Library (NSRL), 146
  PACER (Public Access to Court Electronic Records), 13
  Sedona Conference, 302

Web sites *(continued)*
 Sedona Principles, 79, 137
 Socha Consulting, 152
 Stanford Law School Securities Class
  Action Clearinghouse, 38
 Supreme Court of the United States,
  306–307
 vdiscovery, 152
 WG1, 119
Web-based review platforms, 161–162
Wex, wiki-like legal dictionary, 307
wikis, social networking technology, 53
willful mismanagement of property, 115
wiretap violations, 280
withheld ESI, 212
witness, *Ideal Aerosmith, Inc. v. Acutronic
 USA, Inc.*, 141
witness designation, 295–296
witness testimony, 205
word-frequency lists, 155

work product
 ESI first-pass review, 161
 Hickman v. Taylor, 169
 protections, 169–170
 waiver, avoiding, 173
Working Group on Electronic Document
  Retention and Production, 117–119
Working Group Series (WGS), 302
written document retention, *Keithley v.
 Homestore.com, Inc.*, 124

X-Ways Forensics, 223
X-Ways WinHex, 223

Yelp, 53
YouTube, 53

Printed and bound by CPI Group (UK) Ltd, Croydon, CR0 4YY

27/10/2024

14580182-0002